1994

LEISURE SITE GUIDELINES FOR PEOPLE OVER 55

By George E. Fogg and Robert F. Fulton, Ph.D.

Published by
National Recreation and Park Association
2775 South Quincy Street – Suite 300
Arlington, VA 22206

ISBN 0-929581-80-6 Soft Cover
ISBN 0-929581-81-4 Hard Cover

ACKNOWLEDGEMENTS AND CREDITS

Leisure Site Guidelines for People Over 55 presents information gathered from numerous sources including a survey of people over 55, conversations with recreation leaders, observations of older leisure participants, and the review of many articles and books. The conclusions derived from this data have been combined with the experiences of the authors to come up with many of the recommendations not included in ADA and ANSI requirements.

To all of those who have contributed to the information contained in this book, we give our heartfelt thanks! We would like to single out several people, however, who provided special help.

SPECIAL THANKS TO:

NRPA and Jonathan Howard of the Publications Center for his continuing support and aid throughout the book's preparation.

The people who conducted the survey: Augustine Alvarez, Mary Ellen Donner, Carol Fogg, Michael Fogg, Lavinia Graham, Linda Parrish, Agnes Prestigiorani, Lyn Trembly, Pam Ulsher, Pat Urqhart, Andrea Wheaton and Laura Zimmermann – and the 584 respondents who contributed their time and effort in filling out the survey.

Mary Ellen Donner, recreation specialist, for her detailed review and helpful comments. Steve Brinkman, Director of Collier County, Florida, Parks for his review and comments.

The many people who have provided insights into various aspects of the over-55 leisure needs – Andrea Wheaton, Health Center Director; Agnes Prestigiorani, Senior Center Director; Lyn Trembly, Senior Center Director; Harold Graham, a 91-year-old's viewpoint; Lavinia Graham, an active 79-year-old's viewpoint; Ken Poirier, a 60+ avid golfer's ideas; Bruce Blash, rehabilitation research; John Templer, stairs, ramps, etc.; Rikki Epstein, NRPA's Leisure and Aging Section's Coordinator; Jack Sisk, retirement home leisure director; Jerry Rine, facilities manager, retirement home; and Dr. Joan Erber, gerontologist.

A MOST SPECIAL THANKS TO:

Rebecca Fogg for translating notes, typing, re-typing, editing, re-editing, and typing some more. Without her constant effort, the book would never have been completed.

CREDITS:

Book Layout – Lisa Rice, Computer Consultants of Naples, Inc.
Editing – Mary Ellen Donner, Rebecca Fogg, Robert Fulton
Graphics Design (including cover) – George Fogg
Lighting – Mark Anderson, lighting consultant, prepared the Lighting sec-
tion of Chapter 7 – Utilities.
Photos – All photos by George Fogg unless otherwise noted on the
photo caption.
Typing – Rebecca Fogg

Thank you all!!

DEDICATION

To all of the older people who have had difficulties in
enjoying the leisure facilities they use.

TABLE OF CONTENTS

CHAPTER 9 – ACTIVITIES–INDOOR 163

CHAPTER 10 – DETAILS 179

CHAPTER 11 – OPERATIONS 203

Introduction

Leisure Site Guidelines for People Over 55 is a practical book. It is about what kinds of facilities are needed and how to develop them so they are suitable for use by people as they grow older. It assumes that many people who are involved with the planning, design and/or operation of a leisure facility know relatively little about the leisure interests, needs and capabilities of older people.

What we as design professionals have done in the past for the provision of leisure facilities for older people has been frequently inadequate, if considered at all. We must refocus our attention on the wide range of activities participated in by older people and how we can make these facilities better fit the needs of this often ignored and rapidly growing segment of our society. We must modify our thinking and design for the realities of the users as they pass through their life cycle and demand the leisure facilities to accommodate their special needs.

Chapters 1 and 2 are intended to provide an understanding of many of the issues which establish the need for design and operational modification of leisure facilities to be used by older people. They describe on whom the book is focusing, their capabilities – physically and mentally – and their recreation/leisure time pursuits over a lifetime.

Research by the authors uncovered relatively little accessible information about what are, and how to meet the leisure interests of people over 55. Contact with many individuals and agencies who are actively involved with people over 55 and the elderly, however, has resulted in insights into the problems of older leisure facility users and led to many useful planning, design and operational suggestions.

A survey of individuals over 55 was conducted by the authors in various communities throughout the U.S. to supplement this information. There were 581 respondents providing information on what they do and would like to do for leisure activities, their physical limitations if any, and demographic information. Chapter 2 blends this and other available material into understandable information for use by planners and designers on the leisure needs and abilities of older people. It points the way towards what kinds of design modifications would be helpful to make facilities more older people user-friendly.

Chapters 3 and 4 define "The Problem" through a review of the current U.S. Federal Handicapped Accessibility requirements and relate these federally mandated requirements to the facility needs of older users.

How many, who they are, and what kinds of facilities are needed at a proposed leisure site are the subjects covered in Chapter 5.

Chapters 6 through 10 provide the technical information on what to do to make leisure sites more user-friendly for older people. They have been organized to provide information on groups of facilities/activities for easy reference: Chapter 6 – Circulation; Chapter 7 – Utilities; Chapter 8 – Activities–Outdoor; Chapter 9 – Activities–Indoor; and Chapter 10 – Details.

These five chapters are not intended as a set of new design standards for the many accepted existing site design criteria. They are rather a series of suggestions on how to modify these accepted standards to make them more compatible, more user-friendly for people as they age. Basic criteria for many of the activities can be found in books like *Architectural Graphics Standards* (the latest edition), *Rules of the Game* (1974, Bantam Books, New York), *Handbook of Sports and Recreational Building Design – 4 Volumes* (the Architectural Press, Ltd., London, 1981). For boating, fishing, camping, and other of the "park" type facilities, refer to *Park Planning Guidelines – 3rd Edition* by George E. Fogg, National Recreation and Park Association, Arlington, Virginia.

A final Chapter, 11 – Operations, touches briefly on the needed interface between the provision of physical facilities and how they are operated and maintained.

It is assumed that a typical site design process will be utilized to determine the needed/desired leisure program and the site's capacity to accommodate these uses. For those readers unfamiliar with such a process please refer to *A Site Design Process* by George E. Fogg, also published by the National Recreation and Park Association.

There is no magic formula to make everything work better for use by older people. Understanding their needs, abilities and interests will help. Common sense is another key factor. These two items combined with **GOOD** design practices will go a long way to solving the needs of this special and rapidly growing segment of our population.

This book is a beginning to establishing answers to the leisure needs and their facility requirements for older people. It is, however, only a beginning in setting guidelines for their planning and operation. Your comments and suggestions to the NRPA or to the authors would be greatly appreciated. They will help make future editions of this book more useful for the providers of the leisure facilities. **More importantly, your comments will make it possible to plan, build and operate better leisure facilities for older people**.

Chapter 1 LEISURE LIFE CYCLE

As each of us grows from infancy to older ages, our interests and our capabilities change. Our needs also change, as do our desires. This first chapter provides information which will give structure to the ever-changing and different needs and desires for leisure activities of people in different age categories. It is a brief summary of the human life cycle as it relates to leisure desires and abilities, and the subsequent and appropriate facility needs of people from birth to death. The age categories used here are related to leisure needs and interests, and may vary somewhat from conventional "break points" found in other literature.

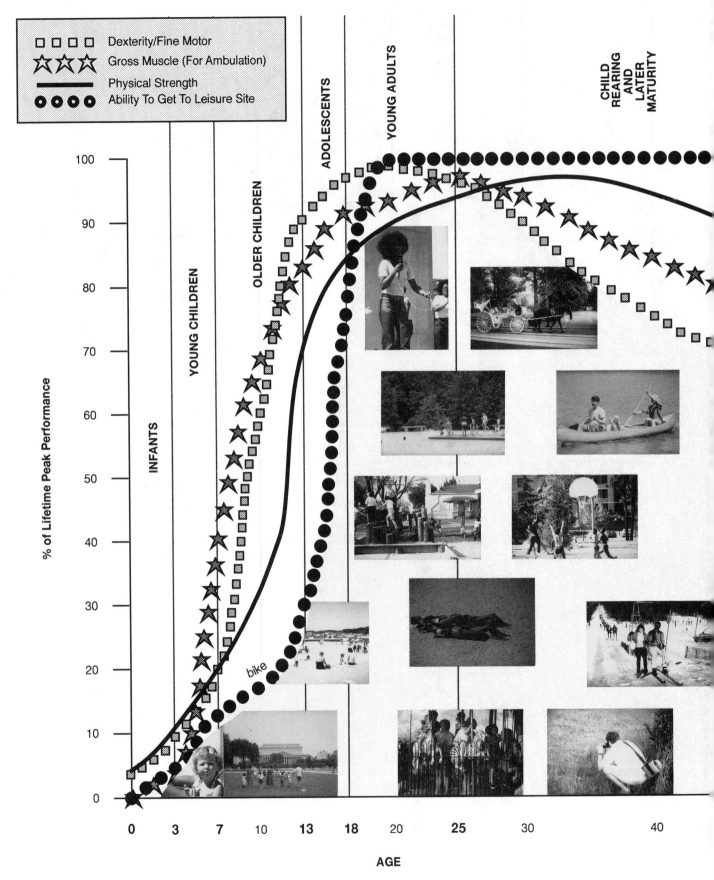

Figure 1.1   *Life Cycle Chart*

Age groups on which this book will focus.

cars & other modes of transportation

PRIME TIMERS

TRANSITION AGES

FRAIL ELDERLY

transport by others

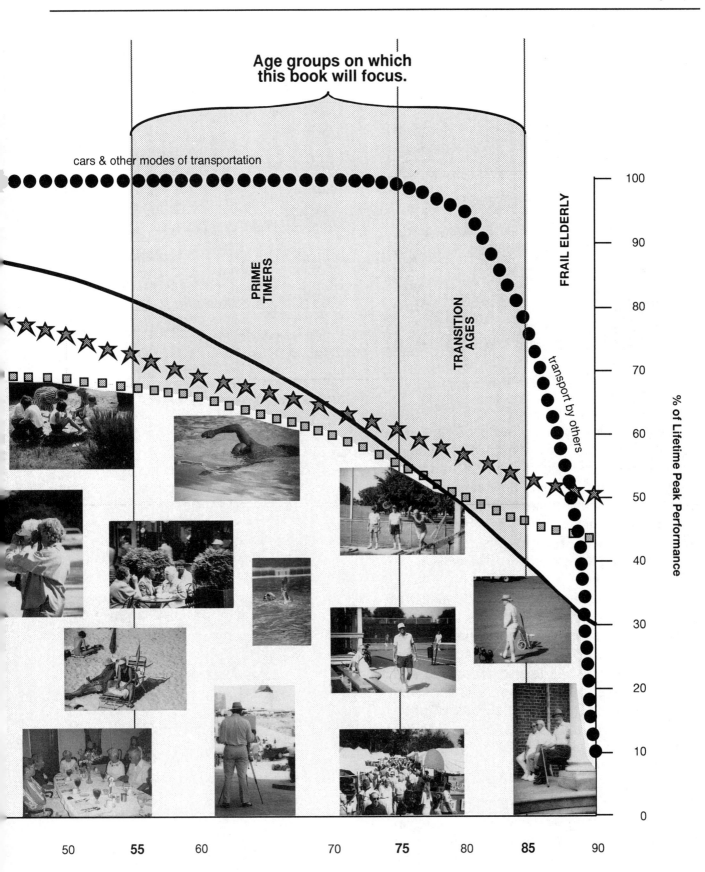

% of Lifetime Peak Performance

100

90

80

70

60

50

40

30

20

10

0

50 **55** 60 70 **75** 80 **85** 90

AGE

INFANTS
0 – 3 YEARS OLD

*Mother and daughter on the beach
– Naples, Florida*

Mobility is limited but improving. Before the age of two (2), much time is spent in developing sensory-motor skills such as hand-eye coordination and learning how safe and predictable is the environment. For example, "if I make a lot of noise, will someone pay attention to me?" **VERY** close supervision is needed during this period.

From the approximate age of two (2) until the end of the third (3rd) year of age, the young person's world has expanded because of increased mobility. Walking skills have improved, and he/she is also expanding and refining levels of mental functioning and understanding. Questions now asked, often privately and to themselves, would include: "If I touch something, is it OK?" "If I cannot touch it, how can I know it?" "Can I taste what I touch?" At this stage they are learning what it is to be a person. And they watch the people around them and look to other cues in the environment to give them the information they need. Mobility has expanded and is still improving, and the need for adult assistance to provide care is total.

Specific Needs And Activities:

• Very close supervision.

• Opportunity to develop fine and gross motor skills.

• Opportunity to explore their surroundings.

• Place for individual play which is done even when other children are present, such as sand digging areas.

• Spaces to be alone, and spaces to interact.

• Controlled environmental conditions, i.e. wind barriers, shade and sun.

• Place for caregivers to sit and talk/visit with other caregivers.

• Easy access for strollers and baby carriages.

YOUNG CHILDREN
4 – 6 YEARS OLD

Wading pool, Codorous State Park – Pennsylvania

Carousel, the Mall – Washington, DC

Although some children may appear to be relatively independent in some respects, continued care by responsible adults is still required. Children in this age range are developing a sense of self-image, gender identity, and learning about who they are as people. These young people need opportunities to explore their limits, which include *encouragement* and *opportunity* to try new activities, and to develop special talents or skills.

Specific Needs And Activities:

- Vigilant supervision.

- Refine gross motor skills, e.g., running, jumping and climbing. Swings and slides become popular activities.

- Refine fine motor skills, e.g., drawing and painting.

- Social play has begun, but is not yet organized. Game rules are beginning to be learned, but are often not understood. Game rules are tested, and often changed by one person or violated. Playmates are often temporary, so social activities may end quickly and individual play is still important.

- Open play spaces with things to see, touch and experience.

- Place for caregivers to sit and talk/visit with other caregivers.

- Safe walks to access park areas, and for bicycles and tricycles to be ridden.

OLDER CHILDREN 7 – 13 YEARS OLD

Children's playground, Sierra School – Sacramento, California

Swimming pool, Little Buffalo State Park – Pennsylvania

Both gross and fine motor skills are well-developed, and the potential for mobility is great. The mobility issue now includes independent or group access **TO** the site, as well as movement around the site itself. Access to the site may be reduced because of lack of transportation options from the home or the school. If the distance and auto traffic allows, bicycle travel may be popular. Adult supervision is still necessary, especially for the lower ages.

Groups are important, but are likely to be small and composed of members of the same sex. Children in this age group are expanding upon experiences from their earlier years, and each is affected very much by his or her family unit. One, two, or a few more close friends may play an important role in a person's life during this time frame, but the family unit is extremely important. Facilities are needed on which individual children and groups of children are able to carry out their activities of physical development, exploration and the expansion of their worlds.

Specific Needs And Activities:

- Larger, more challenging play equipment.

- Open play areas for organized and sports activities such as soccer, basketball, baseball, volleyball, etc.

- Social spaces for noisy gatherings and organized activities that will not disturb other people.

- Sledding and other winter activities.

- Safe walk and bikeway access for the children.

- Paved areas for rollerblading, rollerskating, and possibly skateboarding.

- Places for caregivers to be comfortable while observing the activities.

- Paved areas for court games such as basketball and volleyball.

- Swimming under close supervision.

ADOLESCENTS
14 – 18 YEARS OLD

Sunning on the beach – Naples, Florida

Skiing – Pennsylvania

This age group has greater potential for longer distance access to leisure/recreation sites, but may still be constrained by transportation problems unless they have access to automobile or public transportation. Willingness to use a bicycle is likely to diminish as the members of this age group approach 18. Membership in a peer group is now very important. To be a member of the group to which one aspires to belong is a dominant theme in their lives. There is still a lot of same-sex group behavior, with "best friends" probably males for males, and females for females. The development of male/female relationships now becomes more important than it was earlier, and has an increasing importance in how he or she chooses to spend discretionary time. People in this age range are at the threshold of becoming adults, and are looking for a supportive environment or some significant other person or persons to provide information about what is "OK". We know ourselves by the way other people respond to us, and people in this age range are *very* sensitive to how other people respond to them.

Activities now reflect greater individual choice and freedom. General activities for this age group include both competitiveness, and a high level of peer pressure to conform to group norms. Boys are often socialized to be competitive and to win, and girls are often socialized to be compliant and supportive. There are many exceptions to these general statements about boys and girls among both populations. There is also an ongoing testing of limits, both physical and social. On the surface, pressure to conform and the need to establish one's self as an individual person do not appear to be compatible. For males and females, both needs can be met through individual, group, and team play. People in this age group often wish to include their closest friends in activities, yet want to make their own decisions and demonstrate personal competence in activities of individual choice.

Specific Needs And Activities:

- A full range of competitive facilities for group or team sports, with accommodations for spectators which may include same-sex friends, spectators of the opposite sex, and caregivers.

- Swimming.

- Places to demonstrate individual mastery and compare their skills with those of others, e.g., go-cart racing, a place to race bicycles or motorcycles, rollerblade skating, skateboards, skating, skiing, etc.

- Social spaces, i.e. concerts, dancing, outdoor shows.

- Places to "hang out" with friends which are safe while still offering a sense of freedom and some privacy.

- Solitary activities such as electronic/video games.

YOUNG ADULTS 18 – 25 YEARS OLD

Basketball – Arlington, Virginia

Arts Festival singer – Harrisburg, Pennsylvania

On the average, young adults have a high level of energy and the abilities to engage in a wide range of activities. Sensory and psychomotor functioning are at a peak. There are also stressors in life which may not have been felt at earlier ages. Some people in this age category may be living with parents, or may have moved into a more independent living situation. In addition to earning a living and seeking to establish a career for the future, this time may also include marriage, parenting, divorce, and perhaps the need to maintain a household as a single person. Additional schooling may also be involved. Given the situation wherein most persons have somewhat limited financial resources, leisure activities which are available at a site could be an important element in the quality

of life for that person. This is also true for those people with whom they interact. One example of this is a non-custodial parent with limited financial resources finding activities for weekends or other times when the children are visiting.

Peer pressure is still important, and friendships may continue from earlier years. New friendships also are created from networks of co-workers, neighbors, and other social units, clubs and organizations. Discretionary income, and social and leisure interests vary widely.

Specific Needs And Activities:

- Places for dancing, social activities and parties.

- All organized sports.

- Fishing, hunting and boating.

- Picnicking, swimming, camping.

- Hiking trails and other cross-country activities.

- Thrill activities, e.g., alpine skiing, mountain climbing, water skiing, scuba diving, bungee jumping, etc.

- A place to take children, which is particularly important for non-custodial or single parents.

CHILD-REARING AND LATER MATURITY
25 – 55 YEARS OLD

Canoeing, Presque Isle State Park – Erie, Pennsylvania

Tourism, Independence National Historic Park – Philadelphia, Pennsylvania

Those people who do not live within a family unit larger than two (2) will tend to have greater mobility and often greater discretionary income to spend on leisure activities. For those people who live as a member of a larger family unit, family-related activities often predominate. Generally, friends and relatives become more important as people grow older. There are also physical and sensory changes which are now in process. Vision, taste, hearing, smell, strength, coordination, etc., begin a decline from the levels where they were at younger years. This is often the time when a person's career is a focal point in their life. Occupational stress can become a major factor in health and happiness, and ways to reduce that stress may include participation in a variety of leisure activities.

Specific Needs And Activities:

• Touring by car.

• Swimming, picnicking/barbecue and camping.

Family picnic – Ireland

• Fishing and boating, including a need for docks and ramps.

• Walking/hiking trails and other cross-country activities.

• Some team sports.

• Attending sporting events.

- Attending and/or participating in cultural activities such as plays, concerts, art shows, etc.

- A place to get together with friends and work/business associates.

- A place to spend time with children or adolescents, which is particularly important for non-custodial or single parents.

"PRIME TIMERS"
55 – 75 YEARS OLD

Swimming for exercise – Naples, Florida

The gradual lessening of physical capabilities has continued, but most people in this age range are healthy and capable of a wide range of activities. Also, some people in this age range in the USA today have significant discretionary income and time to engage in a wide range of leisure pursuits. Activities, however, tend to become less "thrill-oriented" than what may have been attractive at an earlier age. Socializing also becomes more important, which includes travel in groups or to places where it is expected that social activities will be a central part of the agenda.

Solitude and the opportunity to do things at one's own pace are also important. Walking

trails and bikeways allow people to engage in activities that are physical, yet allow themselves to pace their own rate and intensity of activity. Watching television is a passive activity in which most people engage throughout their lives. As a person's declining physical limits restrict other activities, television often becomes an increasingly more salient part of a daily agenda. It is also significant to note that people in this age range generally feel and see themselves as being younger than their actual chronological age, and report their health as being "good".

Painting – Mykanos Island, Greece

Specific Needs And Activities:

- Golf, tennis, swimming, horseshoes, shuffleboard, lawn bowling, bocci ball, etc.

Golf, Quail Run Golf Course – Naples, Florida

- Travel, sometimes with groups – especially study tours.
- Attending cultural events such as art shows, concerts, plays, museums, lectures, etc.
- Socializing and dining out.
- Dancing.
- Shopping for pleasure including "window shopping."
- Fishing, including piers and other improved access points.
- Nature study, bird watching, etc.
- Walking and hiking trails with toilets.
- Bicycle trails.
- Opportunity for volunteer activities.
- Television.
- Physical and mental fitness programs and activities, e.g., aerobics, water exercise, board and card games, etc. (both indoor and outdoor games and activities).

TRANSITION
AGES 75 AND ABOVE
(EXCLUDING FRAIL ELDERLY)

Reading at the beach – Naples, Florida

The number of healthy and vigorous people above the age of 75 is growing. The fastest-growing age category in our population is people over the age of 85. Many people in this "oldest of the old" category are very active and independent. Most live alone in their own home or with relatives. Less than 25 percent of the oldest of the old are in assisted living facilities or nursing homes, and approximately 70 percent of the people in this age category are women.

Leisure activities tend to be less vigorous than for younger people. Physical stamina (the "reserve energy" we can draw upon) is considerably reduced, and longer times are needed for resting. Also, transportation to the site now becomes an important issue again. Group travel and appropriate parking facilities are issues for special attention.

Horseshoes – Naples, Florida

Specific Needs And Activities:

- Travel, usually in groups.

- Cards and board games.

- Socializing and dining out.

- Visiting friends and relatives.

- Dancing.

- Shopping for pleasure.

- Fishing, including piers and other improved access points.

- Nature study, bird watching, etc.

*Bird watching, Ding Darling Preserve
– Sanibel Island, Florida*

- Non-impact exercising and swimming.

- Walking trails with frequent rest areas and appropriately located sanitary facilities.

- Sufficient bathrooms and fixtures to accommodate the increased proportion of females in this age category.

- Accessible toilets along trails and at other distant points.

- Opportunity for volunteer activities.

- Television.

- Parking and drop-off areas for vans.

- Physical and mental fitness programs and activities, e.g., low impact exercise, water exercise, board and card games, etc. (both indoor and outdoor game areas and activities).

• Designs should provide for a sense of security, i.e. personal visibility to others, good lighting after dusk, and emergency phones along trails and at other distant points.

FRAIL ELDERLY
(OVER 85 AND AT RISK)

Group tours, Monticello – Charlottesville, Virginia

Some people in this special category live in an assisted living facility or nursing home, and are mostly female. Mobility is limited compared to those who are younger, but there is still a need for activity and to carry out some routine functions. Mental processing and memories may be sharp, but learning new activities may take a bit longer. Although most needs are met within their residential living facility, excursion trips if they are feasible are welcomed changes in routines and environment. Outings are likely to include personnel from the residential facility, and perhaps other family members to help provide transportation and to meet participants' needs.

Specific Needs And Activities:

• Social get-togethers.

• Cards and other board games.

• Television.

• Going out to eat.

Dining for pleasure
– Naples, Florida

• Visiting friends and relatives.

• Non-impact exercising.

- Shaded use spaces including walkways and sitting areas.

- Good lighting indoors, and outdoors after dusk.

- Walkways that are well illuminated, obstacle-free and vision-friendly.

- High security level, including emergency phones.

- Sufficient accessible bathrooms to accommodate the increased proportion of females in this age category.

- Handicapped parking and convenient van drop-off areas.

Chapter 2 PEOPLE OVER 55

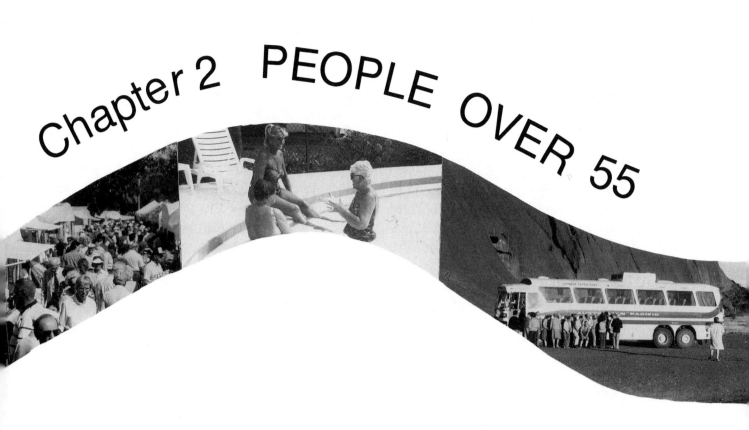

*T*his chapter is intended to expand awareness and to sensitize the reader to special considerations that demand or deserve attention during the planning and implementation processes for provision of leisure facilities. It will also dispel some typical erroneous stereotypes of older people. Although the focus will be on issues involving elderly consumers, many of the same issues could be applied to a variety of handicaps experienced by younger people, and also may be useful in the thoughtful planning of facilities featuring **universal design**. (See Chapter 4 – What is Needed-Universal Design.)

Because of the design and construction expense involved, most leisure facilities are designed to provide functional use over an extended period of time. Time-frames in excess of 25 years are not uncommon. The subject of the **changing** human needs of the consumer population for whom these facilities are designed and intended to serve is one which merits scrutiny and careful consideration by those persons who make the policy, planning, and design decisions. Site supervisors during construction should also be made aware of these broader social issues. Decisions made on site while implementing plans could affect the user-friendly dimensions of the facility. Minor changes during construction can adversely affect the finished project in ways which do not meet the needs of a significant proportion of its intended users.

DEMOGRAPHICS AND THEIR IMPORTANCE

If we look at the people who are in the stores, on the streets, conducting business, and who are generally living and recreating around us, we are likely to notice that larger numbers of them appear to be older than what we remember in the past. The population of the United States is changing in its demographic makeup. There truly is a graying of America in process.

The first U.S. Census was taken in 1790, at which time two (2) percent of the population was over the age of 65. In 1930 (140 years later), only 5.4 percent of the population of the U.S. had attained the age of 65. But in only 50 more years (in 1980) that percentage increased to 11.3 percent, and was 12.6 percent in 1990. By the year 2020, it is projected that 17 percent of our population will be over the age of 65.

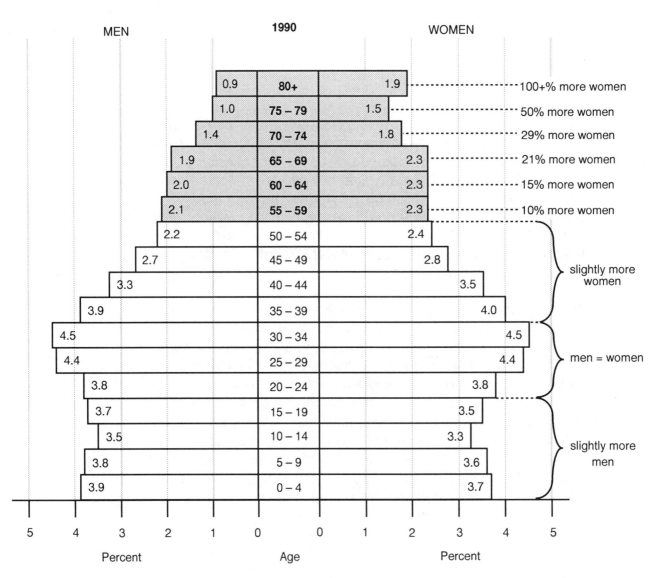

Figure 2.1   *Population Pyramid Chart 1990 (U.S. Bureau of the Census, 1990)*

The 1981 White House Conference on Aging projected that by the year 2050, 62 million people, or 21.7 percent of all Americans will be over the age of 65. The U.S. Bureau of the Census projects that in the year 2050, 10 percent of our population will be over the age of 75. Today, the fastest growing segment of our population is the 85 years old and older group. There are a number of factors which combine to cause this change in our present and projected population makeup, which include improved lifestyles, improved public health and social programs, and advances in

medical technology. The concern is how these changing numbers will impact the planning for facilities which provide access to leisure activities now and into the future.

The change which is occurring is real, and the makeup of the population in which we live will be very different from that of past decades. With a changing population come changing needs. It is important and will be to the reader's advantage to respond in an anticipative and proactive way to the changing needs of the people around us, both today and tomorrow.

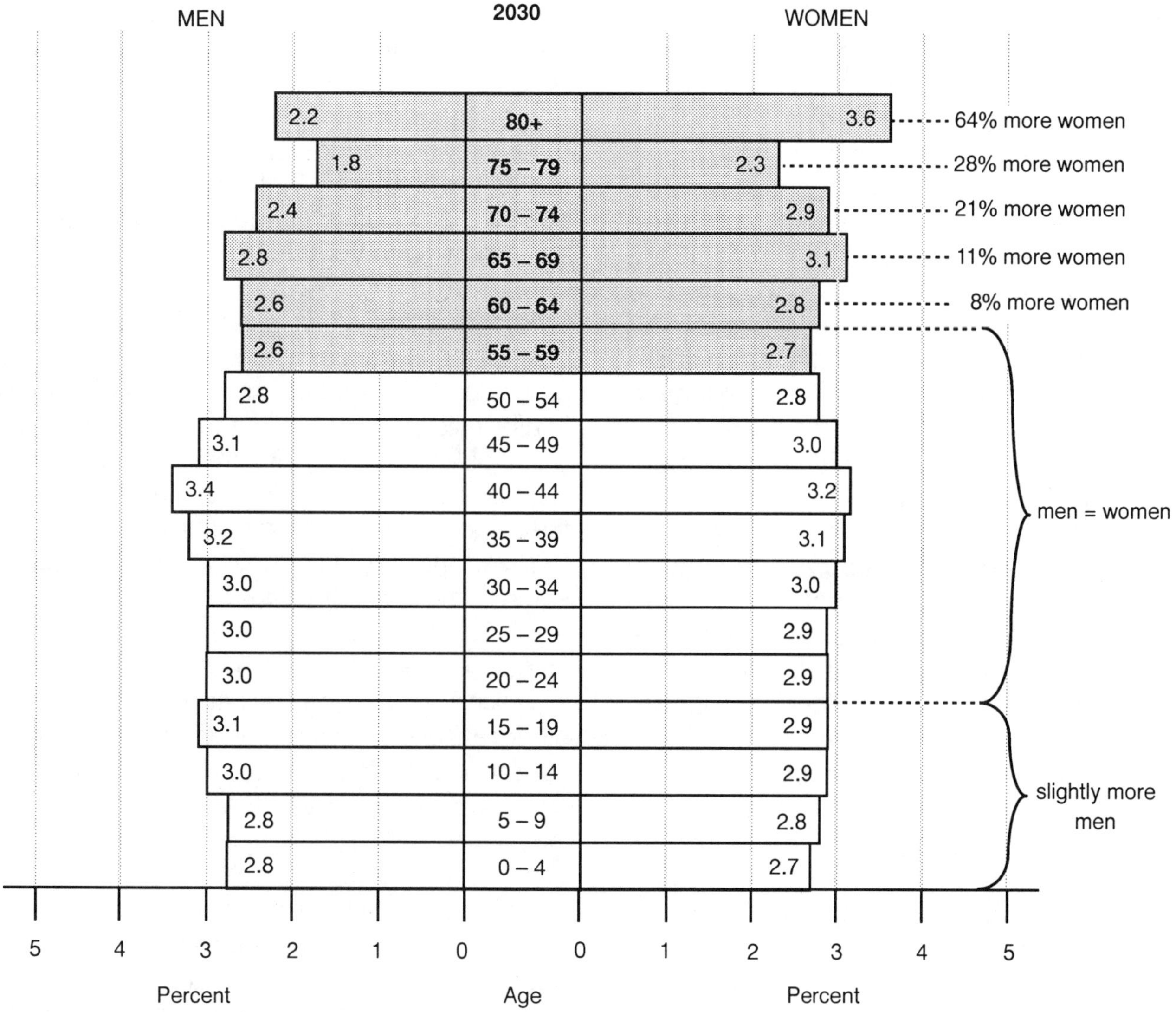

Figure 2.2 *Population Pyramid Chart 2030*
Source: Bouvier, L. Population Reference Bureau, 1980

BELIEFS ABOUT OLDER PERSONS AND THEIR CONSEQUENCES

Stereotypes are sets of **beliefs** that we have about something. The "something" could be an ethnic group, membership in certain religious organizations, age groups of people, etc. We all use stereotypes about people and things, because they make our world an easier place in which to live. Stereotypes are **generalized** beliefs, and are usually **simple**. They give structure to our observations, expectations, and understandings because we believe things which are alike will behave or function in similar ways. This can be very functional, because it is a sort of mental shorthand which allows us to process information more quickly and in greater volume than if we had to consider each element individually.

A stereotype may be wrong, however. Because it generalizes and is simple, it will overlook individual differences and assume that because we call all of the elements by the same name, that they all have the same qualities and characteristics. One example would be that "all elderly people are lonely and helpless." That is an example of potential pitfall. Certainly some elderly people are lonely and helpless, but certainly not all, **and so are some younger people**, but certainly not all. The use of inaccurate stereotypes may lead to less than functional outcomes because the belief system itself is flawed by invalid assumptions and/or incorrect information about a single category of people or things. It follows then that if our belief system about a category of people is flawed, then our decisions, planning, design, and the ultimate outcome of a project which should provide them with the potential for active use of a facility will also be flawed.

What we believe about categories of people, e.g., the elderly, is likely to have a strong effect on how we interact with them as both a social category, and as individual people. Stereotypes of the elderly can be positive or negative. People who live to an old age might be looked upon as being wise, or as having gained the favor of God. Alternatively, they might be seen as a burden, having few if any qualities, skills or abilities of value.

Issues associated with growing older are sometimes avoided because for some people the idea of being elderly brings with it a host of negative stereotyped images. Unlike many other cultures, our culture generally emphasizes youth as being the state which should receive the most positive attention. Messages along that theme are all around us. Youthful images as being desirable bombard us from everywhere from magazine covers, to the story lines and roles assigned to older versus younger people in movie and television scripts. There are relatively few positive, productive images of older persons as compared to youthful roles.

Stereotypes will affect our beliefs about what older persons want and need, and what they are able to do. The way a person is treated is likely to affect his/her own self-image and self-esteem. ". . . if older people receive messages from individuals around them and from the media that they are perceived to be confused, frail, unattractive, and helpless, they are likely to adopt some of these assumptions . . ." (Hooyman and Kiyak, p. 31). A person's self-image or self-esteem is likely to impact the choice of activities in which they engage. Although there may be other reasons or constraints (such as available transportation, etc.), the use or lack of use of leisure facilities which have been designed with the intention of being there for all adults rests to some extent with the self-perception of the potential users. And although choices of leisure activities become more sedentary as a person ages, "compared to a decade ago, older people today are choosing activities far more like those of people twenty years younger than themselves" (Hooyman & Kiyak, p. 363).

Tennis, Fleischmann's Park – Naples, Florida

If the leisure facility is perceived as being a barrier, or in other more subtle ways conveys the message that it is "not intended for me to use," utilization is likely to be low. Examples of these kinds of barriers or messages could include inadequate lighting for older people to see or read menus, instructions, cards, etc., for evening or night-time activities, to an ambivalent or negative attitude toward older users by the operators or attendants of the facility.

From a design standpoint, the ideal and the real must meet in practical ways. To achieve this balance between what *might* be and what *will* be, the planners must understand the needs and desires of those people for whom the leisure facilities are designed. A children's playground, for example, would have considerations which should be mostly related to that age group and their care providers. Facilities designed for adults should be functional, or be, at a minimum, "friendly" for all adults, including those with minor (and perhaps multiple) impairments. In fact, the U.S. Americans with Disabilities Act (ADA) requires that at least some of each type of facility shall be designed for use by the widest range of handicapped users possible. There could be a variety of possible activities which are appropriate for different levels of

fitness and need, such as baseball for some and walking paths for others. In other cases, the special needs of some may be incorporated into the project from the beginning, and will be available for the present and future benefit of all. For example, appropriate lighting configurations could help compensate for problems of people who are visually impaired.

Many problems associated with making facilities user-friendly *begin* when facilities *intended* to be used by specific categories of people do not meet the special needs of some of the users because they were unrecognized or otherwise not included in the planning and design phases. These problems become intensified if those special needs are common among a group of the people the facility was designed to serve, such as older persons. In this case, the lack of understanding by some planners may have a profoundly negative impact on the use of the facility by an increasingly large segment of the public for which the facility was or should have been designed to serve.

Attending cultural events, art show – Naples, Florida

Not everyone likes the same flavor of ice cream. It is reasonable to assume that likewise, different people prefer different types of leisure activities. This becomes evident by noting the wide range of equipment being sold in a typical sporting goods store. Should it be expected that all possible activities be provided at all recreation sites? Of course not. But by excluding particular types of activities which **could** be provided at the site, the planner might also be excluding whole categories of people from using the site as well.

One stereotypical mode of thought about older persons in general is to focus upon what it is believed they **cannot** do, rather than realize how much they **can** do.

Swimming, condominium pool – Naples, Florida

Sightseeing – Ularu National Park, Australia

The healthy, vital, active older person is generally not noticed or remembered. People who are different from the observer are more likely to be noticed and remembered than people who are similar to the observer.

*Stereotype of an old man in the park
– Boston Commons, Massachusetts*

If those noticed differences are then applied to a whole category of people, e.g., older persons, a stereotype has been created which may be correct for a few people, but is being inaccurately and unfairly applied to many others. A worst-case scenario could include implicit beliefs that only people who conform to the stereotypes in the mind of the planner or operator are the "appropriate" users of a recreational facility, and that all others should be excluded by default. This would be a type of modern Social Darwinism where only the "fittest" should be provided services, and the rest should simply stay away. And if they **do** stay away, that is then taken as "proof" that they had no interest in using the facility in the first place, and hence do not need facilities or services to be provided for them. The flawed nature of this type of logic is evident.

The interface between an older person and the environment is often less than satisfactory. One effective way to approach this interface would be to take a more holistic appraisal of how the physical environment and the social needs complement each other. Many unsatisfactory outcomes occur simply because of unknown user needs or mistaken beliefs of the designer and operators. As stated by Hiatt (1986), "Often, there is no advocate or informed **and** vocal supporter of environmental issues. We all feel like environmental experts; [similarly] by referring to our own needs, we feel we can satisfy the requirements of older people" (p. 31). This statement applies to the issue facing a broad spectrum of designers, planners and operators. The willingness and the capacity to be educated and informed about the changing population and the needs of **ALL** of its citizens is critical to all those involved with the provision of user facilities.

Designers, and to some extent operators, are separated from the changing "real world" and the needs of older people. Most design is done by people under 55, and more generally by people between 25 and 40 years old who are in an age group which typically has little or no experience with what older persons want or can do. Their individual experience is likely to be limited to observing some older family members, acquaintances, and strangers from afar, and their beliefs are often reflected in the stereotypes which they have formed or accepted without seriously questioning their accuracy. In an effort to expand upon some of these issues, information will

follow in this and subsequent chapters on special needs and general desires of older people for which planners, designers, and operators should be aware.

SOCIAL AGING

As we move through our life course, the time and place where each of us was born makes an impact upon our experiences. There is a difference in experiences which makes us different than people who were born before us and those who were born later, but similar to those born at the same time and place. In casual conversation we sometimes use the term "generational differences." Another term which allows more precise sociological description and comparison is **cohort group**. A cohort group refers to people who were born at the same time in history. Because of being born at the same time (and sometimes further defined as also including some similar variables relating to culture and society), the members have similar experiences. Because we are all aging, the cohort group to which each person belongs is also growing older as its members occupy the same **age strata** at the same time. Age strata refer to social statuses such as child, young adult, retirement age, etc., as shown in Chapter 1. This aging and changing process of the members of a cohort group is called a **cohort flow**.

Most members of a cohort group will never meet each other, yet their similar experiences often result in shared ideas, values and attitudes. To illustrate, some examples of cohort groups in our society would be: people who were adolescents or young adults during the Great Depression; during World War II; during the 1960's; and draft-related or motivated military service during the Vietnam War. The adolescent and young adult members of each of these cohort groups had different experiences of what it was like to move into adulthood's roles and responsibilities. These often resulted in different values, desires, attitudes and norms through their life cycle.

For example, people who lived during the Great Depression era are more likely to save things, including materials such as string, paper, and worn-out items which "maybe could be fixed," than do people who grew up during the prosperous 1950's and 1960's. Even age at first marriage and childbearing patterns were affected by cohort group membership. People during the Great Depression era postponed both marriage and childbearing far longer than those in the 1950's and 1960's.

Leisure activities may vary significantly by not only gender and culture, but also by cohort group. The activities preferred by older people today are likely to be similar to those activities which they preferred in their earlier adult years. Although more research needs to be done in this area, this is pointed out here to suggest that preferred activities do not necessarily change because of the aging process alone. Transportation and loss of partners for social activities may have an impact. Physiological processes of aging create some changes in perceptual and motor functioning. **More importantly, however, is the fact that the patterns of leisure activity which were established earlier in life are likely to persist so long as there is the opportunity to continue those activities with a successful outcome.** Kelly (1982 and 1987) pointed out that people tend to have a "core" of leisure activities which remain with them throughout their life. Atchley (1991) stated that "Because activity patterns established in early adulthood tend to persist and because what is fashionable in the way of activities varies from time to time and between social groups, it seems safe to assume that no single standard can be used to determine the 'adequacy' of activity pat-

terns among mature adults" (p. 238). It follows then that the method of remaining involved with those activities, and the decision-making process whereby one selects which activities may need to be later discontinued or modified for physical, social, economic or other reasons, will revolve around the continued availability of the facilities for the activities of that core of long-term preferences.

Older minorities' participation in leisure activities parallels the previous statements. One recent nationwide recreation survey by Michael B. Brown, Ph.D. of 1653 older white, Hispanic, American Indian and black adults concluded that "Today's older blacks were shut out of [so many] leisure activities for so long that they just don't even think about such things." He believes skin color and ethnicity will have less influence on future generations' activities. "The whole thing of race is going to disappear for those now in their 20's and 30's." (Brown, p. 9)

SUPPORTIVE RESEARCH

The authors conducted survey research in 1992-1993, collecting data from a sample of 581 people over the age of 55. The majority of respondents were over the age of 65. The mean age for the sample was 70.7, and included responses from males and females from seven states across the United States. Evaluation of the data showed preferences for several types of activities; walking, dining and shopping were the most highly rated across the sample.

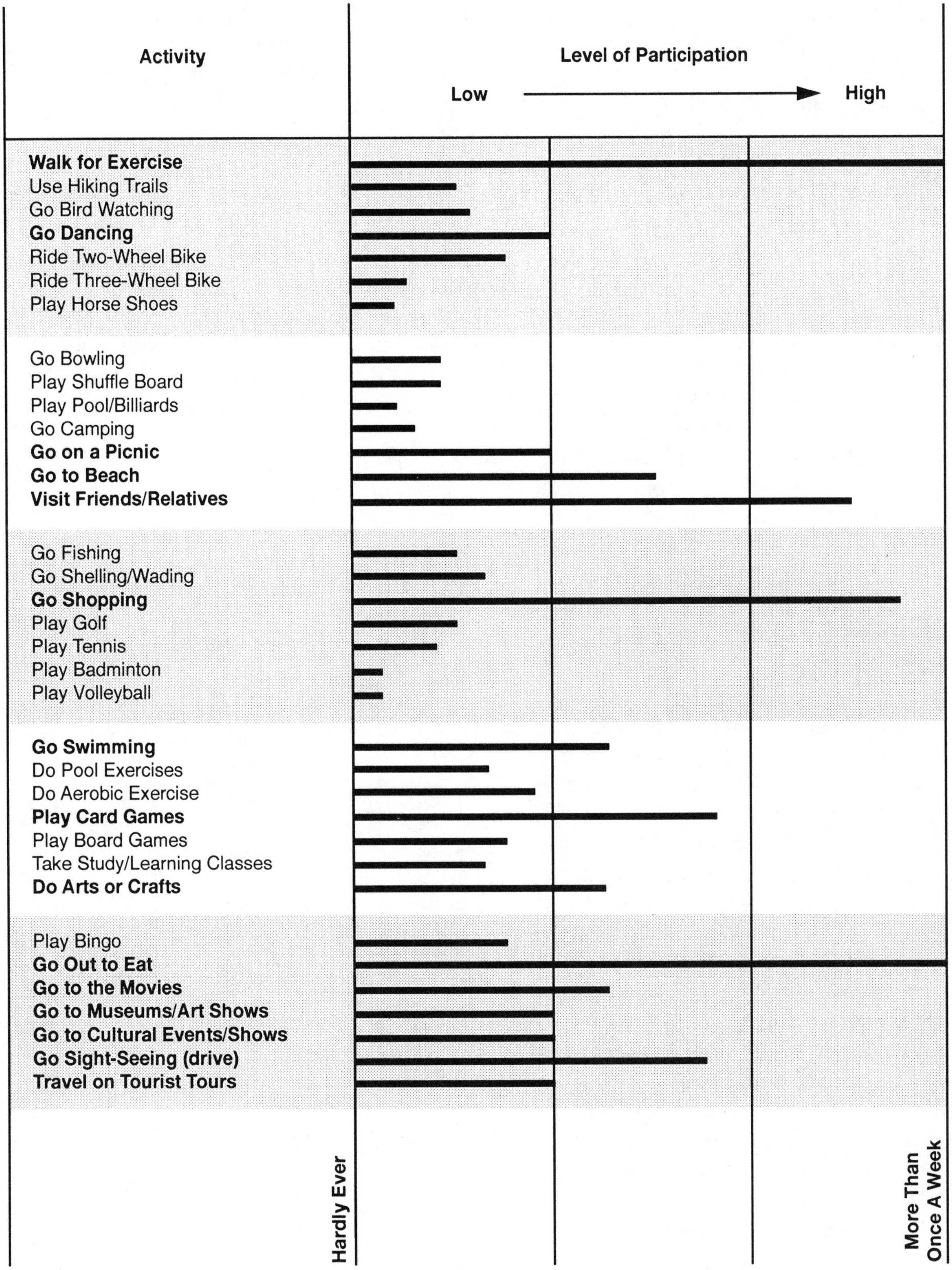

Activity

Level of Participation

Low ⟶ High

Walk for Exercise
Use Hiking Trails
Go Bird Watching
Go Dancing
Ride Two-Wheel Bike
Ride Three-Wheel Bike
Play Horse Shoes

Go Bowling
Play Shuffle Board
Play Pool/Billiards
Go Camping
Go on a Picnic
Go to Beach
Visit Friends/Relatives

Go Fishing
Go Shelling/Wading
Go Shopping
Play Golf
Play Tennis
Play Badminton
Play Volleyball

Go Swimming
Do Pool Exercises
Do Aerobic Exercise
Play Card Games
Play Board Games
Take Study/Learning Classes
Do Arts or Crafts

Play Bingo
Go Out to Eat
Go to the Movies
Go to Museums/Art Shows
Go to Cultural Events/Shows
Go Sight-Seeing (drive)
Travel on Tourist Tours

Hardly Ever

More Than
Once A Week

Figure 2.3 *From unpublished data collected by George E. Fogg and Robert F. Fulton in 1992 – 1993.*

The preliminary evaluation results are consistent with other research published in the field (Lawton, Moss and Fulcomer, 1986-87; and Tinsley, Colbs, Teaff and Kauffman, 1987).

PHYSIOLOGICAL AGING AND SOCIAL/PSYCHOLOGICAL IMPLICATIONS

How well a person can cope with the immediate environment is often what makes one individual stand out in the crowd and another person be barely noticed. A particular elderly person who is having problems with stairs, doors, or other taken-for-granted activities will be noticed because they are different. Perhaps the primary reason they are having difficulties (and are then noticed as being different) is because of how their environment had been designed by its planners, or maintained by its operators.

Physiological situations can spread like a ripple in a pond to affect both social and psychological issues. The subjects become interrelated because most people do not like to be embarrassed. Standing out in a crowd, and especially being perceived in a negative way, is a powerful source of embarrassment regardless of a person's age. (Think about how you feel standing in front of a crowd with all eyes upon you. And then imagine yourself not doing well while you are in that situation.) This is an example of how physiological changes which involve some loss in physical functions may become transformed into a social or a psychological situation with which an older person has to deal with at the moment, and may try to avoid in the future. There is also a sense of asking one's self "who am I right now, and how do I feel about that?" Older people often cope with a partial loss of physical functioning which results in a less-than-positive outcome by giving up activities. The success of the older person in

being able to successfully use the facility is an important variable in measuring the success of the planner and/or operator in providing adequate professional services for the site.

The ages to which males and females can expect to live also vary. On the average, females outlive males in all age categories. Men die at younger ages. As age increases, women outnumber men in increasingly greater proportions. In the year 2000, there will be 78 men between the ages of 65 – 74 for every 100 women. There will be only 60 men between the ages of 75 – 84, and 38 men over the age of 85, for every 100 women in each of those age groups (Atchley, 1991).

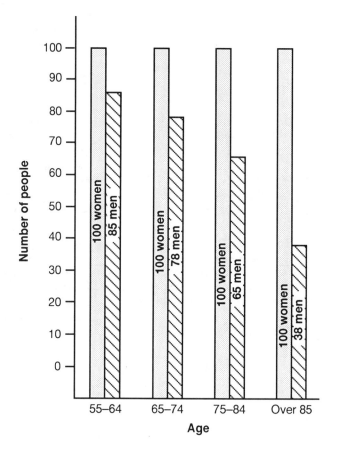

Figure 2.4   *Projected differences in the numbers of men & women over 55 in the year 2000.*

Knowing this, it becomes apparent that sanitary facilities will need to accommodate what will be a changing ratio of male/female users in those age groups. One example of this change in male/female ratio translates into an increased number of sanitary facilities including assistive stalls in the women's rest rooms.

VISION:

Individuals differ, but it is estimated that an elderly person needs anywhere from two to five times more light to see at the same level of illumination than he or she needed at the age of 20. This is because of a thickening and yellowing of the lens of the eye. One general rule of thumb to meet the increased need is: 50 foot-candles for general work, and 100 for close work. But this itself may contribute to a second problem. The elderly tend to be very sensitive to reflected glare and unshielded bright light sources. Glaring light, including bright sunlight off a shiny floor, (wet asphalt roads with oncoming headlights at night, etc.) tends to cause the eyes to tear, headaches, and a general state of discomfort. In a leisure facility, rather than stay in the discomfort caused by bright glare, the person may move to a darker area of the room where there is inadequate light for them to successfully conduct an activity which involves reading or other visual acuity. They may also choose to not drive at night at all for reasons of safety.

The yellowing of the eye lens also creates a change in color perception. Although pastel colors are generally pleasant to most people, when this change occurs soft pastel colors are difficult or impossible to distinguish from each other. Also, the color blue tends to take on a green hue. Using colors as a means of direction, e.g., "the blue door, or the mauve-carpeted hall," may cause confusion. Rather than seeing colors as a younger person might perceive them, the older person is best able to see the bright colors such as red or orange, and to best distinguish contrasts between very light and very dark colors which are placed in juxtaposition.

In addition to a loss in visual acuity, there is a loss in depth perception. Because depth perception has also been associated throughout a person's lifetime with differences in shades of light and dark because of shadows, by placing dark colors next to lighter ones, the contrast might be perceived as a step up or down, or an object to be avoided.

Stairway, Powers Court Estate, 1850's – Ireland

For that reason, patterns which might cause confusion should be avoided on flat or open areas. However, contrast could be used to advantage on stairs, curbs, or other potential hazards. One suggestion might be to use contrasting shades of light and dark on steps and the risers.

For reasons given above, vision at dusk and night can be especially difficult for the older person. Adequate light is necessary, yet bright, unshielded lights cause discomfort. Possible solutions to this problem are provided in Chapter 8.

For written instructions, directions, programs, agendas, etc., to be more easily readable by anyone with a vision impairment, one helpful effort would be increasing the size of the typeface.

This is a 14-point typeface. The larger size may very well make the difference between a person with a vision impairment being able to read, or not being able to read, what is important to them.

HEARING:

The optimal range of human hearing is from 20 – 20,000 hz, and the range of human speech is from 250 – 3,000 hz. The hearing range which is most likely to be reduced or lost as we age begins with the higher-pitched tones. Within spoken communication, sounds in the typical female voice range, and the voice range of most children, are the first to be reduced or lost for both males and females. This is in addition to loss of the high-frequency "consonant" sounds in our language, such as the sounds of *f*, *s*, *h*, *ch*, and *sh*. For example, the word "farm" might be heard as "arm". Some loss of hearing begins at the 8,000 hz range and above at about the age of 40 for most people, then moves lower to the 6,000 hz range and below. This loss is gradual and usually not noticed at first, because there are few occasions where the loss creates an obvious problem. But by the age of 65, both males and females are likely to have a hearing loss for frequencies above 1,000 hz which is significant compared to people of younger ages. One example of planning to deal with this change in hearing is knowing that telephone receivers have a typical range of 300 – 3,000 hz (Favaro, 1993).

Many readers have probably experienced airport, bus or train station announcements which were unintelligible; they simply could not be understood even by someone with good hearing and a knowledge of the language. In contrast to an excellent sound system, in-the-ceiling speakers are more likely to broadcast garbled, lost or confused messages, especially if the announcements are presented above 1,000 hz (Favaro, 1993).

Loss of hearing acuity may also include a reduced ability to separate sounds from each other, e.g., conversation from background noise. Reverberation within a room involves only milliseconds of difference for the sensation of sound echoes, and can be distracting for anyone because of problems created with distortion and discrimination of sounds. For people with partial hearing loss (which is virtually everyone over the age of 40, and progressively worse with increasing age), reverberation becomes a potentially serious problem.

Within buildings, most "noise" is below 1000 hz. Voice conversation and consonants are above 1000 hz, and are at risk of being lost or confused in the background noise.

OTHER PHYSIOLOGY:

As a person moves into old age, there is a tendency for many things to change. A person with **heart or respiratory** problems needs grades which are less steep, and frequent places to stop and rest. The **balance point** of the body may shift slightly forward, especially if there is a tendency toward Parkinson's Disease. An elderly person may also have a tendency to walk on the balls of his or her feet, with a slight forward tilt in posture. Instead of a single balance point which is stable, the balance point may rotate slightly all the while the person is standing upright.

This is a significant insight for the design of ramps. Someone with a slight forward lean is more likely to lose his or her balance while walking down a steep ramp than is someone who is younger. And again, what is comfortable for the designer is not necessarily comfortable for other people. A hand rail on both sides of the ramp would be an added safety feature, and would allow a person to choose the side of the ramp to walk on while descending. See Chapter 2 – ADA for minimum requirements.

Bladder functions also change with increased age. For people over the age of 70, the bladder is less elastic and is able to hold only about 50% of the volume possible at an earlier age. In a practical sense, this means there is more need for bathroom facilities to be available at many locations, rather than one or two central facilities to serve large areas.

The need for *shelter* from the *sun* is often thought necessary simply to avoid the discomfort of sunburn. However, prescription medications often require the avoidance of prolonged exposure to direct sunlight for health reasons directly related to use of the medications. In addition to medication-based reasons, there has been a growing concern of the population in general with prolonged exposure to direct sunlight. Frequent shaded areas are likely to be appreciated by all site users, whether they be young, middle-aged, or older — another example of "universal design" approach.

Ambulation and Grasping Abilities: Older age may also bring with it difficulties in ambulation, and a decrease in the ability to grip with the hands and to twist. Riser tread ratio on stairs should be carefully considered. Doors and other areas of passage not on the accessible way should also allow for people using assistive walking devices such as canes and "walkers," to open the doors eas-

ily. Heavy door closers can create serious barriers. Doors, if they have latches, should have levers rather than knobs. Bathroom spigots should be automatic or have lever controls. Round grips or controls of all kinds should be avoided whenever there is an alternative, even if the alternative is a special order, will take a little longer to get, or is more costly. These are not areas in which to attempt budget reduction; these are issues which will have direct impact upon the ability of the elderly to successfully utilize the area now and in the future.

Quality leisure time is how it is defined by any person at any age. *Walking* is a popular activity among elderly persons, and among people who are younger, also. Along with old age comes an increased need for more time to get from place to place, and perhaps a feeling of less urgency to hurry along. Places to sit indoors at points between long distance areas would be desirable, as well as rest areas on landings on stairways. Numerous shaded outdoor places to stop and sit, especially along walking paths, would likely contribute to the ongoing health and to the increased usage by all visitors.

LONGER TERM IMPLICATIONS:

In looking to the future, it can be reasonably predicted that larger numbers of older people will be looking for ways to be more active in their leisure pursuits as well as ways to maintain their health. Physical fitness has shown itself to be important to our population in general. Many people who are older are currently engaged in leisure and exercise activities, and as the younger cohort groups who are already active move into their older years, there will continue to be a growing demand for these services. ". . . recreation and leisure service delivery systems overall will be held more accountable to meeting the needs of this constituency group at a greater rate in the very near future." (Colston, L., p. 37). Other than the traditional methods of deciding what activities to provide, e.g., water aerobics (especially in warmer climates and indoor pools), the opportunity to be creative and responsive offers challenges and opportunities to planners and operators.

Chapter 3   CURRENT GUIDELINES

*The Americans With Disabilities Act (ADA), one of the newest Federal legislative efforts, and its attendant regulations are the current focus on providing accessible facilities. ADA, Public Law 101-336, was passed in 1990 and signed into law on July 26, 1990. The general purpose of the law is (1) to eliminate discrimination against people with disabilities, (2) to establish national goals regarding people with disabilities, and **(3) to enable all individuals access to every area of American life**. The Act has 5 major areas; Title II–Local Government and Title III–Businesses have the most significant impact on the provision of leisure facilities and services. They, in essence, state that government and businesses shall **not exclude** an individual from participation in or the use of its programs and/or facilities due to their physical limitations.*

*The Act's intent is to make it possible for **ALL** people to enjoy life (and this includes all leisure pursuits) in the most integrated setting possible — a setting which enables the interaction between **all** people to the maximum extent feasible. Provision of accessible facilities is generally based on the Uniform Federal Accessibility Standards (UFAS) – many of which are incorporated into ADA – the American National Standards Institute (ANSI) A. 117.1, and the Design Guide for Accessible Outdoor Recreation by the U.S. Department of the Interior (still in draft form as of this writing). Finally, the ADA Accessibilities Guidelines for Buildings and Facilities published in the Federal Register Volume 56, #144 provides guidance in the needed minimal requirements. A summary of the applicable site guidelines follows with notations on other appropriate factors that should be considered for enhanced older-people accessibility and enjoyment.*

It should be clearly understood that most people when they reach 55 or 65 or even 75 are **not handicapped** and definitely do not consider themselves handicapped. Many of the requirements of ADA will have a beneficial impact on accessibility for older people. Some, unfortunately, will cause problems, i.e. raised toilets for handicapped accessibility which are almost impossible for smaller and older people to use!

FEDERAL ACCESSIBILITY STANDARDS

Accessible Routes

Please refer to the latest published rules in the *Federal Register* for current and complete requirements.

This book focuses on site requirements and is only involved with the interface area on buildings between indoor and outdoor spaces/activities. ADA/UFAS require that all facilities available to the public must have within the site at least one accessible route with a minimum clear width of 914 mm (36") from public transportation stops, accessible parking spaces, passenger loading zones (if provided), public streets and sidewalks to all **public** buildings and facilities. This route shall, to the maximum extent feasible, coincide with the commonly used general public route. It shall be as level as possible with any slopes greater than 1:20 (5%) conforming to the requirements of ramps. Keep accessible ways as short as possible.

Handicapped accessibility – It's the law, The Conservancy – Naples, Florida

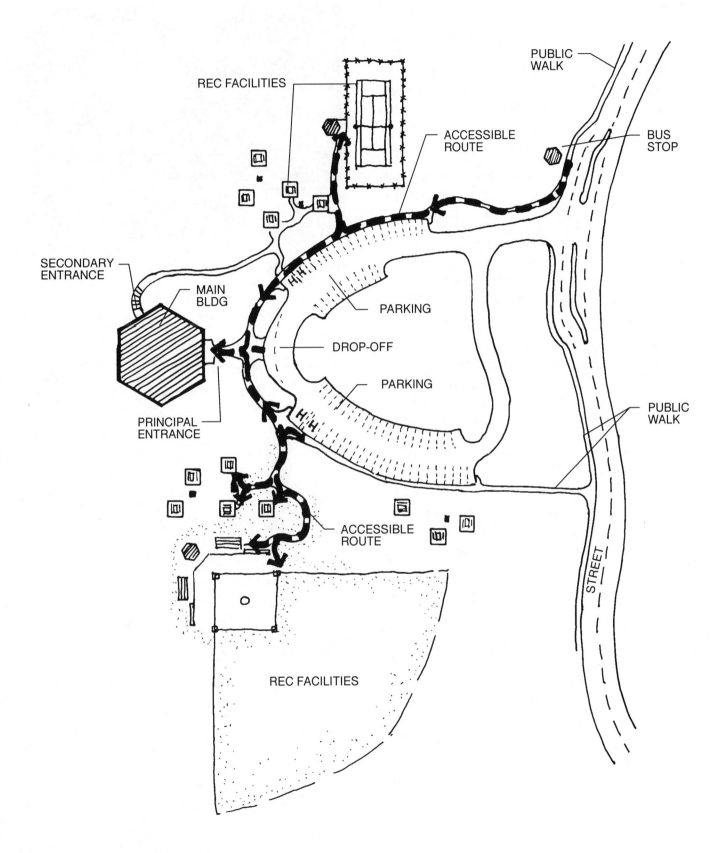

REC FACILITIES

PUBLIC WALK

ACCESSIBLE ROUTE

BUS STOP

SECONDARY ENTRANCE

MAIN BLDG

PARKING

DROP-OFF

PARKING

PRINCIPAL ENTRANCE

PUBLIC WALK

ACCESSIBLE ROUTE

STREET

REC FACILITIES

Figure 3.1 *Accessible Route*

Notes

- Not every part of every area of the site needs to be accessible. A reasonable and usable number of each type of facility or activity space must be available to people with special needs. Please refer to appropriate UFAS standards where available and use common sense on other facilities.

- The accessible walk shall connect all accessible facilities and shall be continuous.

- There shall be no objects protruding into or placed in this accessible way. Any obstacle must be a maximum of 680 mm (27") from the accessible way surface. See Figure 3.1.

- The surface of accessible routes shall be stable, hard, reasonably smooth, skid resistant and have a reasonably level cross slope (2% maximum). Sand, mulch, gravel, cobblestones, etc., are not acceptable.

- Handicapped parking shall be provided on the accessible way. See Figure 3.2.

- Changes in level greater than 13 mm (1/2") shall be considered an obstruction and requires a ramp or mechanical lift to get over it.

- Any running slope in excess of 1:20 (5%) shall be considered a ramp.

- Resting places – benches and wheelchairs shall be located outside of the accessible path right-of-way.

Benches and tables located outside of accessible way – Washington, DC

Total Parking in Lot	Minimum Required Handicapped Parking
1 to 25	1
26 to 50	2
51 to 75	3
76 to 100	4
101 to 150	5
151 to 200	6
201 to 300	7
301 to 400	8
401 to 500	9
501 to 1000	2% of Total
1001 and over	20 + 1 for each 100 over 1000

Figure 3.2 *Required Number of Handicapped Parking Spaces**

*There are exceptions. See the ADA Standards for additional information.

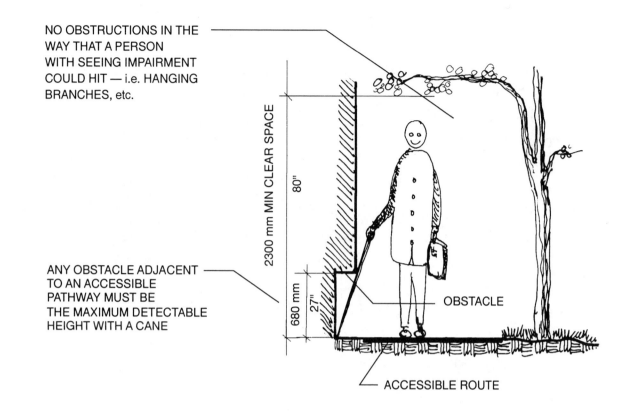

NO OBSTRUCTIONS IN THE WAY THAT A PERSON WITH SEEING IMPAIRMENT COULD HIT — i.e. HANGING BRANCHES, etc.

ANY OBSTACLE ADJACENT TO AN ACCESSIBLE PATHWAY MUST BE THE MAXIMUM DETECTABLE HEIGHT WITH A CANE

2300 mm MIN CLEAR SPACE

80"

680 mm

27"

OBSTACLE

ACCESSIBLE ROUTE

Figure 3.3   *Obstacles/Headroom*

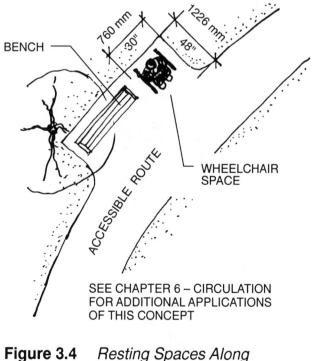

BENCH

760 mm

30"

1226 mm

48"

ACCESSIBLE ROUTE

WHEELCHAIR SPACE

SEE CHAPTER 6 – CIRCULATION FOR ADDITIONAL APPLICATIONS OF THIS CONCEPT

Figure 3.4   *Resting Spaces Along An Accessible Route*

Handicapped parking space design requirements are set up to enable a wheelchair-bound person to get out of the car and onto the accessible way (see Figures 3.4 and 3.5). See Chapter 6 – Circulation for suggested parking lot and parking space modifications from standard designs.

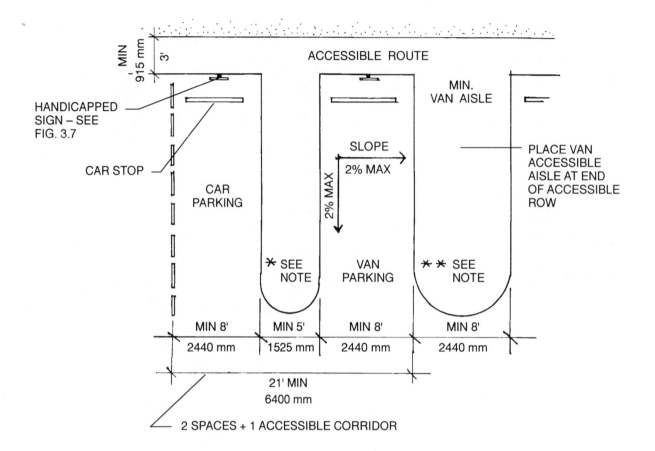

Figure 3.5   *Handicapped Parking
Space Dimensions*

*Note: 12% of handicapped spaces (minimum of 1) shall be van accessible 2440 mm (96") minimum width, with the space located on right side of van.

**Ramp access to get up to curb height is frequently not possible from a van side door. Therefore, if curbing is used around the parking lot, there must be a minimum clearance of 2895 mm (9'6") at right angle to the van.

Handicapped parking sign

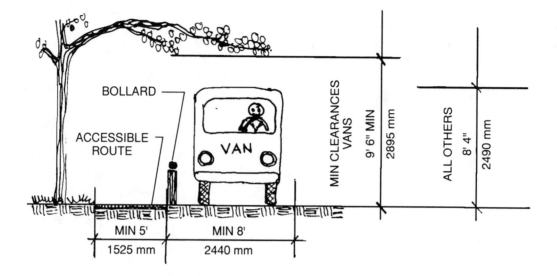

BOLLARD

ACCESSIBLE ROUTE

VAN

MIN CLEARANCES VANS 9' 6" MIN 2895 mm

ALL OTHERS 8' 4" 2490 mm

MIN 5' 1525 mm

MIN 8' 2440 mm

Figure 3.6 *Vertical Clearance in Handicapped Parking & Loading Areas*

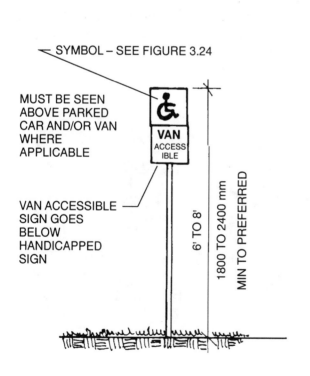

SYMBOL – SEE FIGURE 3.24

MUST BE SEEN ABOVE PARKED CAR AND/OR VAN WHERE APPLICABLE

♿ VAN ACCESS IBLE

VAN ACCESSIBLE SIGN GOES BELOW HANDICAPPED SIGN

6' TO 8' 1800 TO 2400 mm MIN TO PREFERRED

Figure 3.7 *Handicapped Sign Placement*

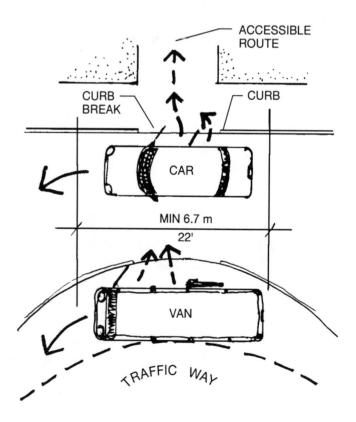

ACCESSIBLE ROUTE

CURB BREAK

CURB

CAR

MIN 6.7 m 22'

VAN

TRAFFIC WAY

Figure 3.8 *Drop-off/Loading Zone*

Wheelchair Requirements Regarding Accessibility

Most accessible route requirements needed to meet ADA and UFAS guidelines are formulated around the needs of wheelchair users.

Wheelchairs need the following minimum spaces.

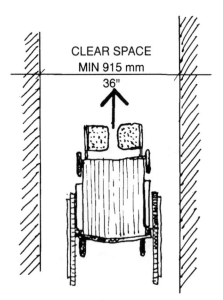

SINGLE DIRECTION CORRIDOR
IS NOT RECOMMENDED FOR
PUBLIC SPACES

Figure 3.9   *Single Direction Corridor or Accessible Route*

Minimum width for 2 wheelchairs to pass is 1525 mm (60") – the same clear space needed for turning around.

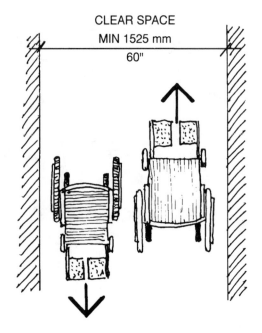

Figure 3.10   *2-Way Accessible Route*

The minimum clear resting space for a wheelchair with occupant is 760 mm (30") x 1220 mm (48").

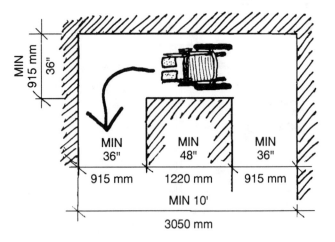

Figure 3.11   *90° Turn Space*

Note: The wider the aisle, the shorter the space needed, i.e. the important measurement is 3050 mm (10').

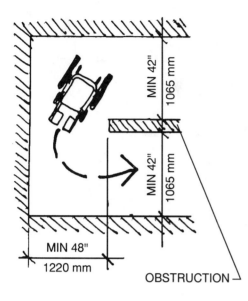

Figure 3.12 *Clearance Around An Obstruction*

Ramps & Curb Cuts

Sites with vertical changes in elevation – natural or manmade – which exceed slopes of 8%

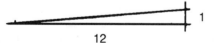

or a 6.5 mm (1/4") vertical rise require ramps.

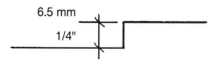

ACTUAL SIZE

Figure 3.13 *Minimum Vertical Rise Requiring Ramps*

These ramps must meet the following criteria: Any portion of the access way over 5% shall be considered a ramp and must comply with the ramp requirements or have mechanical lifts to move people over these obstacles. These same criteria also apply to ingress and egress to swimming pools, and to some extent to natural beaches (see Chapter 8).

Curb Cuts

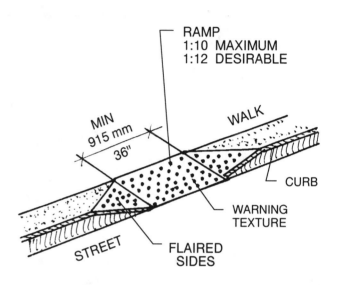

Figure 3.14 *Curb Cut Detail*

Typical warning texture for visually impaired at walk/road intersection – Florida

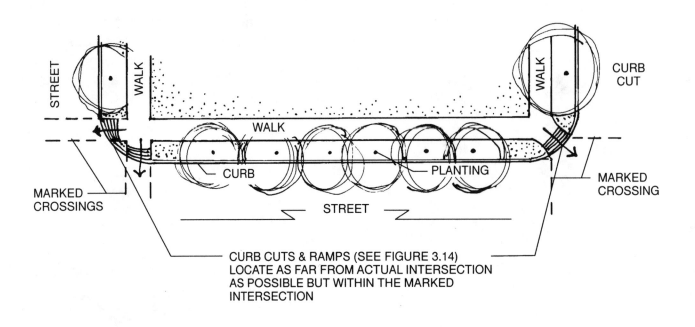

Figure 3.15   *Curb Cut Locations*

Curb cuts that infringe on the adjacent walkway are not desirable unless the walk is sufficiently wide to have a 915 mm (36") minimum clear way in addition to the ramp.

A built-up curb ramp can be used in parking lots where the ramp does not interfere with traffic or does not serve as access for van parking. A built-up curb ramp is generally not a good solution for most parking lot situations.

Ramps

The design of any outdoor spaces will require the use of ramps. They take a lot of room and frequently are a major visual feature. Ramps, therefore, must be carefully considered from the earliest design stages. See Chapters 6 and 10 for suggested additions for people over 55.

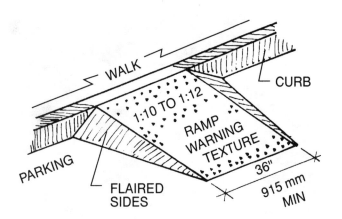

Figure 3.16   *Curb Ramp*

"Handicapped Ramp", ADA required and usable by all – Lee County Sports Complex, Florida

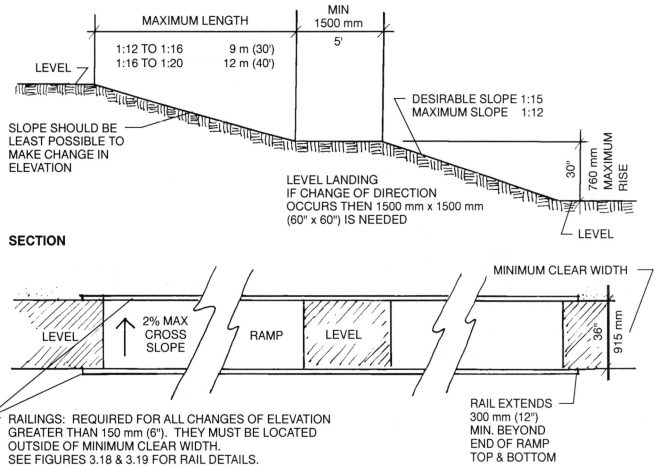

MAXIMUM LENGTH

MIN
1500 mm
5'

1:12 TO 1:16   9 m (30')
1:16 TO 1:20   12 m (40')

LEVEL

DESIRABLE SLOPE 1:15
MAXIMUM SLOPE   1:12

SLOPE SHOULD BE
LEAST POSSIBLE TO
MAKE CHANGE IN
ELEVATION

30"   760 mm MAXIMUM RISE

LEVEL LANDING
IF CHANGE OF DIRECTION
OCCURS THEN 1500 mm x 1500 mm
(60" x 60") IS NEEDED

LEVEL

SECTION

MINIMUM CLEAR WIDTH

LEVEL

2% MAX
CROSS
SLOPE

RAMP

LEVEL

36"   915 mm

RAILINGS: REQUIRED FOR ALL CHANGES OF ELEVATION
GREATER THAN 150 mm (6"). THEY MUST BE LOCATED
OUTSIDE OF MINIMUM CLEAR WIDTH.
SEE FIGURES 3.18 & 3.19 FOR RAIL DETAILS.

RAIL EXTENDS
300 mm (12")
MIN. BEYOND
END OF RAMP
TOP & BOTTOM

PLAN

Figure 3.17 *Ramps*

Railings

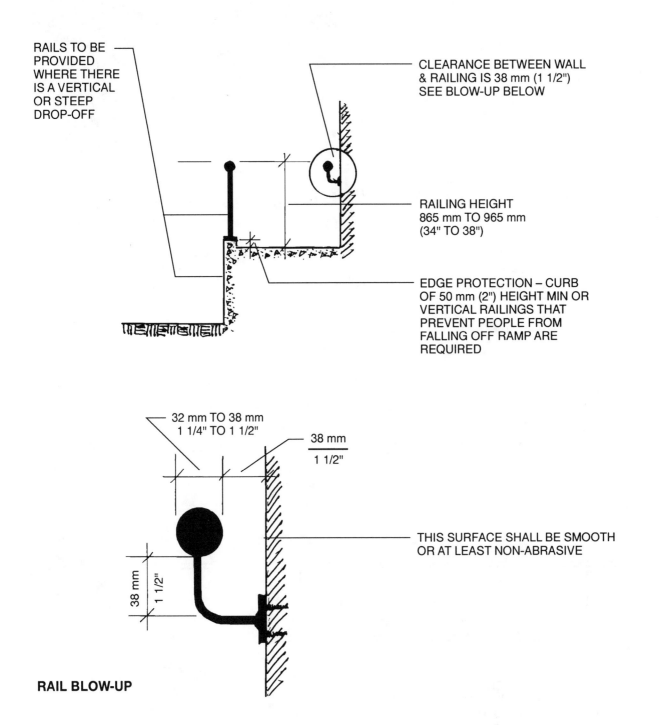

RAILS TO BE PROVIDED WHERE THERE IS A VERTICAL OR STEEP DROP-OFF

CLEARANCE BETWEEN WALL & RAILING IS 38 mm (1 1/2") SEE BLOW-UP BELOW

RAILING HEIGHT 865 mm TO 965 mm (34" TO 38")

EDGE PROTECTION – CURB OF 50 mm (2") HEIGHT MIN OR VERTICAL RAILINGS THAT PREVENT PEOPLE FROM FALLING OFF RAMP ARE REQUIRED

32 mm TO 38 mm 1 1/4" TO 1 1/2"

38 mm 1 1/2"

38 mm 1 1/2"

THIS SURFACE SHALL BE SMOOTH OR AT LEAST NON-ABRASIVE

RAIL BLOW-UP

Figure 3.18   *Railings*

There are many variations of this detail but all must incorporate these features and dimensions. The object is to make the railing easy to grab and hold, thus the 32 mm - 38 mm ϕ (1 1/4" - 1 1/2"). Also there shall be nothing to scrape the hands or jam the fingers.

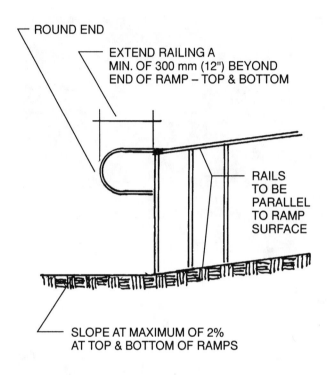

ROUND END

EXTEND RAILING A
MIN. OF 300 mm (12") BEYOND
END OF RAMP – TOP & BOTTOM

RAILS
TO BE
PARALLEL
TO RAMP
SURFACE

SLOPE AT MAXIMUM OF 2%
AT TOP & BOTTOM OF RAMPS

Figure 3.19 *Rail Endings*

Stairs

ADA/UFAS guidelines give much detailed guidance regarding stairways and other means of moving from one elevation to another elevation.

General:

- All steps on any flight of stairs shall have uniform riser heights and tread widths.

- All stairs and approaches shall be designed so no water accumulates on walking surfaces.

- Treads shall be no less than 280 mm (11") wide riser to riser.

- Nosing – maximum depth 38 mm (1 1/2").

See Chapter 6 – Circulation and Chapter 10 – Details for additional input on stairs, etc.

HANDRAILS – SEE RAMPS
RAILING – THE ONLY CHANGE
IS AT THE BOTTOM OF THE
STAIR FLIGHT

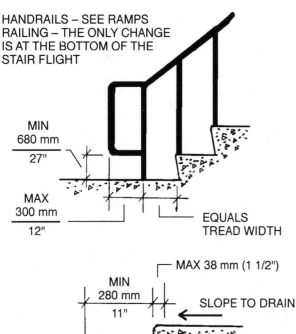

MIN
680 mm
27"

MAX
300 mm
12"

EQUALS
TREAD WIDTH

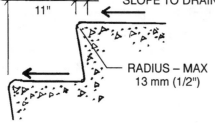

MAX 38 mm (1 1/2")

MIN
280 mm
11"

SLOPE TO DRAIN

RADIUS – MAX
13 mm (1/2")

ALT "A"

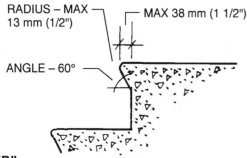

RADIUS – MAX
13 mm (1/2")

MAX 38 mm (1 1/2")

ANGLE – 60°

ALT "B"

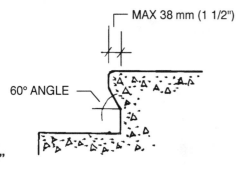

MAX 38 mm (1 1/2")

60° ANGLE

ALT "C"

Figure 3.20 *Stair Detail*

Outdoor Performance / Assembly Area / Sports Seating

A handicapped person shall be able to get to all assembly areas from an accessible route. In addition, if fixed seating is provided, then wheelchair space must be provided as follows:

"Handicapped" wheelchair seating at Lee County Sports Complex – Florida

Total Capacity of Seating	Number of Wheelchair Locations
4 to 25	1
26 to 50	2
51 to 300	4
301 to 500	6
over 500	6 + 1 additional space for each total capacity increase of 100

Figure 3.21 *Required Wheelchair Spaces Needed In Assembly Areas.*

In addition, 1% of seats (minimum of 1) shall be aisle seats without arm rests, or of design suitable for wheelchair users. Finally, where certain conditions exist (i.e. over 50 fixed seat capacity, an audio system is provided, etc.), it will be necessary to have permanently installed assistive listening systems. See ADA 4.1.3 (19) Assembly Areas (b).

Signs

Signs shall comply with the following ADA requirements (4.30.1, 4.30.2, 4.30.3, 4.30.4, 4.30.5 and 4.30.6) where applicable. Individual characters, numbers and letters shall have a width-to-height ratio of between 3:5 and 1:1.

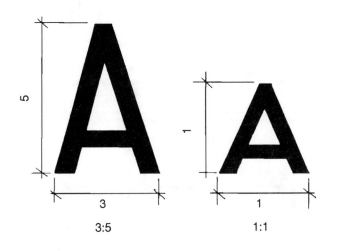

Figure 3.22 *Width-to-Height Ratio of Letters and Numbers*

The line width (stroke) shall have a width-to-height ratio of between 1:5 and 1:10.

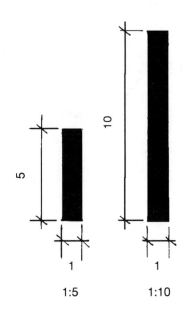

Figure 3.23 *Line Width of Letters*

The height of the letters shall be determined by the viewing distance from which they are to be read. Seventy-five millimeters (3") is a normal height for sign letters that are approximately 2050 mm (7') above a walkway. The signs should be eggshell white with a matte or other non-glare finish with a strong contrasting color — i.e. black, blue, brown, green, red. Please note that best readability results from light characters on a dark background.

Braille information signs are generally not as useful as guides or audio devices.

Accessibility signs shall use the international symbol of accessibility. Use grid (17 units x 18 units) to establish appropriate proportions. Note: Signs shall be blue on white or white on blue.

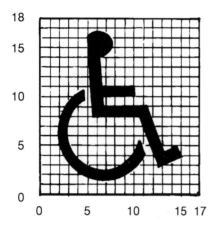

Figure 3.24 *Proportions for International Symbol of Accessibility*

Sanitary Facilities (Reference ADA 4.17)

Handicapped accessible sanitary facilities, when provided, shall comply with the detailed ADA requirements. In addition, many states may have specific, more strict handicapped requirements – i.e. Florida adds a lavatory in each handicapped accessible stall. These facilities shall, of course, be located and reachable from the site's accessible way and are the minimum required for all projects to be used by the public.

The provision of access to handicapped facilities goes a long way towards making sanitary facilities more easily usable for people as they age. See Chapter 5 for additional suggested requirements.

The size of handicapped toilet stalls/water closets depends in part on the location of the access door. See Figure 3.25 for several examples.

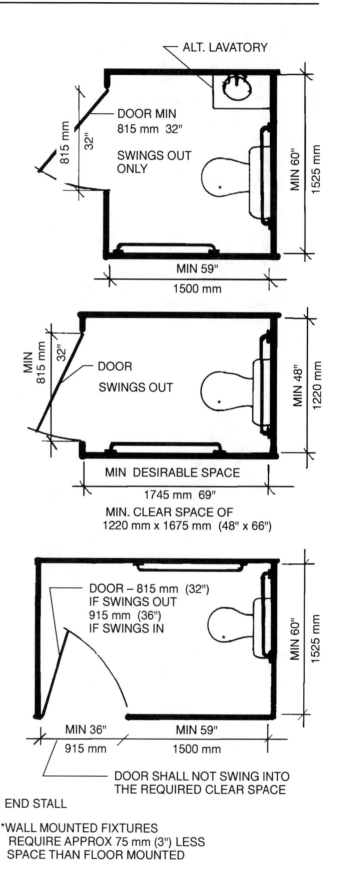

END STALL

*WALL MOUNTED FIXTURES
REQUIRE APPROX 75 mm (3") LESS
SPACE THAN FLOOR MOUNTED

Figure 3.25 *Handicapped Toilet Stalls/ Water Closets*

Urinals – See ADA 4.18

Urinals, if provided, shall have at least one with clear floor space in front of 760 mm x 1220 mm (30" x 48") to allow a wheelchair approach.

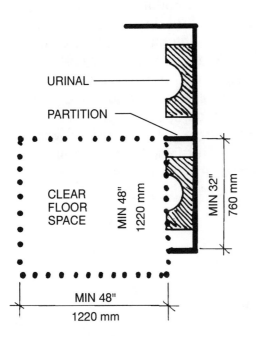

Figure 3.26 *Urinals*

Showers

If showers are provided, at least one shall be accessible and located on an accessible route. See ADA 4.23.

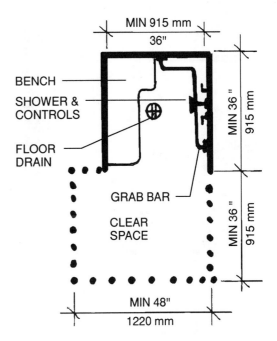

Figure 3.27 *Showers*

Telephones

Public telephones, if provided, are required to be accessible, therefore, they must be located on an accessible way. Clear space of 760 mm x 1220 mm (30" x 48") minimum shall be provided at the phone for wheelchair access. The phone shall be set between a minimum of 850 mm off ground and a maximum of 1370 mm (27" to 54") high for all people for operable parts, i.e. phone, coin slot, dialing mechanism.

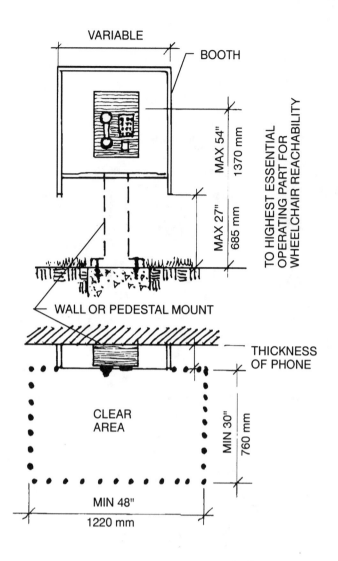

Figure 3.28 *Telephones*

SUMMARY

The following is a summary of suggested accessibility guidelines for accessible outdoor recreation facilities. It is a modified version of the Summary Chart in the U.S. Department of Interior/U.S. Department of Agriculture Interim Draft of "Design Guide for Accessible Outdoor Recreation." Although these are not "required" UFAS standards, all public facilities are required to meet accessibility standards to ensure their usability for most people with disabilities without assistance. The facilities in this summary chart meet UFAS standards as shown earlier in this chapter.

SUMMARY OF MINIMUM ACCESSIBILITY TO MEET ADA REQUIREMENTS

Function/Facility	Minimum Requirements	

PARKING

No. of Spaces

Total	Access
1-25	1
26-50	2
51-75	3
76-100	4
101-150	5

See Fig. 3.1 for additional details.

Car and Van
12% van, min. of 1
88% car.

Space Width
2440 mm (8 ft)

Aisle Width
1525 mm (5 ft) auto,
2440 mm (8 ft) van.

TRAILS & PATHWAYS

Running Slope
1:20 (5%) max.

Cross Slope
1:50 (2%) max.

Width
1220 mm (4 ft) 1-way
1525 mm (5 ft) 2-way.

Rest Stops
Level rest area every 61 m (200 ft) max.

Edges
Curbs at drop-offs.
Railings if drop more than 760 mm (30 in).

Surface
Hard, smooth with textured finish.

RAMPS

Slope
<1:12 (min.)
<1:16 (better)

Landings
Every 760 mm (30 in) of vertical rise.

Edges
Curbs and/or railings.

PICNIC AREAS	Accessible tables & grill, (if provided). Hard surface. Nearby accessible adjacent parking. Parking – 50% vans, 50% cars desirable.
CAMPING	Accessible tables, grills and storage facilities (if provided). Accessible hard surface tent pad. Adjacent parking.
TOILETS & RESTROOMS	In accessible areas there must be sanitary facilities on the accessible way.
BEACHES	
Inland	Firm, hard walking surface to water – extend into water where possible.
Coastal	Method of getting users to water, such as large-tired chair, movable panels, etc. Firm, safe access into water, if appropriate.
POOLS	Access ramp into pool or self-operated assistive device that will enable a wheelchair-bound person to get into water. All support facilities to meet UFAS.
BOATING FACILITIES	Docks, piers, gangways meet accessible pathways and ramp requirements.
	Curbs and/or railings required on accessible dock.
	Safety equipment.
	Boat transfer aids similar to pool access aids.
FISHING FACILITIES	Access way and materials meet accessible guidelines.
Deep Water Fishing Area	Curbs and/or railings.
Shallow Water Fishing Area	Curbs.
EQUESTRIAN FACILITIES	When provided, support facilities such as drinking fountains, corrals, and gates, shall be accessible.

PLAYGROUNDS

Play areas and support facilities, such as restrooms and drinking fountains, shall be accessible.

Accessible facilities including a waiting/ watching area for caregiver needed.

Low-level challenges must be provided in addition to traditional equipment where site conditions permit.

AMPHITHEATERS

Grade site to provide wheelchair access at more than one location, site permitting.

Firm, hard surface paths.

Chapter 4 WHAT IS NEEDED?

Chapter 3 has summarized the ADA and other requirements for making facilities accessible to people with disabilities. Chapters 1 and 2, however, clearly point out that most people over 55 do not have disabilities — they just have less of the physical abilities that they had as younger people. To verify this point for yourself, look at the number of handicapped parking spaces that go unused even at the local senior citizen centers and note how far away many people who even look handicapped park and walk, or check out the unoccupied handicapped parking spaces at the "mall" and note the number of older people shopping.

What then is needed to make the facilities that are likely to be used by older people more older-people friendly? Basically, designers must consider all facilities likely to be used by older people in light of the users' capabilities and constraints. This means more consideration must be given for people with less than optimum capabilities but who are not "HANDICAPPED."

Many of the issues and subsequent facility modifications for older people will also address the needs of the many of all ages who have some physical limitations but who are not "handicapped." Also, some people involved with the provision of built facilities have been exploring the concept of universal design as discussed in some detail at the end of this chapter.

Multi-generational outing, Playground in Chinatown – Boston, Massachusetts

Basically those involved with the provision of leisure facilities for older people need to pay more attention or consideration to (1) safety, (2) visual clarity, (3) accessibility, and (4) environmental modifications.

SAFETY

Safety, **actual and perceived**, is of importance to most people and becomes of more concern to many as they reach their older years. Safety for this book is divided into three components.

First is the **safe design of the physical facilities**. Are they properly designed for the intended use — i.e. is the tread/riser ratio correct? (See Chapter 10 – Details.) Are the barriers around raised platforms the right height and width? (See Chapter 10 – Details.) Is there adequate passenger drop-off space at the destination? (See Chapter 6 – Circulation.) Are the walk surfaces obstacle-free and non-slip? (See Chapter 6 – Circulation and Chapter 10 – Details.)

Second is **safety from criminal activity**. Personal safety was frequently mentioned in the authors' survey as an area of concern. This concern can be mitigated through design, and through operation and maintenance. Security measures such as boundary fencing and entrance controls should be an integral part of any design. Operational procedures should include such practices as roving security patrols to provide a sense of security. (See Chapter 11 – Operations.)

Third is **emergency care**. At a minimum, first aid needs to be available on site. In addition, an operational plan for quickly securing more highly trained response is needed together with easy access for emergency vehicles. (See Chapter 11 – Operations.)

VISUAL CLARITY

Facilities and actions needed to make it possible for older people to see things better, easier, and with more clarity are a necessity. These measures fall into three groups.

First, evenness of light — including artificial and natural. (See Chapter 6 – Circulation and Chapter 7 – Utilities.)

Second, legibility of graphic information — particularly signs of all types. (See Chapter 10 – Details.)

Third, understandability of design — dealing in particular with depth perception. (See Chapters 6 – Circulation, 7 – Utilities, and 10 – Details.)

Legible sign, Lava Beds National Monument – California

ACCESSIBILITY

Some of all facilities are now legally required to be accessible as per ADA rules and regulations. From the time a person enters the site and/or is dropped off and/or parks his/her car, until reaching the final destination within the facility, there should be NO obstacles to impede progress through the site and enjoyment of the site and its amenities. For the most part this is now true, but as mentioned previously, older people are generally not handicapped, therefore, they do not have special parking spaces. Frequently standard parking consists of 2.7 m (9') bays or even as narrow as 2.5 m (8.5') wide making it difficult for older people to get out of their cars. For people with mobility impairments these spaces are virtually impossible to use, particularly if they are driving a large-model automobile, and older people have a tendency to drive larger cars. After exiting the car there is frequently an obstacle course to negotiate in the typical parking lot to get to the destination — such things as wheel stops and planting beds. In addition, there is a constant stream of cars across the primary pedestrian access way which almost invariably separates the parking from the destination.

Chapters 6 – Circulation, 8 – Activities–Outdoor, 9 – Activities–Indoor, and 10 – Details address these issues and many other similar problems dealing with accessibility.

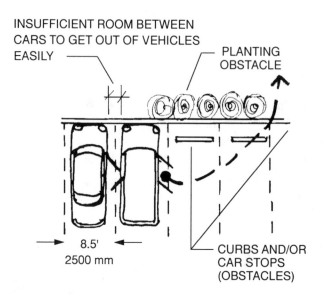

Figure 4.2   *Parking Obstacles*

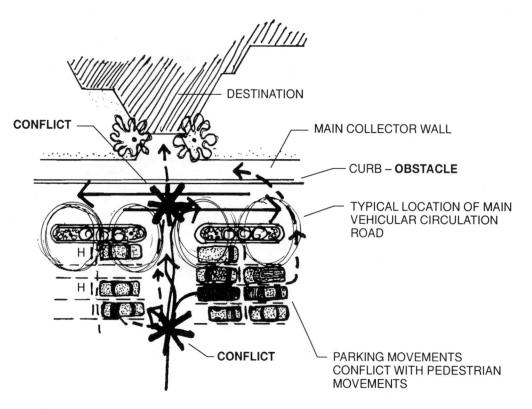

Figure 4.1   *Parking Lot Conflicts*

ENVIRONMENTAL MODIFICATIONS

Making the environment more climatically comfortable for the users will make the facilities more user-friendly. Here we need to modify mother nature in ways that will be environmentally sensitive. Examples of such modifications are: providing shade at resting areas and where possible along heavily used walks for those who cannot be in direct sunlight, making wind protected pockets, cool shaded areas for warm weather, and providing warm, sunny areas for cold weather. (See Chapters 6 – Circulation, 8 – Activities–Outdoor, and 10 – Details.)

Shaded rest area – Cypress Gardens, Florida

Arbor shaded walkway – Athens, Greece

UNIVERSAL DESIGN

As mentioned earlier in this chapter, some people who are involved in the provision of facilities have been exploring the idea of *universal site accessibility* or *universal site design*. Basically, the concept is to design **ALL** facilities (within reason) so that they are accessible/usable by **ALL** — not just the average. This is philosophically and conceptually a desirable goal. Implementing universal site design will require thoughtful and creative solutions to a number of difficult realities.

People have varying capabilities, both physically and/or mentally. Some are stronger or faster or smarter, etc. The challenge here is to make **ALL** facilities accessible and usable to the least capable while maintaining the challenge and stimulation for the more able. Optimally, facilities could be designed and built with multiple levels of difficulty and challenge. Chapter 8 – Activities–Outdoor–Trails, shows one solution that appears to work. The first part of the trail is designed to serve all levels of abilities. A second section of the trail is designed to provide more challenge, and a third, more remote section, is intended to serve and challenge the most capable.

Different preferences of people may put a real strain on a project's acceptance and subsequent use. One example of this phenomenon is cultural activities. Some people like classical music, some country/western, and some rap, etc. Ideally, different kinds of music could be planned and scheduled for different times. But acoustical design and physical accommodation needs may differ, i.e. a small orchestra needs more room than a jazz combo. The solution to designing to fit the aesthetics and cultural tastes of **ALL** the likely range of users is a real challenge, i.e. background music in stores and elevators!

A far different problem is that of physical size. Humans vary from small children and babies to typical adult size to jumbo size like football players, basketball players and sumo wrestlers. Stairs, as a case in point, do not readily lend themselves to use by varying sizes of users. Ramps, however, can be easily used by all.

In summary, good design for older people, like good design for all people, should be kept simple. Decisions by facility users of what they should do, which way they should go to reach their destination, etc., should be obvious. Obstacles to access by any age group and use by people with varying abilities should be minimized and, wherever possible, eliminated. Where supplemental directions and/or instructions or information are needed, they should be easily read by people with less than perfect eyesight, and readily understood by people with as wide a range of capabilities as possible.

It should be clearly understood that modifications to existing design and development criteria may entail some additional costs. You cannot add special features to facilities without incurring costs. Modifications for ADA requirements do not come free, especially when retrofitting existing facilities. Time and creative thinking can reduce these ADA costs substantially. The creative application of new ideas for site design for use by older people can provide better facilities in a more cost-effective manner.

The remaining chapters will expand on these four points and will provide suggested guidelines and ideas for making a wide range of leisure activities more enjoyable – more user-friendly for people over 55.

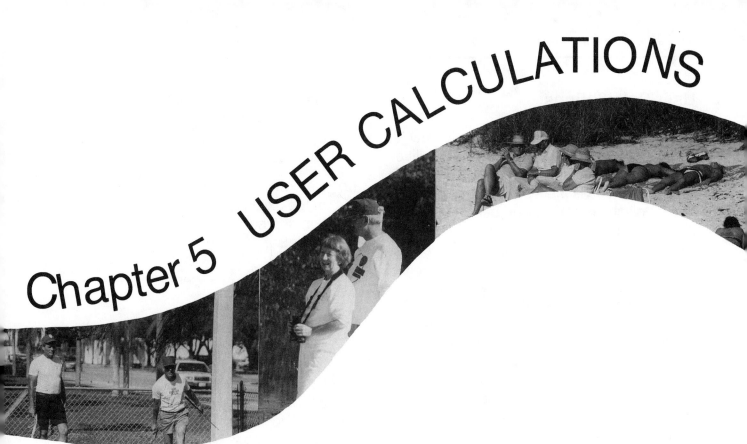

Chapter 5 USER CALCULATIONS

*W*ho and how many are going to use the proposed leisure facilities? *This is always a difficult question to answer when planning any facility. It is no different for facilities which are intended to serve people over 55. The answer to the question of what are people over 55 likely to want to do in the year 2000, 2010 or any other year is perhaps a little easier to determine.*

As Chapter 3 of this book points out, people continue to participate in their current leisure activities (sometimes at facilities that have been modified to meet their changing abilities, i.e. a closer tee to the green in golf, softer surfaces on tennis courts, etc.) as long as they are physically able. Therefore, if you are preparing a leisure development proposal for older people for completion five or ten years (or even more for some very large projects) in the future, you should consider what people of 50 or 45 years old, or even younger, are doing now. Take this activity mix and participation rate and project it into the future project time frame. As an example, if the project is proposed for 55 to 65-year-olds and is to be completed 7 years into the future, look at people who are in their late 40's to late 50's. This methodology may not give the developer and/or the designer the exact user mix but it certainly will provide a realistic idea of how many of what kinds of facilities are needed. The data on current use should be collected in the vicinity of the proposed project to make it as site-specific as possible. If this is not possible or practical, a "comparable demand" type analysis should be used (see Section titled Number of Users in this chapter).

User Calculations

Before entering into the details of how to modify standard site and leisure facilities guidelines to make them more older people user-friendly, it is necessary to understand how to calculate (1) the number of users, (2) the size of parking lots (where space is not a limiting factor), (3) the numbers of facilities that are sustainable on a given land area (i.e. carrying capacity), and (4) the numbers of users for various kinds of activities. With this information available the number of the various kinds of facilities needed can be determined.

The following summary of user/facility calculations is presented for your quick reference. See Chapters 2 and 3 of *Park Planning Guidelines, 3rd Edition* for a more in-depth discussion of these matters.

NUMBER OF USERS

The number of users of a leisure facility is determined by one of two methods – maximum carrying capacity or comparable demand.

Maximum Carrying Capacity – Used in areas where heavy use is a probability. It is based on designing the site to its maximum sustainable capacity without deteriorating. This approach assumes a thorough knowledge of the users and their needs and desires and the site's capabilities to sustain use.

Comparable Demand – This approach compares one, or preferably more, existing similar recreation facilities with the proposed facilities. The use at the proposed facility is computed by analogy with these comparable projects.

(1)   Determine the population of travel-time zones around the proposed leisure facility and the existing comparable leisure facilities.

(2)   Determine the per-capita recreation use at the existing area from the total population served and attendance figures from the leisure facility.

$$\frac{Use}{Population} = \text{per capita use}$$

Check attendance trends at the comparable leisure facility and population trends in the proposed service area. If specific activity use figures are available, an even more accurate projection tailored to the specific proposed program would be possible.

Multi-generational beach use – Naples, Florida

Example

150,000 population within 1/2 hour's driving time of the facility (the area served by the neighborhood park) and 10,000 within 15 minute's walk – number of users is 1,500 on a maximum day or a per day, per capita use of 0.01.

(3)   After establishing a ratio using the population and attendance of the existing lei-

sure resource, apply this to the proposed facilities. The resulting figures will give a projected attendance for the new facility.

Example

If the population in the proposed service area is 100,000, then the number of users would be 100,000 x 0.01, or 1000.

(4) Adjust the figures to account for the influence of existing and proposed competing leisure developments in the zone of influence (the area from which users might be expected to come). Please note that the results of these findings may show that the facilities planned are not needed!

The reliability of this method depends largely upon the degree of comparability between the two resources, both as to intrinsic recreation potential and as to distribution and type of population.

FACILITIES DETERMINE DEMAND AND/OR LEADERS DETERMINE DEMAND

It is believed by some resource researchers and planners that the provision of recreation/leisure facilities and/or recreation leaders themselves can create visitor demand. This is particularly true for organized sports and other supervised recreational/leisure activities. In the private sector, the use of promotional programs can greatly increase the number and kinds of users. This approach may also be the only way to increase usage by members of minority groups and age groups in the service areas which are underrepresented in site usage.

DETERMINATION OF VISITOR DAY CAPACITIES AND PARKING LOT REQUIREMENTS

Most large leisure areas can be reached only by car or bus. Therefore, the daily capacity of these facilities can generally be determined by multiplying the number of cars times the average turnover rate times the number of people per car or, conversely, the number of parking spaces can be determined by taking the capacity of the site to accommodate users and dividing that number by the appropriate number of people per car. If buses (mini or standard size) are likely to be used for access to the leisure facility, their much larger per vehicle unit loads (mini vans @ 10 people ± and buses up to 50 people) must be included in the calculations. It should be clearly understood that a visitor day usually consists of more than one activity day.

Formula

Number of cars + turnover x's number of people/car = daily capacity or, conversely, number of users (instant capacity) ÷ by the number of people per car = the number of parking spaces needed. See Figure 5.1.

Examples

1000 cars + 0.05 turnover = extra cars that would use the facility for a total of 1050 cars.

1050 x 2.2 = 2310 people

Type of Activity	No. of People per Car	Average Turnover Rate*
Sightseeing	2	Variable (1–10 or more)
Family Picnic	2.2	1.0 to 1.5
Family Camping	2.4	1.0
Group Picnic	2.4	1.0
Group Camping	4.0	1.0
Boat Ramp	1.5 to 2.0	1.0 to 2.0 for parking 4.0 for ramp
Freshwater Beach/Pool Areas	2.0 to 2.5	2.0 (for pool or beach only – not for multi-use beach/ picnic, etc. areas)
Coastal Beach Areas	2.0 to 2.5	1.3 to 2.0
Boat Concession	2.0	2.0 or more
Overlook	2.0	Variable 1 – 10 or more
Golf (during main use season)	1.5	1.5 – Private 2.0 – Public
Restaurant	2.2	2.0 per meal time
Stables	1.5	2.0 to 3.0
Equestrian Area	1.5	1.0
Fishing	1.5 to 2.0	1.0
Hiking	2.0	1.0 to 1.5 depending on trail length

Figure 5.1 *Number of People Per Car for Various Activities*

* The turnover rate is the number of times a specific facility is used in a given time period – i.e. a boat launching ramp can be used 40 times, or a picnic area may only be used by one group in one day. Careful judgment should be used in applying the turnover rate. The numbers shown here have not been accurately verified.

The number of people/car has been declining steadily (along with family size). In the 1960's approximately 4 people per car was the accepted norm. By the 1970's the number had decreased to 3.3. In Pennsylvania in the late 1970's it was down to 2.8 per car. More recently, unpublished studies in Pennsylvania by the Pennsylvania State Park staff in 1990, and in Lee County, Florida, by George Fogg in 1991, have shown the average number of recreation users per car was down to 2.2/2.3

NUMBERS OF FACILITIES NEEDED

The numbers of facilities of various kinds needed in any leisure area is determined by a combination of factors. These include the activity mix or cluster of uses a person or group does while at the facility. A leisure visit will normally include doing 2+ activities. As examples, a shopper for pleasure will probably eat while out and may use the sanitary facilities; a bird watcher may also hike and have a picnic lunch or eat at the concession stand and use the sanitary facilities; a group going to the beach would probably do some sun bathing, reading, picnicking and/or use the food stand, play in the sand, play in the water, go shelling, go for a walk along the beach, do some people watching, play games, possibly even do some swimming, and use the sanitary facilities

How do you calculate then the number of facilities and the amount of space needed in any given recreation area? First, determine the number of people at the site at maximum use at a given point in time (does not include turnover) – i.e. instantaneous capacity (2.2 ± x number of parking spaces plus people who come by other means such as bus, on foot, or bicycle). Second, allocate all of the users to their various destinations – i.e. beach space, 250 users; walking, 100 users; bird

watching, 25 users, etc. Please remember that most people participate in more than one activity when they are on a leisure outing. Third, multiply the number of users by their respective activity space requirements. Each activity requires "X" amount of space – i.e. beach use on shore requires 4 sq. m to 8 sq. m (45 sq. ft to 90 sq. ft) of space per person, depending on density of use. In addition, you will need (1) sanitary facilities sufficient to meet codes (modified to meet the needs of older users – see Chapter 7 – Utilities), (2) possibly eating space at the food concession preferable on or with a view of the beach and/or in an adjacent picnic area, (3) a 3 m to 5 m (10 ft to 15 ft) wide space to walk along the shore, (4) possibly a boat rental area and/or bicycle rental area, etc.

One effective way to organize the site-specific space needs calculations is to list the facilities and their site requirements and multiply that number times the projected instantaneous users.

See the Sample Program/Relationship Chart adapted from pages 68-69 of *Management Planning for Park and Recreation Areas*.

Activity and/or Facility	Who	How Many
Administration	Staff/public	5/10
Marina In water storage	Boat owners & guests	400 boats 4m to 15m max length
Dry storage { Covered (powered)	Staff	250
Open (sail)	Staff/Owners	200
Sales { Boat Rentals Major Items Supplies	Fishermen All boaters	50 15 people + display space
Service/Repairs	Staff	3
Food Service { Bar Snacks Restaurant	50 + 3 staff 100 + 4 staff 100 + 10 staff	
Parking { Visitor { Boat launch All others Staff		
		25
Buffer Space*		
Circulation { Vehicular**	Cars Cars/trailers Service	60% of stored boats will be used @ one time 300 – separate
Pedestrian	Internal to site & from adjacent housing	
Bicycles	Visitors Staff	
Boat Launching { Public Private	Power boats Sail boats Staff & boat dock Rental owners	200 100 Maintenance – 10 Dry Covered – 120
Maintenance	Staff only	10
Picnic & children's play	Boat owners & guests Primarily boat launchers	
Sanitary Facilities	Staff Visitors	25 2200

*   Normally not able to be determined other than in a general way, i.e. usually separate visitor entrance from service area.

** Usually takes more (sometimes **much** more) space than expected, especially if there are adverse site conditions.

Figure 5.2   *Sample Program/Relationship Chart*

Unit***	Total	Relationships****
10 m² per staff (100 ft² ±)	50 m² + 40 m² + Service 25 m²	Lobby reception space needed for public – up to 10 people @ 4m² (40 ft² ± per person)
40m² per boat (450 ft² ±)		Amount of space is dependent on boat size + parking for 200 cars must be within 200 m + parking for 175 cars parking for car/trailers 200
		25 Boats needed Fishing tackle & supplies 4 Boats/motors etc.
		Located adjacent to private boat launching
		View of in-water boat storage for all users Separate service access
30 m² (350 ft²)		Separate parking for lessees ajacent to docks
28 m² per car (300 ft² ±)		Divided into small spaces near appropriate work areas
As needed.	Visually	Separate service areas from adjacent non-compatible uses
		Access control needed to public boat ramp for fee collection – 3 lanes of launching needed within 60 m to 70 m of car trailer parking
		Minimize pedestrian vehicular conflicts
		Will need bicycle parking – separate from other circulation desirable
Forklift		Separate launching for power boats & sailing boats Must be directly accessible to dry land storage and service and repairs
		Could be combined with service and repairs – visually separate from view of marina users

*** Unit sizes are available in a number of resource books.

**** These activity/facility relationships form the basis for the space diagrams, the first step in actual site design. This step is not necessary in determining number of users.

Therefore, a typical beach/picnic area would require the following space for 2200 people. Provision of 1000 car parking needs 1000 x 2.7 m^2 or 2700 m^2 (1000 x 30+ sq. ft or 30,000 sq. ft, beach space of between 4 m^2 to 8 m^2 (45 sq. ft to 90 sq. ft) per person x 1700 (approximately 80% of 2200 people) – some people are going to and from cars, some at picnic site, etc. – or approximately 6800 m^2 to 13,600 m^2 (80,000 sq. ft to 160,000 sq. ft). They would also need a water area for approximately 700 people (30% of the users), or 1900 m^2 to 2900 m^2 (20,000 sq. ft to 30,000 sq. ft), plus possibly another 3 m to 5 m (10 ft to 15 ft) wide space for a beach walking area. In addition, as an example, there may be need for an active play area for volleyball and/or frisbee of approximately 375 m^2 (4000 sq. ft) x 2 the number of courts (approximately 1 per 1000 beach users) or 750 m^2 (8000 sq. ft). It may also be desirable to have space for equipment rental for boating and/or bicycling requiring another 100 m^2 ± (1000 sq. ft ±) of space. Of course, sanitary facilities including change rooms will be required. Additional space for buffering and aesthetics will also be needed and could amount to two or three times the required space for the above activities. A total of approximately 14,000 m^2 to 26,000 m^2 (150,000 sq. ft to 260,000 sq. ft) then would be necessary to provide for the recreation facilities described above, with an additional 40,000 m^2 to 95,000 m^2 (310,000 sq. ft to 1,040,000 sq. ft) possibly needed for screening and buffering.

ANNUAL CAPACITY

The annual capacity of a park can be determined by multiplying the daily capacity by the number of capacity days per year. Different geographic regions of the country have different numbers of capacity days per year per facility. In Central Atlantic States a typical park might enjoy fifty capacity days of use determined as follows: three days of use per week (40 percent during the week, 20 to 25 percent on Saturday, and 35 to 40 percent on Sunday) x 13 weeks summer season + 30 percent off-season use (3 x 13 + 30 percent = 51). In milder areas there might be as many as 100 capacity days or more, while in colder climates only 40 days. These figures must be adjusted to take into consideration differences in traveling time, variety and kinds of facilities and local weather.

Example

(people/day x number of capacity day/year)

+ off-season use = Annual use

(4000 x 50) + 30% =

200,000 + 60,000 =

260,000 ± people/yr. would use the facilities.

Description	# of People	# of Units	m²	Unit Space Required ft²	Space in m²	Space in ft²
Parking	2200 (All)	1000	2.7	30	2700	30,000
Beach	1700 (80%)	1700	4 to 8	45 to 90	6,800 to 13,600	80,000 to 160,000
Water Area	440 to 880 (20% to 40%)	440 to 880	3 to 6	30 to 65	1,900 to 2,900	20,000 to 30,000
Beach Walk Space	440 ± 20% ±	440	3 to 5 x length of beach	10 to 15 x length of beach	1,400 to 2,800	15,000 to 30,000
Play Space*					750 to 1000 or more	8,000 to 11,000 or more
Equipment Rental & Concessions					100 ±	1100 ±
WC					100 ±	1100 ±
Subtotal					13,750 to 23,850 ±	155,000 to 260,000
Buffer Space		2 to 3 x's the required space			27,000 ± to 47,700 to 40,000 to 71,550	310,000 to 520,000 to 465,000 to 780,000
Total Space					40,000 to 71,000 to 54,000 to 95,000	465,000 to 780,000 to 620,000 to 1,040,000

* As needed to meet expected user mix – possibly 2 sand volleyball & 1 children's play & frisbee throwing area.

Figure 5.3 *Summary of Calculations for a Sample of Numbers of Facilities and Users and Space Requirements*

Chapter 6 CIRCULATION

*G*etting to and from a site is one of the first items to be considered in the planning and design of any leisure facility. Access can be by any means, from bus service, trains, boat, bicycle, on foot or by cars. Most leisure facilities, with the exception of some urban sites, are normally accessed by cars. The first part of this chapter then will concentrate on vehicular access/egress to and the necessary storage (parking) of the vehicles at the site while the passengers are pursuing their leisure activities.

After arrival at the drop-off area and/or parked vehicle area, users must be able to get to the desired facility(ies). The focus of the chapter at this point changes to pedestrian circulation. Here ideas are presented for walks, drop-off points and site/facility accessibility in general. Finally, Chapter 6 explores the special needs for bicycle, 3-wheel bikes and other forms of non-powered movement used by older people.

VEHICULAR CIRCULATION

As in traditional site design, vehicular circulation used by older people should, wherever possible, be separated from pedestrian, bicycle/3-wheeled bikes and equestrian ways.

Walkers, 3-wheeler bike in roadway
– Naples, Florida

Some factors to consider that will make roads more enjoyable and safer for older drivers are:

• Access to site should be provided with ample stacking lanes plus acceleration and deceleration lanes.

• All signs to be clearly visible and easily readable – basically larger lettering and well lighted. See Chapter 3 – Current Guidelines, Chapter 7 – Utilities–Lighting, and Chapter 10 – Details–Graphics.

• Direct access to a drop-off point on the accessible route. See Chapter 3, Figure 3.1 and the following Figures in this chapter: 6.2 Van & Handicapped Drop-off, and 6.6 Parking Lot Layout and Pedestrian Patterns.

• Drop-offs must be so designed as to permit ingress and egress from the right (passenger) side of the vehicle. Provision of shaded sitting at the drop-off is desirable for people waiting to be picked up.

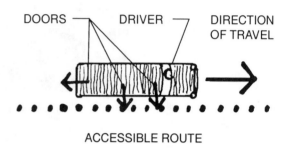

Figure 6.1 *Accessible Route*

• Arrival areas should be shaded – the minimum desirable is canopy planting, with a structurally covered arrival that keeps off precipitation more suitable.

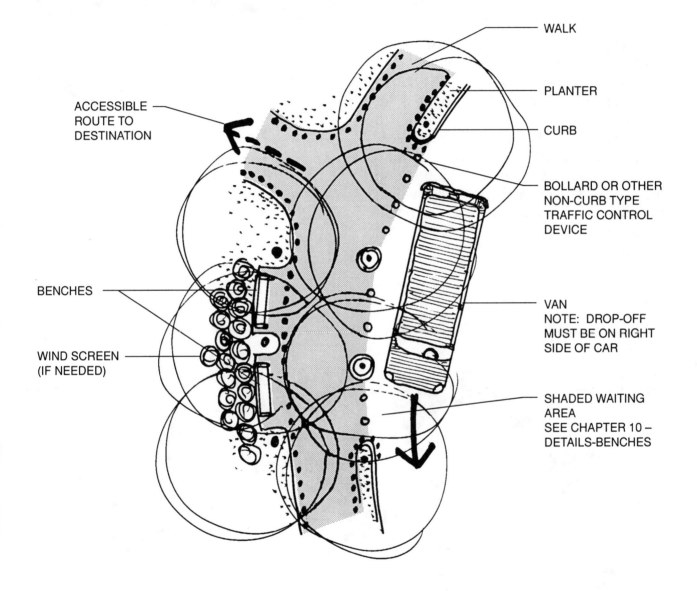

WALK

PLANTER

CURB

BOLLARD OR OTHER
NON-CURB TYPE
TRAFFIC CONTROL
DEVICE

VAN
NOTE: DROP-OFF
MUST BE ON RIGHT
SIDE OF CAR

SHADED WAITING
AREA
SEE CHAPTER 10 –
DETAILS-BENCHES

ACCESSIBLE
ROUTE TO
DESTINATION

BENCHES

WIND SCREEN
(IF NEEDED)

Figure 6.2   *Van & Handicapped Drop-off*

• Aesthetics are an extremely important aspect of the vehicular circulation system. Every care should be taken to enhance the arrival and departure experience as well as the visual aspects of moving about within the site. (See Chapter 8 – Activities–Outdoor-Driving for Pleasure for additional details.)

• Roadway plantings are desirable from an aesthetic standpoint. Intermittent sun/shadow patterns, however, can cause many older people to have periods of reduced visual acuity as their eyes try to adjust to the contrasting light intensities. All roadside plantings that cause sun/shadow patterns should be avoided. Long stretches of shaded and open areas would be acceptable and, where possible, continuous tree shaded areas would be most desirable.

Alternating sunlight shadows on the road – North Carolina

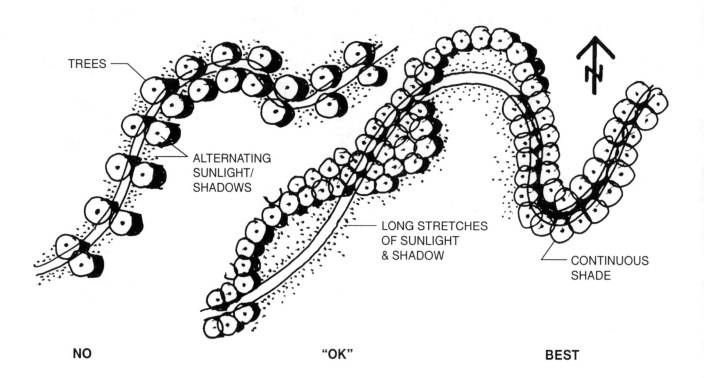

TREES

ALTERNATING SUNLIGHT/ SHADOWS

LONG STRETCHES OF SUNLIGHT & SHADOW

CONTINUOUS SHADE

NO   "OK"   BEST

Figure 6.3   *Roadside Planting*

• Sight distance – provide **extra** sight distances at intersections so that there is sufficient time for slower-reacting drivers to be able to make the required movements safely.

• Signaling devices – where there is heavy traffic (where normal drivers would experience some difficulty in making the necessary vehicular movements), consider installing traffic lights.

• Pull-offs – needed on 2-lane roads at one to two hour intervals for slower cars to pull off roads to let traffic pass.

PARKING

The generally accepted standard design criteria for parking will work for use by older people. The following modifications will, however, make the parking easier to use.

• Access – direct, easily identifiable vehicular route to drop-off area(s).

• Parking space – make approximately 2.9 m to 3.0 m (9.5' to 10') wide – wide enough to open doors completely, but small enough to discourage extra car parking.

• Shade – wherever possible, all parking spaces should be shaded for summer use. In northern and colder areas, winter sun would be desirable, i.e. in the north use deciduous trees, and in the south use broad leaf evergreens or deciduous trees.

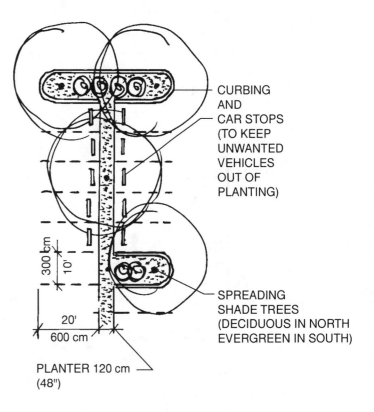

CURBING AND CAR STOPS (TO KEEP UNWANTED VEHICLES OUT OF PLANTING)

300 cm
10'

20'
600 cm

PLANTER 120 cm (48")

SPREADING SHADE TREES (DECIDUOUS IN NORTH EVERGREEN IN SOUTH)

NOTE: DO NOT USE CURBING WHERE OLDER PEOPLE MIGHT WALK.

Figure 6.4 *Parking Details*

Parking and the older person

- Grades – sufficient slope for good drainage – 0.5% minimum, 1% desirable minimum. A maximum slope of 2% is desirable so that car doors can be opened easily. Where possible, slope the lot at 90° to the parking so that cars will not roll backwards accidentally. All handicapped spaces must not exceed 2% slope in any direction.

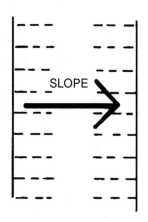

NOT ACCEPTABLE

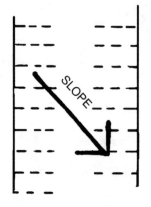

ACCEPTABLE

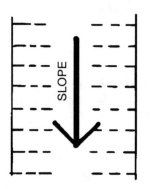

BETTER

0.5% MINIMUM
1% DESIRABLE
2% DESIRABLE MAXIMUM
5% MAXIMUM

Figure 6.5   *Parking Lot Grading*

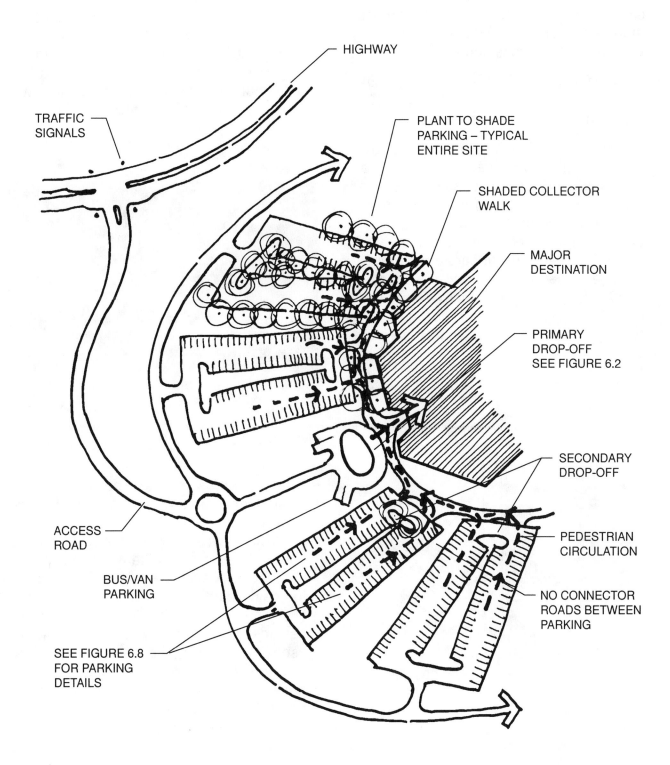

HIGHWAY

TRAFFIC SIGNALS

PLANT TO SHADE PARKING – TYPICAL ENTIRE SITE

SHADED COLLECTOR WALK

MAJOR DESTINATION

PRIMARY DROP-OFF SEE FIGURE 6.2

ACCESS ROAD

SECONDARY DROP-OFF

PEDESTRIAN CIRCULATION

NO CONNECTOR ROADS BETWEEN PARKING

BUS/VAN PARKING

SEE FIGURE 6.8 FOR PARKING DETAILS

Figure 6.6 *Parking Lot Layout and Pedestrian Patterns*

- Minimize pedestrian and vehicular conflict points. This is especially true on larger sites such as shopping centers, amusement parks, etc. See Figure 6.6 – Parking Lot Layout and Pedestrian Patterns.

- Keep parking layout simple. Make all parking either angle (60°) or right angle (90°). Do not mix the two. It confuses people!

- Orient large parking lots so that the rows are perpendicular to the destination. See Figure 6.6. Personal observations over many years have shown that most people get out of their cars and walk to the back and down the vehicular circulation way. Walks between rows of cars are generally not used when provided and the space is needed for planting for shade. This is usually the case unless the destination is directly in front of the parking. See Figure 6.7.

- All larger destination areas and any that might have users arriving by large vans, small buses or standard buses must have the access, drop-off, and at least some parking designed to accommodate these larger vehicles. These vehicles are not able to utilize the standard car parking lots, drop-offs, and turning radiuses. See Figure 6.6 – Parking Lot Layout and Pedestrian Patterns.

Mini bus at Monticello – Charlottesville, Virginia

- ***Parking areas should be barrier-free*** wherever people are likely to walk. Essentially, this means **NO** curbs where people are likely to walk between the parking area and walk system. Where car stops are used by the visually impaired, they should, for easy identification, be colored a distinctly contrasting color to the surrounding pavement – i.e. white or light grey on asphalt and grass, and black or other dark color on concrete or compacted stone. In areas subject to use during snow season, alternate, more visable colors for car stops should be considered.

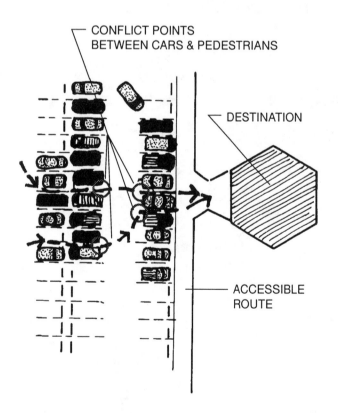

Figure 6.7   *Pedestrian Patterns in Small Parking Lots*

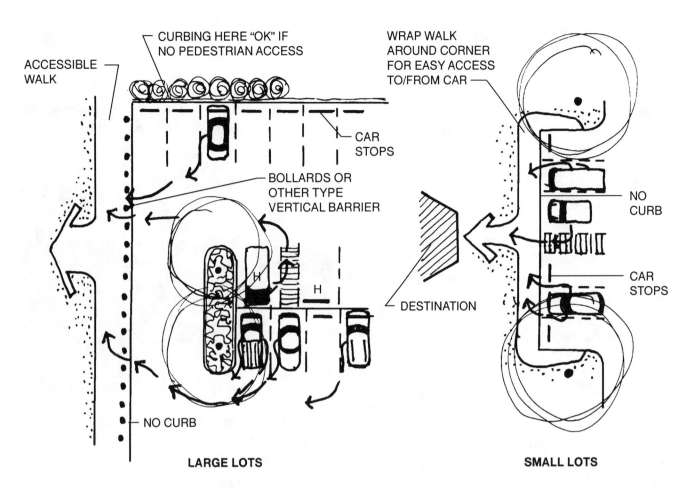

ACCESSIBLE WALK

CURBING HERE "OK" IF NO PEDESTRIAN ACCESS

CAR STOPS

BOLLARDS OR OTHER TYPE VERTICAL BARRIER

H

NO CURB

LARGE LOTS

WRAP WALK AROUND CORNER FOR EASY ACCESS TO/FROM CAR

DESTINATION

NO CURB

CAR STOPS

SMALL LOTS

Figure 6.8 *Barrier Free Parking Lots*

- Snow removal is a major problem in many cold climate areas. It is critical that parking lots and pedestrian entrances to leisure facilities (especially buildings) used during the snow season be designed to accommodate the storage of snow removal from the parking area in an easy manner.

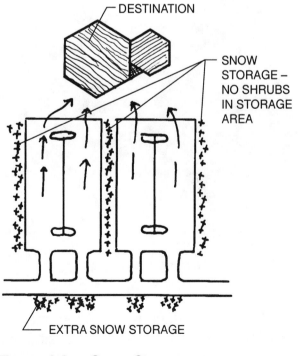

DESTINATION

SNOW STORAGE – NO SHRUBS IN STORAGE AREA

EXTRA SNOW STORAGE

Figure 6.9 *Snow Storage*

BICYCLE CIRCULATION INTRODUCTION

High-speed bicycles and pedestrians utilizing the same space place all users at great risk. This is especially true when dealing with older people whose reflexes and sensory capabilities are declining and for whom even minor accidents may cause serious injury. It, therefore, stands to reason that wherever space and finances permit, bicycles and pedestrians should be separated. Within the bicycle community there are two frequently incompatible types of bicyclists – the high-speed (15 to 25 ± mph) commuters and the serious bike enthusiasts in one group, and the more numerous and slower touring and leisure bicyclists. The two types of bicycling are incompatible; high-speed bicycling must be separated from slower bicyclists. High-speed cycling can best be accommodated on paved shoulders where on-street parking is not permitted. See Figure 6.10 – Bicycleway Plan.

more important than speeding to some destination. Bicycling is also used by both groups as exercise.

Within the more leisurely user group there is a growing sub-group, the 3-wheelers.

3-Wheeler on pedestrian way – no problem! – Naples, Florida

Bike race – Harrisburg, Pennsylvania – High-speed biking is very similar.

For most older bicyclists, speed is not normally the criteria for enjoyment. Seeing and experiencing what is around you and talking to your bicycling companion(s) normally are

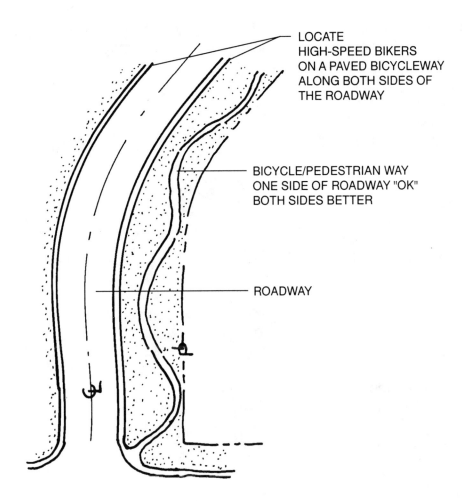

LOCATE
HIGH-SPEED BIKERS
ON A PAVED BICYCLEWAY
ALONG BOTH SIDES OF
THE ROADWAY

BICYCLE/PEDESTRIAN WAY
ONE SIDE OF ROADWAY "OK"
BOTH SIDES BETTER

ROADWAY

Figure 6.10 *Bicycleway Plan*

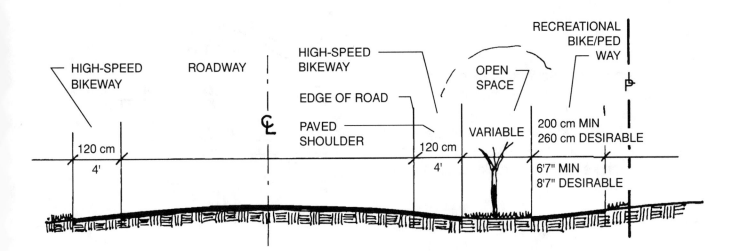

RECREATIONAL
BIKE/PED
WAY

HIGH-SPEED   ROADWAY   HIGH-SPEED
BIKEWAY   BIKEWAY   OPEN
                                                       SPACE
                    EDGE OF ROAD

                    PAVED   VARIABLE   200 cm MIN
HIGH-SPEED   SHOULDER   260 cm DESIRABLE
BIKEWAY

120 cm   120 cm

4'   4'   6'7" MIN
                                                                    8'7" DESIRABLE

Figure 6.11 *Bicycleway Section*

The 3-wheelers are generally slower moving and require a minimum of 1 m (3.3') of usable one-way paved pathway. If the bikeway is for two-way traffic and also pedestrian use, it is necessary to have as a minimum a 2 m (6.7') wide pathway. For 3-wheelers, it is preferred the path be a minimum of 2.60 m (8'5") wide.

Horizontal alignment

- Sufficiently curved to discourage high speed biking.

- A shaded way would be most desirable. If continuous shade is not possible, then shade for portions of the way is acceptable. The shade should be continuous for sections of the trail. Alternating shaded with sunlit spaces will cause the riders continual visual problems in adjusting from the bright sun to shade, making accidents more likely. See Figure 6.3 this chapter.

Vertical alignment – In areas subject to snow and/or icing, bikeways should be designed to maximize winter sun on the pathway surface for rapid melting. Flat to gently rolling alignment is preferred. If short stretches of steeper grades are necessary, they should be shaded for warm season use. Further, a shaded rest area should be provided at the top of the grade.

Surface – All bikeways need hard, all-weather surfaces. Asphalt and compacted crushed stone choked with fines are recommended as both are relatively inexpensive to install and maintain. Concrete pathways are also good, but more expensive and are subject to uneven settling and cracking if not correctly installed.

Lighting – All bikeways that will be used in the evening/night time must be well lighted. This can be done easily for lighted roadways with minor street light fixture modification. If the bikeway is on an unlighted roadway or separate from the vehicular system, it will require special lighting. See Chapter 7 – Utilities-Lighting for more information.

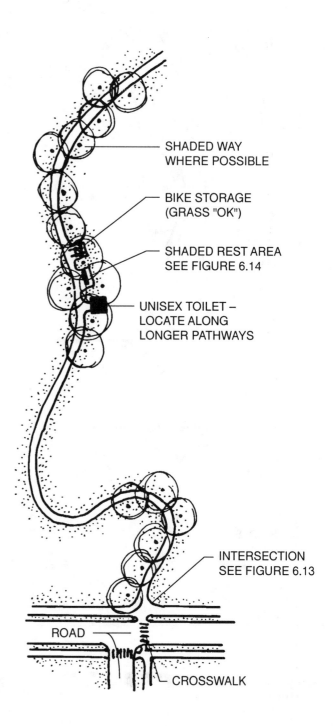

SHADED WAY WHERE POSSIBLE

BIKE STORAGE (GRASS "OK")

SHADED REST AREA SEE FIGURE 6.14

UNISEX TOILET – LOCATE ALONG LONGER PATHWAYS

INTERSECTION SEE FIGURE 6.13

ROAD

CROSSWALK

Figure 6.12 *Bikeway Ideas*

Shade – Bikeways, like walks, should be shaded wherever possible. The pathway should avoid intermittent shade/sun areas and should strive for continuously shaded stretches. See Figure 6.3 Roadside Planting.

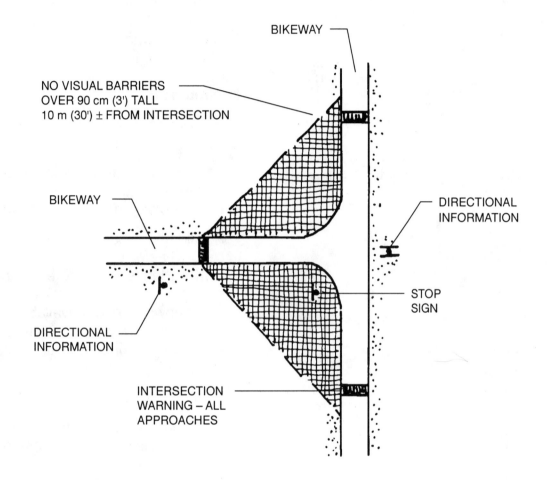

Figure 6.13 *Intersection Design*

Rest areas – locate at appropriate intervals along bikeway at a minimum of every 3 to 4 kilometers (2 miles ±). If the bikeway is combined with a walkway, rest areas every 1 to 1.5 kilometers (1 mile ±) should be more than sufficient so long as an open place off the pathway is available to park the bikes/3-wheelers. A small unisex toilet would be desirable at rest areas on longer bikeways – perhaps every 4 kilometers (2 miles ±). These might be combined with existing sanitary facilities at parks or other compatible public facilities.

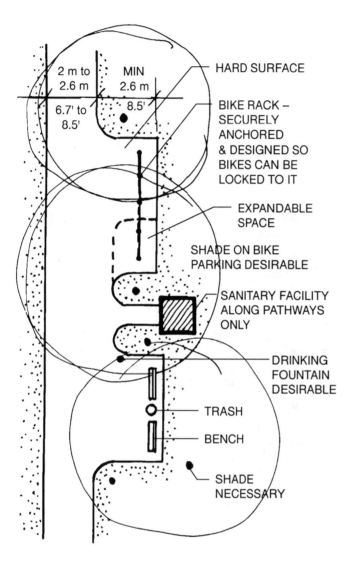

PLAN

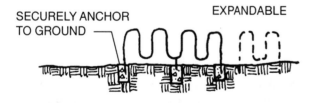

SECTION

Figure 6.14 *Bike/3-Wheeler Parking*

Bicycle Parking

All primary and secondary destinations where the rider will be out of sight of his bike, there should be a parking area with suitable space for storing and locking bicycles and 3-wheelers. The space should have adequate equipment for storing the expected numbers of bicycles and be capable of expanding if future use warrants such expansion. The design should include:

Minimum

- Easy access off of the bikeway or bicycle path.

- Parking for 3-wheelers and bicycles. Please note that 3-wheelers take 2 to 3 times the parking space of bicycles.

- A solid and secure support to which a bicycle/3-wheeler can be locked. See Figure 6.14. Please note there are many other configurations of bike racks available. The type shown is readily available from a number of manufacturers, easily expandable, and has a minimum visual impact on the surrounding landscape.

- Space approximately 3 m x 6 m (10' x 20').

- Surfaces – hard, weed free, no sharp stones and/or edges which could damage tires.

- Shaded sitting space.

- If pathway is used at night, parking must be well lighted.

Desirable

- Summer shade is desirable for bike parking to keep metal and dark bicycle/3-wheeler parts cool.

- Drinking water.

- Trash container.

- Space for expansion of bicycle/3-wheeler parking.

• One unisex toilet every 4 kilometers ± (2 miles ±).

PEDESTRIAN CIRCULATION

Walking for exercise – Naples, Florida

As stated in the Introduction to this chapter, walks are necessary to get from the vehicle parking and/or drop-off area to and within the destination point(s). At least one of these walks must be a handicapped accessible way. See Chapter 3 – Current Guidelines.

In addition, more and more people are walking for physical fitness and pleasure, especially older people. This type of use often takes place in the neighborhood where the person lives. In many communities there are no physical places to walk or safe places to walk security-wise (real or perceived), especially in poorer urban areas. Many communities have no walks at all, especially in some suburban developments. Also walking during temperature extremes can be a serious health hazard for older people.

Besides walks, there are trails and trail systems which are almost exclusively used in parks and other natural type areas. Also, some malls have opened their public spaces to walkers on a regular basis before normal store opening hours. Many people avail themselves of this opportunity, especially when a recreation agency or health center staff person is involved. These enclosed spaces provide an excellent opportunity for year-round use. It also brings potential shoppers to the mall and makes it possible for older people to enjoy one of their favorite activities – window shopping. See Chapters 9 – Activities–Indoor and 11 – Operations–Programming for more details on this activity.

Walkways, including their stairs, ramps, railings, benches, benchwalls, graphics and lighting are all part of the pedestrian circulation system. Information on stairs, ramps, railing, benches, benchwalls and graphics can be found in Chapters 7 – Utilities–Lighting and 10 – Details.

Layout/Location

All **public** facilities must have an accessible way to at least some of each leisure facility available for public use. Handicapped accessibility assures older people accessibility to at least some recreation areas which may in the past have been difficult to get to. In addition, trails and similar pedestrian oriented activities should be designed, where possible, to accommodate people with diminishing abilities. The following guidelines will assist in improving pedestrian way usability for older people.

Design Criteria

- Keep vertical alignment as level as the site will permit. Where grades over 10% and/or stairs are necessary, place climatically tempered benches at the top of grade. If the vertical separation is greater than 3 m (10'), consider intermediate rest stops. Slopes over 5% are considered ramps when used on an accessible way and must be treated as such.

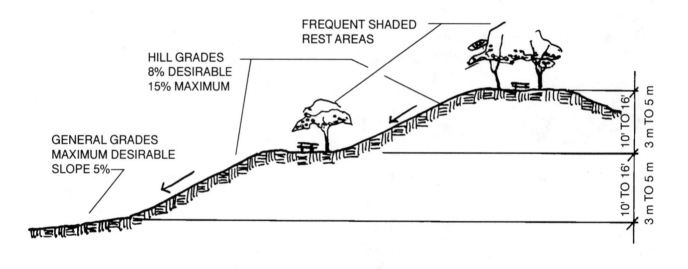

Figure 6.15 *Walk and Trail Slopes (Not Handicapped Accessible)*

- All walks to be used during darkness must be well lighted. This is particularly necessary for stairways. See Chapter 7 – Utilities -Lighting.

- Access walks should be designed to get people where they want to go in the most direct way possible commensurate with good design practices. Minimum clear way width with no obstacles is 1200 mm (48")

so a minimum of two people can walk side by side. Desirable minimum is 1500 mm (60"), the minimum for wheelchairs to pass and/or turn around in the walkway.

- Shade all walkways where possible with plant material, deciduous in the north and evergreen or deciduous in the south.

- Screen walkways from cold winds.

Tree shaded walkway – Lisbon, Portugal

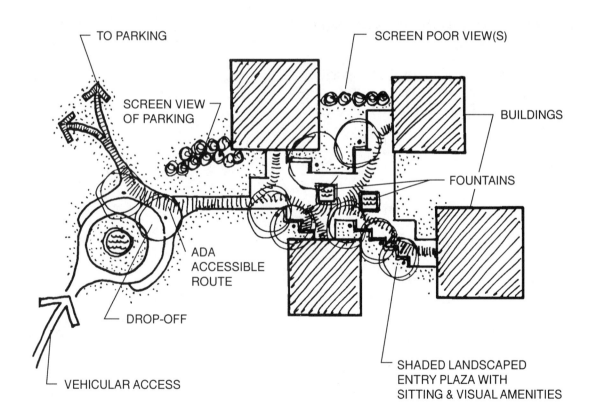

Figure 6.16 *Access Walkway Plan*

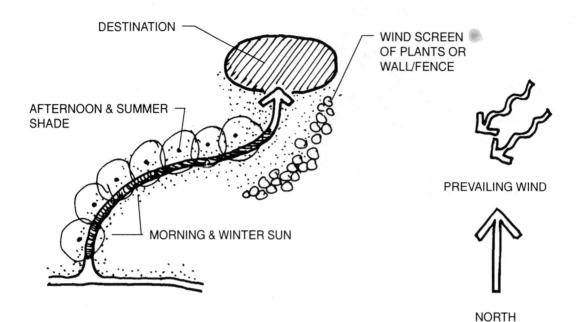

DESTINATION

WIND SCREEN
OF PLANTS OR
WALL/FENCE

AFTERNOON & SUMMER
SHADE

MORNING & WINTER SUN

PREVAILING WIND

NORTH

Figure 6.17 *Environmental Modifications to Walkways*

• Walk surfaces should be hard finished (concrete, pavers with obstacle-free surfaces, asphalt). See Chapter 10 – Details.

Chapter 7 UTILITIES

*F*or the most part, utilities are utilities and are usually out of sight, out of mind. They follow standard engineering practices and are not of concern for older people unless they affect their ability to use the leisure facilities. Important exceptions to this general statement are explored throughout this chapter.

Sanitary facilities, their location and design are of critical importance. They are one of the key elements in making leisure facilities more older-people friendly. Other utility items which, when properly located and designed, such as drinking fountains, communications (phones and sound systems), and lighting can considerably enhance user enjoyment. The problem of background noise is of critical importance in many leisure pursuits. This affects the location of (1) all noise generating mechanical equipment (air conditioners, pool pumps, lift stations, etc.), and (2) building entrances and building/site areas, transition/gathering areas, outdoor theaters, campgrounds, etc.

SANITARY FACILITIES

Current guidelines for the design of sanitary facilities are comprehensive and detailed. *Park Planning Guidelines 3rd Edition* has suggested fixture requirements for many recreation activities. All accessible sanitary facilities must comply with ADA and must include the necessary modifications to make standard toilet stalls wheelchair accessible, sinks with easy to operate faucets, etc. (See Chapter 3).

Most public facilities currently make an attempt to provide these requirements. In addition, please note state and local requirements could be even more restrictive and detailed. The authors suggest that some additional considerations be given to facility layout and numbers of fixtures for men and women. First and most important, the toilets for use by handicapped should be immediately available on entrance to the building. Older people and people with sight problems should be able to find easily and quickly the object of their relief!

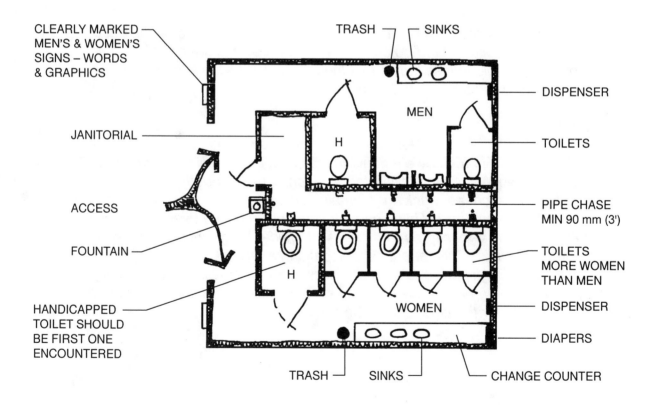

Figure 7.1 *Toilet Facilities*

Please Note – Number of fixture units – toilets and urinals. Where approximately the same number of men and women are expected, then more fixtures (toilets) are needed for the women than the men (toilets and urinals combined). This may not be considered in local building requirements, but it is necessary to prevent waiting lines for women. This design modification is sometimes known as "potty parity."

The demographic charts in Chapter 2 graphically illustrate the skewing of the male/female ratio to the women as the cohorts age. It is therefore **necessary** to provide more fixture units for women than men for facilities that serve older people. The number of extra facilities needed can be determined by separately calculating the number of men and women and then providing the appropriate fixture count for each sex.

As people age, their bladder capacity and/or control are frequently diminished. It is desirable therefore to provide sanitary facilities closer together and/or in more locations. The logical outgrowth of the solution to this problem is more strategically located, smaller-in-size sanitary facilities. See Chapter 6 – Circulation plus individual activities in Chapters 8 and 9 for location suggestions.

WATER

The design of water systems is not affected by age except in minor ways such as availability of drinking water, ease of being able to utilize water faucets, and, where irrigation is used, keeping the water off walk areas.

Drinking Water

Drinking fountain

Frequent sources of drinking water, located especially in areas where older people are likely to congregate, would be much appreciated. Such points, in addition to those normally provided, would be at (1) selected rest areas along walkways and trails, especially at tops of stairs on long grades, (2) tennis courts, golf courses, and other active recreation sites, (3) tourist features such as community piers (docks), and (4) shopping areas and malls, especially those that permit early morning exercise walking.

Fountains should be located where they are out of the circulation path but can be easily seen by the users. Use of handicapped type

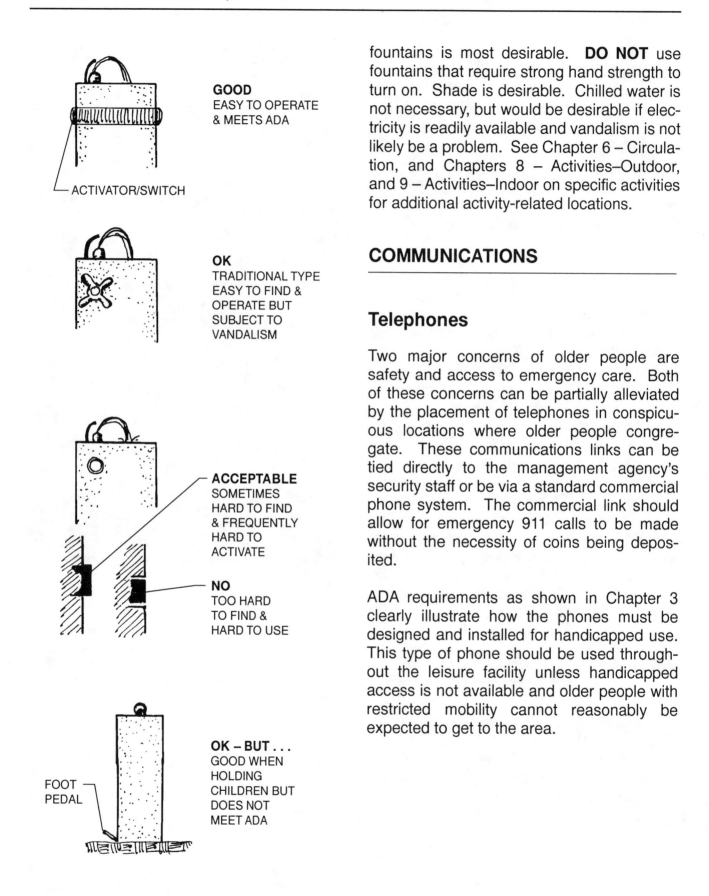

GOOD
EASY TO OPERATE
& MEETS ADA

ACTIVATOR/SWITCH

OK
TRADITIONAL TYPE
EASY TO FIND &
OPERATE BUT
SUBJECT TO
VANDALISM

ACCEPTABLE
SOMETIMES
HARD TO FIND
& FREQUENTLY
HARD TO
ACTIVATE

NO
TOO HARD
TO FIND &
HARD TO USE

OK – BUT . . .
GOOD WHEN
HOLDING
CHILDREN BUT
DOES NOT
MEET ADA

FOOT
PEDAL

Figure 7.2 *Drinking Fountains*

fountains is most desirable. **DO NOT** use fountains that require strong hand strength to turn on. Shade is desirable. Chilled water is not necessary, but would be desirable if electricity is readily available and vandalism is not likely be a problem. See Chapter 6 – Circulation, and Chapters 8 – Activities–Outdoor, and 9 – Activities–Indoor on specific activities for additional activity-related locations.

COMMUNICATIONS

Telephones

Two major concerns of older people are safety and access to emergency care. Both of these concerns can be partially alleviated by the placement of telephones in conspicuous locations where older people congregate. These communications links can be tied directly to the management agency's security staff or be via a standard commercial phone system. The commercial link should allow for emergency 911 calls to be made without the necessity of coins being deposited.

ADA requirements as shown in Chapter 3 clearly illustrate how the phones must be designed and installed for handicapped use. This type of phone should be used throughout the leisure facility unless handicapped access is not available and older people with restricted mobility cannot reasonably be expected to get to the area.

Telephone Booth

Provision of emergency communications is a must in areas of perceived danger – i.e. isolated areas of any kind and high crime areas, real or perceived. Communications are also necessary wherever older people participate in strenuous physical activities for summoning emergency health care personnel – i.e. beaches, pools, tennis courts, exercise locations, etc. Consider phones also at rest stops along trails, bikeways and at the tops of strenuous climbs or grades.

Sound Systems

An area frequently overlooked by designers is the need for special types of sound equipment for older people. As Chapter 2 points out "by the age of 65, both males and females are likely to have a hearing loss for frequencies above 1,000 hz..."

Many leisure facilities utilize overhead speakers, especially in trams, buses, passenger loading areas, etc., which normally have at best poor quality sound reproduction even for those with good hearing. These systems must be upgraded to the best level possible if it is desired that older people are to understand and/or enjoy what is being transmitted.

Background Sound

In addition, older people may have a reduced ability to separate sounds from each other, especially conversations from background noises. Every effort should be made to reduce the reverberations within the site, especially where people gather. This is particularly true in the transition/interface areas between indoor and outdoor activities and at building entrances.

Reverberations can be reduced by:

(1) Avoiding fully enclosed spaces where possible.

(2) For all areas which are enclosed, use sound deadening techniques such as –

- Textured sound absorbing ground plane, i.e. groundcovers, grass, textured paving.
- Building surfaces to be sound absorbing or at least not highly sound reflective, i.e. textured wall material, possibly vines on walls, uneven wall planes, etc.
- Walks of textured concrete pavers, decks of wood, not smooth stones or concrete.

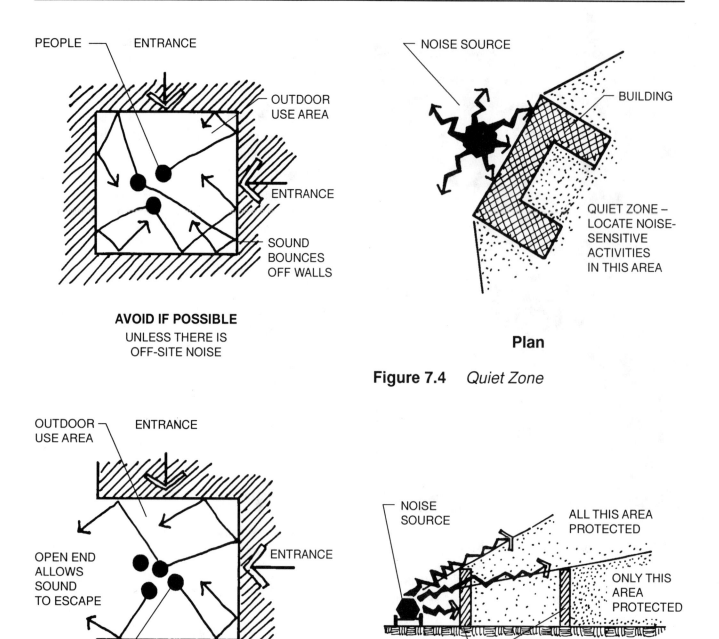

PEOPLE — ENTRANCE

OUTDOOR USE AREA

ENTRANCE

SOUND BOUNCES OFF WALLS

AVOID IF POSSIBLE
UNLESS THERE IS
OFF-SITE NOISE

NOISE SOURCE

BUILDING

QUIET ZONE –
LOCATE NOISE-
SENSITIVE
ACTIVITIES
IN THIS AREA

Plan

Figure 7.4 *Quiet Zone*

OUTDOOR USE AREA — ENTRANCE

ENTRANCE

OPEN END
ALLOWS
SOUND
TO ESCAPE

PEOPLE —

BETTER

NOISE SOURCE

ALL THIS AREA PROTECTED

ONLY THIS AREA PROTECTED

BARRIER

Section

Figure 7.3 *Avoid Fully Enclosed Outdoor Use Areas*

Figure 7.5 *The Closer the Solid Barrier to the Noise Source, the Larger the Quiet Zone*

All entrances and people use areas should be so located that they are in a quiet zone. See Figures 7.4 and 7.5 from *Park Planning Guidelines 3rd Edition.*

Tree and/or shrub screen

Sound screening with walls and berms

Noise travels in a straight line. Only two things significantly affect noise reduction – distance (the farther away, the less noise) and solid physical barriers such as walls, mounds and buildings. Plant material, however dense and nice it might look, **DOES NOT** significantly reduce sound. This means that if there is a noise source, all people entrances, transition and use areas need to be located in quiet zones. This is particularly true for functions and activities that cater to older people. See Figures 7.6 and 7.7.

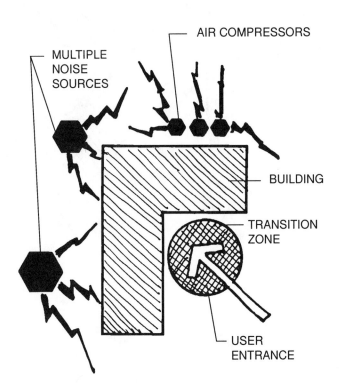

Figure 7.6 *Use of a Building to Create a Quiet Zone at Primary People Entrance*

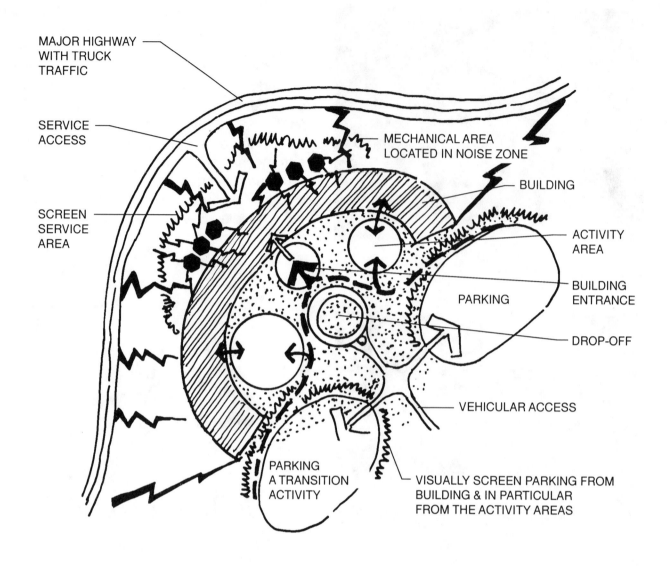

Figure 7.7   *A Noise-Sensitive Site Plan*

LIGHTING

As we mature, lighting plays an increasingly important role in our ability to perceive visual cues and information. Physiologically, a decline in visual acuity generally begins in our twenties and continues throughout our lifetime. The muscles of the eye become less elastic, the lens changes, and as a result it becomes more difficult for the eye to make adjustments to bright and dark environments. This can result in "adaptive" problems.

The retina contains two kinds of light-sensitive cells – rods and cones. The cones are receptors of higher levels of illumination and color. The rods help us to see under low light conditions and are color-blind. The rods are the cells that our brain uses for night vision. Unfortunately, the rods do not provide us with very clear and distinct vision. To illustrate, go to a dark room and focus on a specific object within that space. You will find that moving your glance slightly "off-center" will improve the visual impression of the particular object. This is because we are using less efficient rods for seeing. With more illumination on the object, our cones come back into play and our visual image improves dramatically. Because of these two factors, lighting for older people must consider more uniform lighting designs, i.e. avoid the "pools" of light and provide increasingly higher levels of quality, uniform illumination.

Providing higher foot-candles (unit of illumination) is only one factor of lighting design. Control of glare is of major importance in providing good visual environments and cannot be over-emphasized. A lighting design that calls for relatively low lighting levels without debilitating glare and shadows can be achieved at both low initial and operating costs. The key here is to select the proper equipment which must be installed in accordance within specific design parameters.

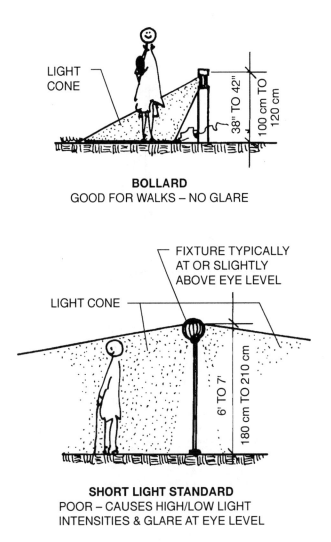

BOLLARD
GOOD FOR WALKS – NO GLARE

SHORT LIGHT STANDARD
POOR – CAUSES HIGH/LOW LIGHT
INTENSITIES & GLARE AT EYE LEVEL

Figure 7.8 *Walk Lighting Fixtures*

As we all have observed, an evening stroll under a full moon is very pleasant and yet the lighting level is quite low. The illumination from the moon is perhaps a couple of foot-candles, but the "quality of light" is good, i.e. uniform and glare-free, and allows us to see obstructions with ease. By comparison, at noon on a sunny day it would not be unusual to measure 10,000 foot-candles. As a matter of fact, these sunny-day conditions are typically too bright for some. That is why we wear sun glasses and find it more comfortable to read under the shade of a tree, a perfect example of "quality" illumination.

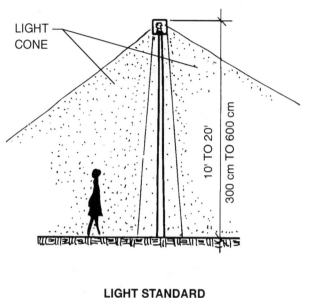

LIGHT CONE

10' TO 20'

300 cm TO 600 cm

LIGHT STANDARD
PROVIDES UNIFORM
LIGHT DISTRIBUTION

Figure 7.9   *3 m to 6 m Light Standards for Uniform Light Distribution*

For exterior use, where temperature extremes and maintenance are a consideration, H.I.D. lamps are the best choice. Without getting into a technical discussion, ***metal-halide*** H.I.D. lamps offer the best balance of efficacy, long lamp life, good color rendition (white light), and operating cost. This type of light is best also for people with visual problems.

Another H.I.D. light source is ***high-pressure sodium***, the amber or yellow light used predominantly for roadway lighting. Because of poor color rendition, H.P.S. sources are not recommended for purposes of this discussion for either interior or exterior use.

Horizontal vs. Vertical Lighting

Lighting requirements differ for various activities. Shuffleboard for example requires, for the most part, horizontal foot-candles. A walk through an interpretive facility with signage, a parking lot, or an art class requires vertical foot-candles. The success and full utilization of the intended purpose of the activity demands consideration of these fundamental design elements.

LIGHTING RECOMMENDATIONS FOR SELECTED LOCATIONS

Parking Lots

Recently, security has become a major concern to people of all ages. Leisure activities are not limited to between the hours of nine to five. Poorly lighted parking lots are very often a concern to people who might otherwise have no concerns during daylight hours. If evening hour activities are planned, well lighted parking lots and walkways are critical to high utilization and security. H.I.D. light sources are best.

Tennis and Sport-Court Lighting (Exterior)

In many climates the most enjoyable time for vigorous sports, e.g., tennis, is after sunset. Lighted outdoor tennis courts permit enjoyment of the sport into the evening hours thereby expanding access and opportunity. In order to provide proper court lighting, it is only considerate and neighborly to restrict the light to the court surfaces, eliminating "direct light" into bedroom windows of adjoining residences. This can be accomplished by using "cut-off" lighting fixtures on 6 m to 7.3 m (20 ft to 24 ft) davit arm posts. This design limits the lighting to the courts only.

Signage (Illumination)

As discussed in a previous section, size of letters and graphics, and in particular, contrast, play an important role in the legibility of signage. Additionally, if night-time use is anticipated signage must be illuminated, remembering that in most cases, a vertical plane is involved. Illumination level shall be 100 to 300 lux (10 to 30 foot-candles).

Stairways, Curbs and Passageways

Between structures the designer must pay particular attention to stairways, curbs, individual steps, or any other change in elevation. Proper illumination is critical for safe passage, especially for those wearing corrective lenses such as bifocals and trifocals, and for older adults with less mobility. Lighting for good depth perception is frequently more difficult to design for older people. The perception of depth cues is directly related to lighting and shadows produced by the lighting system. Careful placement of lights to show clearly the changes in elevation is critical.

Roadway lighting, if provided, should be uniform with no pools of light. If budget constraints do not permit uniform lighting, then provide quality lighting at intersections only, and no lights for the remainder of the roadway. Where pedestrians and/or bicyclists share the same roadway, street lighting is a necessity.

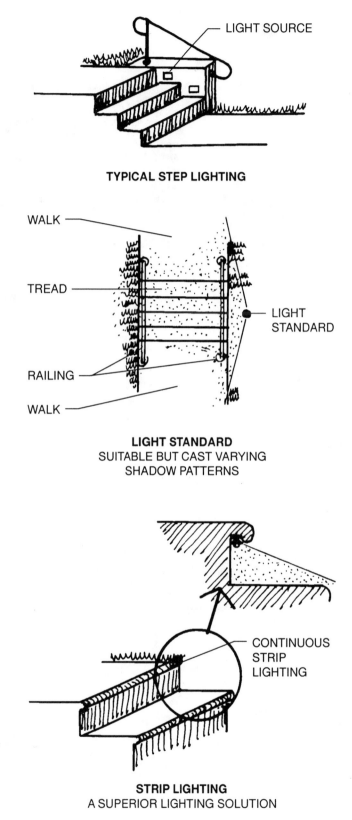

TYPICAL STEP LIGHTING

LIGHT STANDARD
SUITABLE BUT CAST VARYING
SHADOW PATTERNS

STRIP LIGHTING
A SUPERIOR LIGHTING SOLUTION

Figure 7.10 *Step Lighting Roadways*

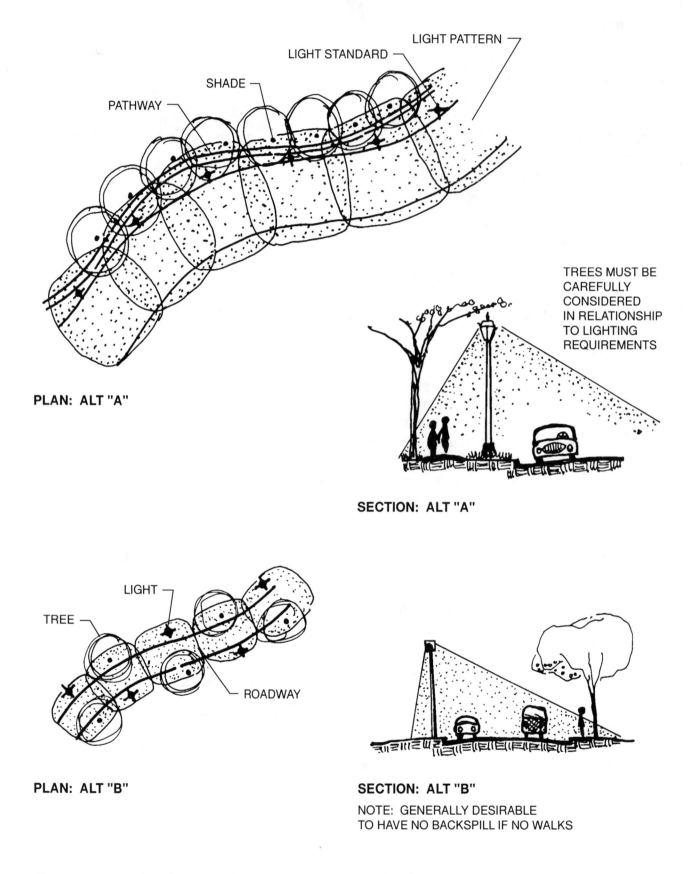

PATHWAY   SHADE   LIGHT STANDARD   LIGHT PATTERN

PLAN: ALT "A"

TREES MUST BE CAREFULLY CONSIDERED IN RELATIONSHIP TO LIGHTING REQUIREMENTS

SECTION: ALT "A"

TREE   LIGHT

ROADWAY

PLAN: ALT "B"

SECTION: ALT "B"

NOTE: GENERALLY DESIRABLE TO HAVE NO BACKSPILL IF NO WALKS

Figure 7.11 *Roadway Lighting*

Parking Lots

A minimum of one foot-candle is necessary at any point, with maximum to minimum foot-candle value ratio not to exceed seven to one. (Shopping centers are typically designed for minimum levels of 3 to 5 foot-candles.) High light standards (light poles) are preferred to insure uniform lighting levels, however, this may conflict with parking lot planting and must be carefully studied.

Walkways

Particular care must be paid to adequate levels of good quality lighting on all walkways used by older people. A minimum of one-half foot-candle with good uniformity of lighting is required, i.e. no pools of light.

Building Entries

A minimum of five foot-candles is needed at building entries.

Shuffleboard and Basic Recreational Lighting

A lower source of lights should be adequate to illuminate the court surface – 20 foot-candles. Make sure that lighting spill will not cause problems with neighbors.

For recommended levels of illumination of other facilities/sites refer to the Illuminating Engineering Society's recommendations: *I.E.S. Lighting Handbook – Reference Volume.* This resource is published by: Illuminating Engineering Society of North America, 345 East 47th Street, New York, NY 10017.

It is strongly urged that a qualified lighting consultant be utilized in the lighting design aspects of a project.

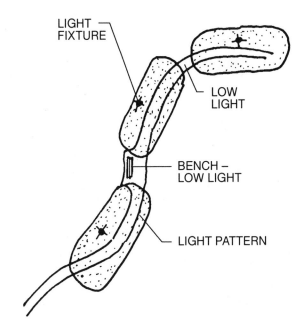

NO

TYPICAL LIGHTING – AESTHETICALLY PLEASING BUT HARD FOR EYES TO ADJUST TO VARYING LIGHT LEVELS

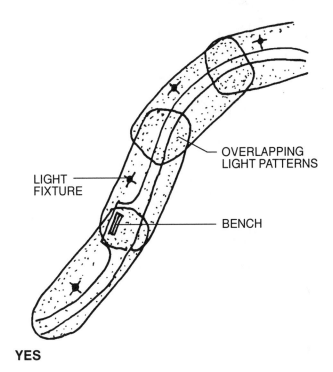

YES

OVERLAPPING LIGHT PATTERNS CREATE UNIFORM LIGHT LEVELS

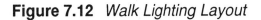

Figure 7.12 *Walk Lighting Layout*

Chapter 8 ACTIVITIES–OUTDOOR

Many leisure facilities have specific rules, criteria and/or dimensions that need to be followed. These core characteristics of the physical facilities should not be changed if at all possible.

As we have discussed previously, people's abilities/capabilities change over their lifetimes.   The dilemma then is in designing the basic facilities which should not have to change while people are constantly changing. The question then is: What can be done to make the leisure experience more enjoyable, and in some cases make it even possible, for people to do as they age?

*The following are activity specific recommendations on how to modify facilities without changing their basic rules, criteria and/or dimensions. Many of these ideas could fit into the concept of "**UNIVERSAL DESIGN**" and will make the facility more usable and enjoyable for a wide range of users, not just people over 55.*

Creativity and care should be taken in site specific application of these modifications to minimize their costs.

TENNIS

Tennis – Naples, Florida

A 1992 tennis industry survey showed participation in tennis by people age 50 and over nearly doubled from 1988 to 1992 from 971,000 to 1,813,000, or approximately 13 percent of all tennis players. There was a 60 percent/40 percent men/women ratio.

Tennis court users in general can benefit from a number of modifications which will make the courts better for older users.

(1) Resilient surfacing – for less impact on legs.

(2) Sitting area(s) – resting, visiting, waiting, watching.

(3) Environmental modifications – i.e. wind screens on the courts and shade and windscreens at the sitting areas. Both are desirable for enhanced user enjoyment while shade is necessary for health reasons for many older people.

(4) Use of black or other dark colored permafused vinyl coated fencing against which the ball can be better seen.

(5) A communication link to a manned emergency response center for health emergencies.

(6) Easily accessible sanitary facilities within 60 m (200') of courts.

Shade should preferably be by man-made structure or clean-type trees rather than trees which drop small leaves/needles, sap and/or insect droppings on the court surface. The shade device(s) should be located so as to provide adequate afternoon sun protection. (See Chapter 10 – Details–Shade Structures.)

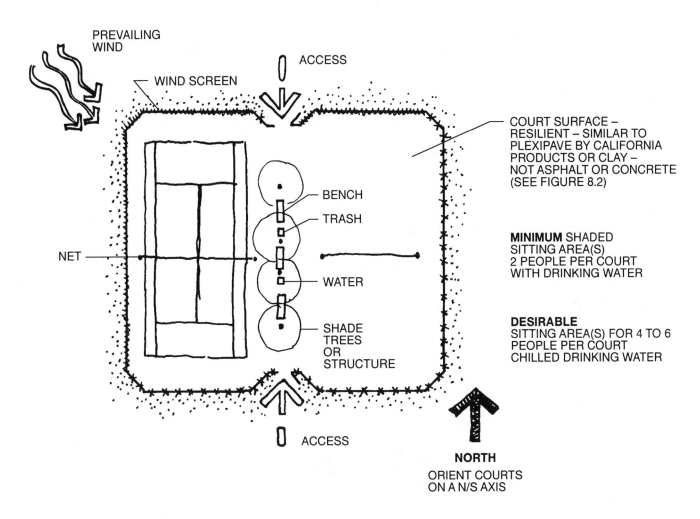

Figure 8.1 *Tennis Court Layout*

Extra shaded sitting space for spectators is desirable wherever space permits. The problems of debris on the court surface are not apparent here, therefore, the sitting area can be shaded by trees or vine covered trellises. There are some older people who would like to watch even though they are not able to play. This space must be located on the accessible route and must, at a minimum, be shaded for summer sun and protected from cold winds.

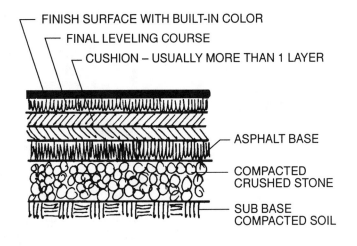

Figure 8.2 *Tennis Court Surfacing*

GOLF

Golfing continues to grow in popularity even though it is an expensive leisure activity. Many upscale residential developments utilize golf and its attendant clubhouse, dining and social spaces as their primary sales enhancement, and also as a portion of its legally required community open space component. Since so many new people are taking up golf as the opportunities for golfing expand, it is necessary to understand who these users are and their needs. The following demographic information is from 1987 data by the National Golf Foundation.

According to data furnished by the National Golf Foundation, older golfers play golf twice as frequently as younger golfers. Many older golfers play more for fun than the competition. It therefore stands to reason that as populations age, there will be proportionately more older users on the courses.

By household income:

3.8% of golfers	less than 10,000
12.9%	10,000 to 19,999
17.7%	20,000 to 29,999
20.5%	30,000 to 39,999
44.9%	40,000 per year or more

By age:

4.0%	5 to 14 years old	11% of golfers and
7.2%	15 to 19	they play 6.7% of rounds played
27.3%	20 to 29	73% of golfers and
22.2%	30 to 39	they play 62% of
14.1%	40 to 49	rounds played
10.2%	50 to 59	15% of golfers and
5.4%	60 to 65	they play 31% of
9.6%	over 65	rounds played

By sex:

77.4%	men
22.6%	women – however, 41% of the new golfers in 1987 were women which could, if the trend continues, have a major long-term impact on increasing the percentage of women playing golf.

Golf, Quail Run Golf Course – Naples, Florida

As stated in Chapter 2, people continue their leisure pursuits of earlier years into their maturity and older years. These activities are modified, however, to meet the limitations placed on people by the aging process.

Park Planning Guidelines characterizes golf as "a game of power, skill and judgment – power to hit the ball as far as possible, skill to hit it where it is needed to go, and the judgment to decide where to hit the ball and what club to use to accomplish it. Of equal importance for most golfers, it is a place to meet and socialize." (p. 121)

The ability to "hit the ball as far as possible" declines with age. To compensate for this reduced distance capability, it is recommended that an additional tee(s) be added closer to the green. See Figure 8.3.

Other factors that are important to older golfers are:

- Sanitary facilities – diminished bladder retention capability requires the addition of sanitary facilities. These facilities should be located between the 4th green and 5th tee and again between the 13th green and 14th tee. (See preceding figure.) Facilities should be unisex in design and handicapped accessible. One or two fixture units per location should be adequate.

- Golf carts are a major revenue generator for golf courses. For those courses serving older people they are also a necessity. Care should be taken in laying out golf courses to ensure that all playable parts of the course are golf cart accessible. Some areas such as greens may be marked as "off limits" to all carts (except those with certified physical handicaps as defined by ADA).

Golf carts – for older people they can make the game more enjoyable and, in some cases, they are a necessity

- Courses with significant natural rough areas (wetlands and habitat areas) may need to establish "No Hunt Areas" – areas where you cannot go into the rough to hunt for your ball. This would tend to speed up play if people are not going too far off the course.

- According to a number of "older" golfers, the course aesthetics become more important as you age – possibly to compensate for reduced ability and increased scores.

- Older people need to have special attention paid to them during weather extremes (cold and especially hot weather). This might mean that a patrol should be established during hot days, or that rules be established restricting play when temperature/humidity exceed a danger threshold.

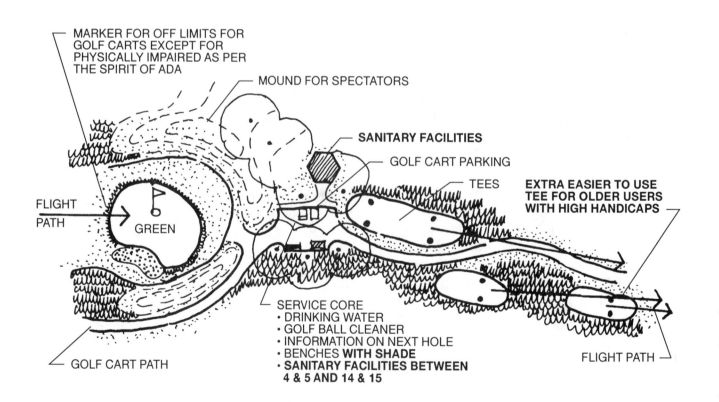

Figure 8.3   *Player service core at greens/tees*

Golf course aesthetics, Pebble Beach – Carmel, California

SWIMMING AND RELATED ACTIVITIES

Many older people go to the beach or pool frequently – on the average of once a month, with a significant percentage going much more frequently. Swimming is normally only a portion of their water-related activities. Except for the avid exerciser, it is probably only a minor part of the beach/pool experience. Other things (or activities) take up most of the time: visiting with friends, relaxing, reading, people watching are the norm. In all swimming-related activities though there are some constants.

Parking – Locate as near as practical to the water activity with maximum distances of 100 m to 150 m (330' to 500').

Access – Utilize the accessible route or other walks and paths designed as per Chapter 6 – Circulation–Pedestrian.

Shade – A necessity and can be by permanent structures, trees and/or movable umbrella-type shade devices. See Chapter 10 – Details–Shade Structures.

Sanitary facilities – Located within 60 m (200') of activity area and at least one on the ADA access route.

Water – Drinking water (chilled where possible) should be as close to the beach as feasible and within a maximum of 60 m (200') and 40 m (125' ±) of the beach users. Best location is on the access walk system.

Communication (health and safety) – Free telephone service needs to be available for medical emergencies and the feeling of safety with a link to emergency and security help. Locate at sanitary facilities on the primary accessible route.

In addition:

Food service – Desirable where economically feasible. The eating area should be placed in a location with a view of the water.

Chairs – A very desirable amenity which reduces the amount of material needed to be carried from the car to the beach.

Pool

Many pools in small communities (especially condo and home owner association pools) have become centers for older people to gather.

Access – A ramp is required by ADA and can be very useful for the more elderly and those suffering mobility difficulties. See also Figure 8.6.

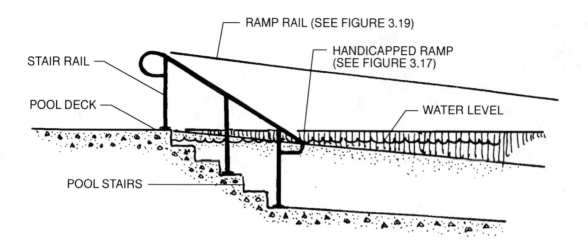

Figure 8.4   *Access Ramp and Stairs*

In-Pool Sitting – A desirable amenity for leisure pools is in-pool sitting. It provides a comfortable place for visiting with friends, both in the pool and on the deck. The seating could also be combined with a pool-side bar.

Note: The addition of in-pool sitting is not suitable to competition pools! Separate sitting bollards should not be placed in the lap section of any pool.

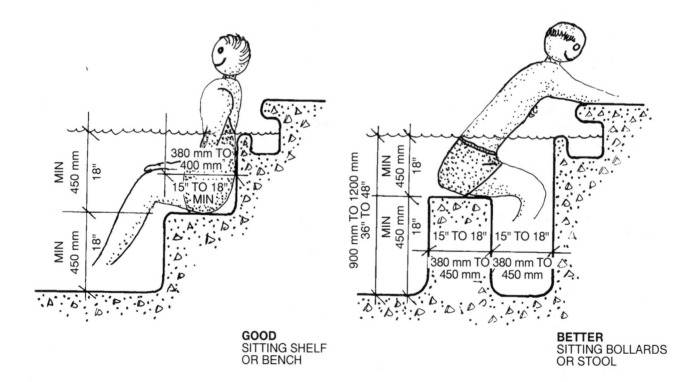

Figure 8.5   *In-Pool Sitting*

Lap Lanes – Provide lap lanes for the people who swim laps for exercise – preferably separate from other pool "play" type space.

Water Aerobics or Aquasizing Area – A 1000 mm to 1200 mm (40" to 48") deep area for in-pool exercising. An electrical outlet and table nearby for a music system are necessary. Please note that a good quality sound/speaker system is a necessity for older people to hear.

Pool used for water aerobics – N. Fort Myers, Florida

Orientation – Lap lanes should be oriented on a north/south line or as close to it as possible. If there will be no "lap" swimming, any orientation is suitable with the exception that all pools need to have maximum sunlight during the cooler parts of their season – spring and fall in the north, and winter in the far south.

Lighting – Many pools are used in evenings – quality lighting is essential, both in the pool and on the surrounding deck. Parking and pedestrian accessways would also need lighting. See Chapter 7 – Utilities–Lighting.

Outdoor Cooking / Eating – A nearby cooking and eating space is desirable. It is generally not desirable to have eating on the pool deck due to staining and attracting yellow jackets.

Spa/Jacuzzi – A desirable, heavily used addition to pool areas for older people. A user-activated pool pump control with an automatic shut-off would be a desirable cost-saving feature.

Fencing and Gates – All pools must be fenced for safety. In private pools, condos, etc., the gate latches must be easy to operate, but the opening mechanism must be high enough that small children cannot reach them. A better solution to both unauthorized use and small child safety is a key operated, self-closing and locking gate(s).

Aesthetics – Older people may spend a great deal of time at the pool aquasizing, swimming, sunning, reading and, most importantly, visiting with friends. Good aesthetic surroundings will enhance the users' enjoyment, i.e. plantings, views (of the golf course, mountains, etc., and possibly other activities).

Deck Area – Most people do not swim and many do not even go into the pool. A 2:1 or 3:1 pool deck space to water space is needed for sunning, lounging, pedestrian circulation, and most importantly, visiting with friends. Shade and sun areas are both needed. Sunny, warm deck areas are needed where the pools are used during cool weather. Cool season use may also necessitate wind barriers.

Pool Heating – Warm (tempered) water is needed to make pools enjoyable and, in fact, even usable for people as they age. This can be done efficiently and cost-effectively with solar heating if it is considered early in the design stages.

Pool deck – a multipurpose space for visiting, lounging, sunning and circulation – N. Fort Myers, Florida

Beach

In addition to the normal water play, visiting, etc., there is a great deal of walking along the beach in singles, but more likely by couples and in small groups of friends. General nature observation is very common, and shelling is very common along the coast. The beach is a frequent location for multi-generational gatherings.

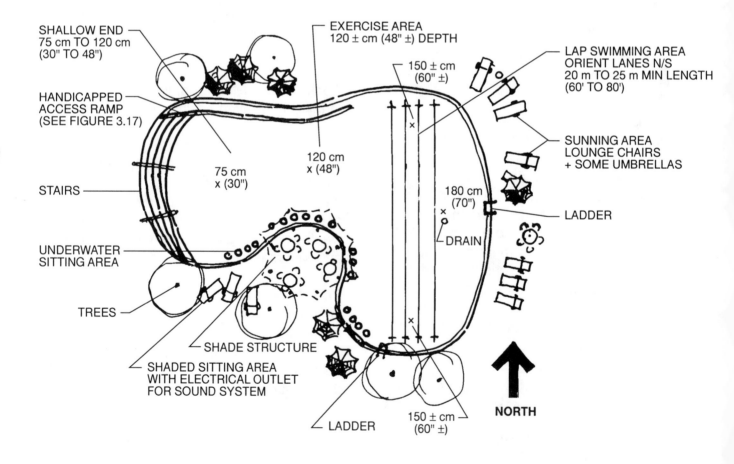

Figure 8.6   *Pool Layout*

Coastal

Beaches – Foot washing facilities are needed – showers are desirable.

Shade! – This usually requires shade structures due to coastal ecology. Structures must also meet severe storm condition requirements, especially on the Gulf and Atlantic coasts.

Access – Dune walkovers to coastal beaches are becoming the rule, rather than the exception. They are necessary for dune protection and present a desirable location to include interpretive information. Sensitive environmental situations may require parking to be remote (greater than 150 m (500')) from the beach. Under these conditions, consider the provision of a tram service, either free or for a small fee.

Nature study trails – Self-guiding trails along the shore and in areas behind the primary dune are a desirable addition for older beach users. Information on the trails can be made available on the dune walkover or at beach sanitary facilities.

Concession – A desirable addition for beach users. Normally they provide food service, equipment rental, especially umbrella and lounge chairs, and miscellaneous beach items.

Chairs – Desirable to have durable, movable chairs available at entrance to beach. Staff will be needed to pick up chairs daily.

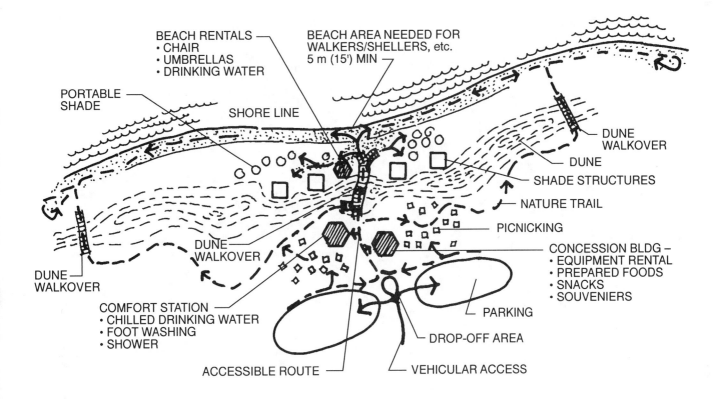

Figure 8.7 *Coastal Beach Area*

Inland (Usually Fresh Water)

Shade – Normally trees will already be existing at the inland beach site. With good design, they can be saved and utilized in place. If not existing, bring in large 5 m± (15') x 2 m (6'±) tall spread trees.

Nature trail – Self-guiding trails along the shore and inland. Information about the trails should be located on the beach access or at the beach sanitary facilities.

Concession – Same as coastal beach.

EQUESTRIAN FACILITIES

Older people ride horses. Generally few modifications would be needed to make equestrian activities more suitable for older riders.

Proof that horseback riding after 55 is possible – Naples, Florida Photo: Sharon Kurgis Ginter

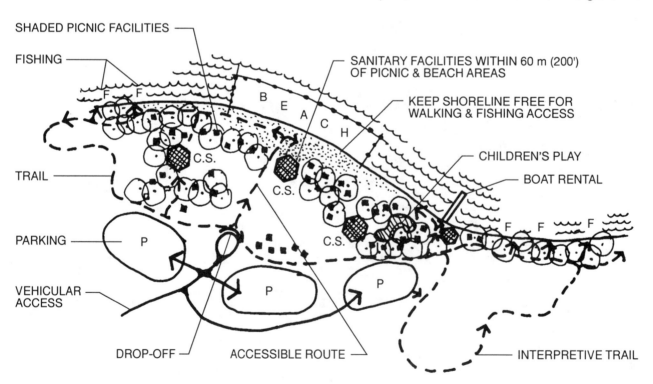

Figure 8.8   *Inland Beach Area*

Some suggestions:

Riding

• Provide sanitary facilities at stables, trail-head parking and at one-hour intervals along heavily used trails.

Consider a mounting ramp – this could be used for handicapped accessibility. See Chapter 3 – Current Guidelines–Ramps.

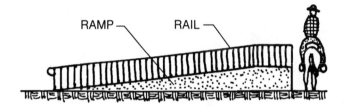

Figure 8.9 *Equestrian Mounting Ramp*

• Drinking water is needed.

• Provide loop trail system similar to pedestrian system (see Chapter 6 – Trails) with shaded rest areas at one-hour intervals.

Spectator Areas

• Shade and other environmental modifications.

• Drinking water.

• Sanitary facilities.

• When provided, at least some of the benches should have backs.

DRIVING FOR PLEASURE

Driving for pleasure and sightseeing are activities that all who have access to transportation can enjoy with ease. For some older people, this may be one of the few things in which they can participate throughout their entire life. It is also one of the most participated-in leisure activities in the U.S. As such, it is desirable then to provide special considerations for cultural and aesthetic (enhancement) and appreciation to roadway designs. All highways, roads and byways should be designed with aesthetics in mind – i.e. views, not just corridors for moving cars and other vehicles. At the very least, roads which serve resort areas, leisure complexes, and internal park and forest roads should be designed and their rights-of-ways managed for maximum visual enjoyment of both natural and cultural features.

Fall color from the road – Pennsylvania

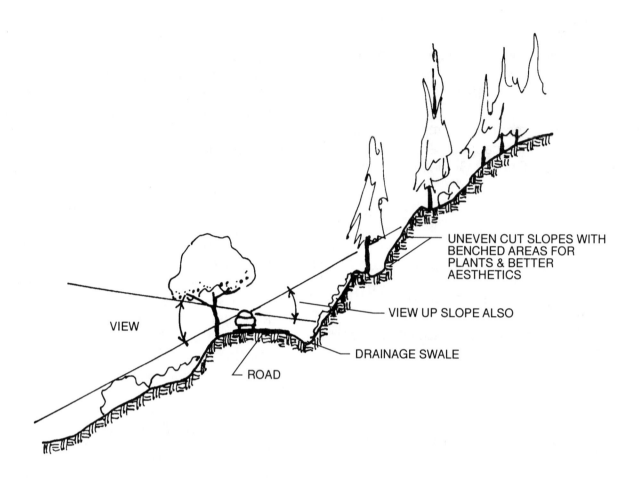

UNEVEN CUT SLOPES WITH BENCHED AREAS FOR PLANTS & BETTER AESTHETICS

VIEW UP SLOPE ALSO

DRAINAGE SWALE

VIEW

ROAD

Figure 8.10 *Road section for a side hill cut*

Things to consider for leisure/aesthetic enhancement of roadways:

- Horizontal and vertical alignment – maximize fit to ground and view opportunities. Minimize cuts and fills and unattractive views – i.e. power line crossings and landfills, some industrial developments. It should be noted, however, that some industrial activities such as oil refineries, steel mills, etc., can be very interesting viewing and could make good interpretive stops.

- Road alignment should avoid damaging visual features – physically or with noise pollution.

- Enhance views through selective clearing, carefully framing with plants. Screen undesirable views with berming and planting.

- Overlooks and educational stops should be provided.

Overlook along road
– Tidaughton State Park, New York

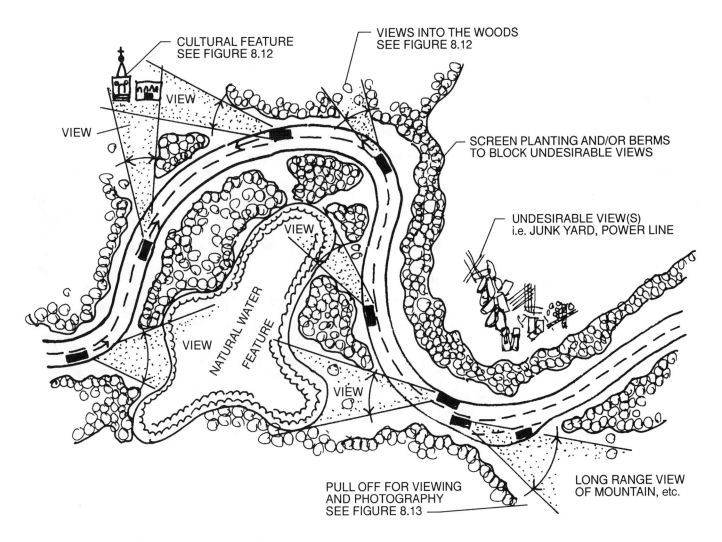

CULTURAL FEATURE
SEE FIGURE 8.12

VIEWS INTO THE WOODS
SEE FIGURE 8.12

VIEW

VIEW

SCREEN PLANTING AND/OR BERMS
TO BLOCK UNDESIRABLE VIEWS

UNDESIRABLE VIEW(S)
i.e. JUNK YARD, POWER LINE

VIEW

NATURAL WATER FEATURE

VIEW

VIEW

PULL OFF FOR VIEWING
AND PHOTOGRAPHY
SEE FIGURE 8.13

LONG RANGE VIEW
OF MOUNTAIN, etc.

Figure 8.11 *Views along a roadway*

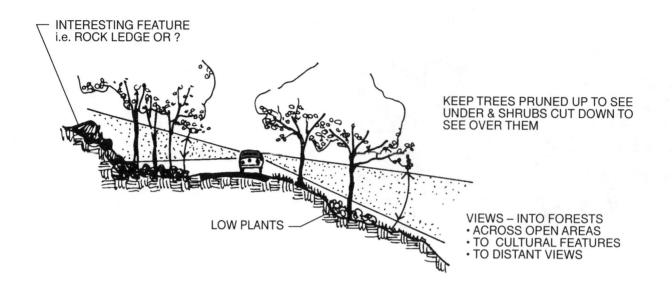

INTERESTING FEATURE
i.e. ROCK LEDGE OR ?

KEEP TREES PRUNED UP TO SEE
UNDER & SHRUBS CUT DOWN TO
SEE OVER THEM

LOW PLANTS

VIEWS – INTO FORESTS
• ACROSS OPEN AREAS
• TO CULTURAL FEATURES
• TO DISTANT VIEWS

Figure 8.12   *Clearing for views*

Overlooks / Interpretive Stops

Long drives are tiring. Places to stop along the way are useful from a safety standpoint, but their location and design are seldom considered from an aesthetic standpoint. Overlooks and interpretive stops would not be intended as a substitute for roadside rests, but rather as supplements to these rest stops and an integral part of enhancing the leisure driving experience. They should be considered for inclusion on all scenic road designs and for all leisure facility projects.

Overlooks/interpretive stops should feature views, both natural and cultural, and areas or features which lend themselves to short informational stops (5 to 10 minimum typical)

Overlook – Grand Canyon National Park, Arizona

In all cases, where stops are provided, consideration should be given to the following:

- Ease and safety of ingress and egress from both directions – this is especially necessary for older drivers with diminished perceptions.

- Viewing areas with informational signs and/or displays – use of large print in graphic displays (see Chapter 10 – Details).

- Shaded places to sit – see Chapter 10 – Details.

- Trash receptacles.

- Where possible, drinking water should be available.

- Sanitary facilities should be provided where room permits, utilities are reasonably attainable, and the time from last available public toilets is greater than 1-hour's driving time.

- Some informational displays may be desirable to be read from the car if site permits their suitable location. This is especially true for minor informational stops – i.e. historic markers and minor view areas.

Where possible, at least some of the view should be able to be seen from the parking area, especially the handicapped parking space.

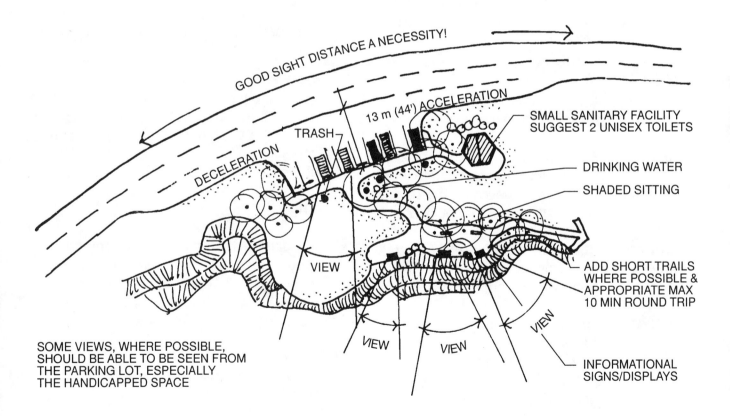

Figure 8.13 *Overlooks and interpretive stops*

WALKING/HIKING/JOGGING

Walking, hiking and jogging, together with bicycling, are all activities which utilize facilities that are basically linear in nature. All can be accommodated within most parks and recreation areas, in large-scale commercial leisure facilities, in utility rights-of-way, and in most road rights-of-way. Most, except hiking and high-speed biking, can be accommodated on the same pathway if it is appropriately designed. Chapter 6 – Circulation–Bicycle and Pedestrian Section provides much of the information on urban linear facilities that are part of the function of the circulation system. The additional recreation activity specific information presented here for walking/hiking/jogging/nature trails/interpretive trails/etc., is intended to supplement Chapter 6. As a reminder, safety, rest areas, shade and sanitary facilities discussed in Chapter 6 need to be included in the various recreation activities pathway's suggested design criteria.

Combined Activities Pathway

Combining linear recreation activities makes sense from a space and cost standpoint. There are some constraints, however, in the design criteria when these facilities are combined.

Pathway Width – Sufficient for a bike and 3-wheeler to pass – minimum 180 cm ± (6'-0"); desirable minimum of 250 cm ± (8'-0").

Pathway Alignment – Vertical – no grades over 10% and probably less (5%) where 3-wheelers are likely. Sufficient run-out at bottom of grades to gradually slow bikes. Horizontal – gentle, no sharp turns or switchbacks.

Pathway Surface – Must be obstruction-free with hard, all-weather surface.

Hiking Trails

(See *Park Planning Guidelines* – Trails, pp. 31-35.)

In addition to walkways, older people can often be found on most trail systems. Unlike walks, special design consideration need normally only be given for those trails that would typically serve older people engaging in activities such as bird watching or natural/historic and interpretive trails. These topics are covered under the appropriate sections in this chapter.

The following are some factors to consider in the design of trails which older people might frequent. These factors will also be useful for a wide range of users.

Grades

• Keep pedestrian circulation to maximum grades of 10%.

• Where steeper grades are necessary, provide frequent shaded and climatically tempered rest areas at 3 m to 5 m (10' to 16') of vertical grade change. See Chapter 6 – Circulation–Walks and Chapter 10 – Details for material on rest areas.

Signing

Clear, visible – at start include information on trail length and difficulty (a map similar to the following Figure 8.14 would be helpful).

Trail Section

Typical – no obstacles on Types I and II. Type III obstacles with considerable difficulty "OK."

Width – minimum Type I and II 100 cm (3.3') – desirable 120 cm (4'). Type III minimum 60 cm (2') - desirable 90 cm (3').

Trail Surface

- Easy to walk on such as compacted stone, or compacted native soil (if it is of good construction quality), or possibly wood chips. Wood chips and loose stone should not be used on steep slopes.

- No loose stones, especially small, round stones on trails for Levels I and II which could cause slipping.

- Clear out all roots or other possible tripping hazards on trails for Levels I and II.

Environmental Considerations

- Shade all or as much of the walk/trail as is possible. Use shrubs to reduce effects of prevailing cold winds.

Universal Trail Design

The U.S. Forest Service designates at least some of its trails by degree of difficulty. A system like the Forest Service's or one similar would be desirable. For example, in the Conceptual Universal Design Trail Layout, Figure 8.14, there are three types of levels of difficulty.

Accessible – Type I – UFAS Handicapped Accessible – modified as to width, rest areas and edging to relate to the conditions commonly found on trails, wheelchair usable surface, maximum grades 7%, with numerous shaded rest stops. Suggested maximum time between shaded rest areas is 1/2 hour, or approximately 1 kilometer (0.6 miles). These areas should have water if possible. Intermediate small rest areas with a bench at intervals of 90 m (300') are desirable as well as water and sanitary facilities at one-hour intervals, or approximately 2 kilometers (1.2 miles) if trail is longer. These rest areas should also have benches and be shaded, preferably structurally. Recommended approximate length of this Type I trail is 2 kilometers (1.2 miles). Type I would have accessibility signs. Provide tactile warnings at all potentially dangerous areas.

Challenge Level 1 or Type II – Older people and people with limited fitness ability. Maximum grades should be 8%, with frequent shaded rest stops. Suggested time between stops is 2 to 4 hours, with water and sanitary facilities every two hours, or approximately 4 kilometers (2.4 miles). Approximate length of the trail should be from 8 to 12 kilometers (5 to 7.5 miles). **"NOT ACCESSIBLE"** signs should be provided.

Challenge Level 2 or Type III – Demanding – highly difficult. Grades may be to 12% or more in some instances, and there may be some obstacles. Rest stops will be scattered or infrequent, usually only at view points or other features. There is no actual maximum grade limit. Water and sanitary facilities should continue to be no less frequent than every 4 kilometers (2.4 miles) and at all overnight stops.

A trail system designed as described above and as shown in Figure 8.14 would be said to be following the universal design approach.

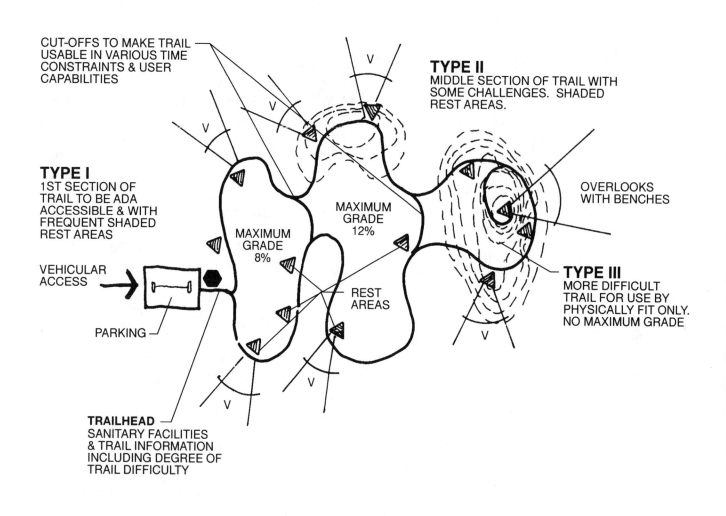

CUT-OFFS TO MAKE TRAIL USABLE IN VARIOUS TIME CONSTRAINTS & USER CAPABILITIES

TYPE II
MIDDLE SECTION OF TRAIL WITH SOME CHALLENGES. SHADED REST AREAS.

TYPE I
1ST SECTION OF TRAIL TO BE ADA ACCESSIBLE & WITH FREQUENT SHADED REST AREAS

VEHICULAR ACCESS

PARKING

MAXIMUM GRADE 8%

MAXIMUM GRADE 12%

REST AREAS

OVERLOOKS WITH BENCHES

TYPE III
MORE DIFFICULT TRAIL FOR USE BY PHYSICALLY FIT ONLY. NO MAXIMUM GRADE

TRAILHEAD
SANITARY FACILITIES & TRAIL INFORMATION INCLUDING DEGREE OF TRAIL DIFFICULTY

Figure 8.14 *Conceptual Universal Design Trail Layout*

Cultural Walks

Older people are frequently more interested in seeing and learning about nature and history than many younger people. This factor, therefore, skews the demographics of the users of interpretive and nature walks, pathways and trails towards older users. Educational trails design, both conceptually and in its details, therefore, must take the needs of older users into consideration. Interpretive trails, both cultural and nature, can be self-guided and/or guided.

Cultural walks allow the user to see and learn about archeological, historical and cultural features. All trails of this type should have, as a minimum, the following:

Alignment – Dictated by the features being interpreted. All grades and other alignment factors must be done in a manner which will accommodate the older users.

A loop system is a necessity with a one-way system which is preferable to keep the story line sequential and understandable.

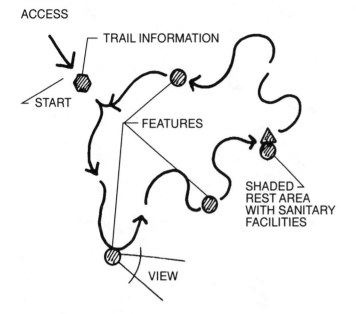

ACCESS

TRAIL INFORMATION

START

FEATURES

SHADED REST AREA WITH SANITARY FACILITIES

VIEW

Figure 8.15 *A Loop Trail*

Information – Must be provided at the start (trailhead) of the trail. The trail's length, difficulty and what can be seen are the minimum information needed.

Graphics – All signs, interpretive displays and self-guiding information guides must be prepared with large enough type and graphics that people with less than perfect eyesight will be able to read them.

Interpretive/information stations should be located at various points along the walkway. The information presented should be appropriate for the stopping point/station. If signs are utilized to convey the story line, the text size and legibility should be as noted under graphics. Sufficient space is needed at each station to allow the expected number of users to stop, read, see and experience, while others should have the ability to continue on the walk. Gathering or stopping space is especially needed where guided walks/tours are given.

Rest stops – Sufficient climate-modified rest areas should be provided as per Chapter 6 - Circulation. These might be combined with interpretive/information stations.

Sanitary facilities – Trailhead areas should be provided with sanitary facilities. All trails that would normally require more than two hours to complete should have identifiable toilets at one to two-hour intervals along the way.

The pathway surface should be free of any obstacles, including stones and roots. It should be built so that slipping on loose, rounded stones and plant parts will not occur. The best surface for interpretive walks would be a compacted stone base choked with a compacted fine finish, i.e. decomposed granite, quarry waste, crushed shell. See Chapter 10 – Details. Other finishes to consider are concrete, asphalt, and possibly wood chips. The choice of walk finish is dependent on the subject being interpreted and should fit the trail theme. Keep in mind that hard, smooth surfaces such as concrete and asphalt are more appropriate for wheelchair use than are looser surface composition.

Trail width – 90 cm (3') minimum for a one-way single file trail – 120 cm (4') minimum desirable – allows two people to walk side by side.

Nature Walks/Trails

See Cultural Walks above and Non-Consumptive Natural Area use later in this chapter for additional information. Quality natural features – animal, plant, geological and/or palentological – are the focus of these walks and trails. The design and construction of nature walks and trails should be even more sensitive to the natural environment than normal walk and trail facilities. They should disturb the site as little as possible. The trail and attendant support and informational features should look like they belong to the natural environment. To make trails as inconspicuous as possible, the trail should, wherever possible, be constructed with "natural" material. The trail surface must still, however, be easy to use – obstacle-free, non-slippery and firm. Wood chips, although more difficult to walk on than other surfaces, can be utilized here.

All other features discussed in Cultural Walks apply equally to Nature Walks/Trails.

Jogging/Running

These two activities are primarily related to physical fitness. Normally they can be carried out on any *safe* linear pathway system and would not need additional design modifications to accommodate older users if their needs have been previously considered.

There are some joggers/runners who believe, with good cause, that concrete and asphalt are too hard on the legs (knees and shins) and that softer, more resilient surfaces would be more desirable. Ideally, a resilient surface, similar to that recommended for tennis courts, would be used. If these surfaces have not been provided, the joggers/runners will frequently run alongside the paved way where space will permit.

If a long – over 6 kilometers (3.7 miles) – jogging/running trail is provided as a separate function or is provided on a pathway not modified for older-people use, then, as a minimum, sanitary facilities should be added at the half-way point, or at 6 kilometer (3.7 mile) intervals.

Please note that exercisers will frequently use the pathway system during early morning (sometimes before sunrise) or late evening hours (after sunset). This would necessitate security lighting throughout the pathway length. In addition, **ALL** places where potential assailants might hide must be removed.

Rollerblading/In Line Skating

This activity has become very popular in a short time span even for the over 55 age group. Its functions can be accommodated on the combined activities pathway described earlier in this section and on bikeways and walkways discussed in Chapter 6 – Circulation. If there are many rollerbladers of any age anticipated on any pathway, it will be necessary to provide additional width. Other criteria would be the same as paths for bicycles.

High-Speed Biking

(See Chapter 6 – Circulation–Biking) This type of activity is far too dangerous when combined with other trail activities and has no place on walking/hiking/jogging trails!

SOCIAL SPACE

Spaces where people young and old can meet and visit are a desirable amenity to any community.   These spaces can be both indoor and outdoor.   They would consist primarily of places for sitting and multi-use spaces.   With some exceptions – spaces for large events, i.e. art shows, performances, exhibits, etc. – these areas are best designed as intimate gathering spaces. The mini park in New York City is a perfect example. People come here, rest, visit, use the toilets, and possibly buy food at the food concession stand, or eat their bag lunches.

Urban mini park – New York City, New York

The key ingredients for a successful outdoor gathering space are:

• People – there must be sufficient numbers of potential users to make it feel like a place to be.

• Protection from harsh environmental conditions.

• Places where small groups of people can sit and talk.

To make a typical outdoor space into a better place for older people, consider the following:

• Sanitary facilities – a nearby necessity. Approximate distance – minimum, none. Maximum suggested 50 m± (150'±).

• Environmental modification – wind barriers for strong and/or cold prevailing winds (summer breezes are delightful and should not be blocked!) See Chapter 10 – Details for shade structures.

• Drinking water with a suggested maximum distance away of 25 m (75'±).

• Seating in conversational clusters (see Chapter 10 – Details for benches, etc.) – fixed and/or movable as appropriate for the site. At least some with seat backs and arm rests.

• Board game area for cards, checkers, chess, etc.

• Screening off of background noise.

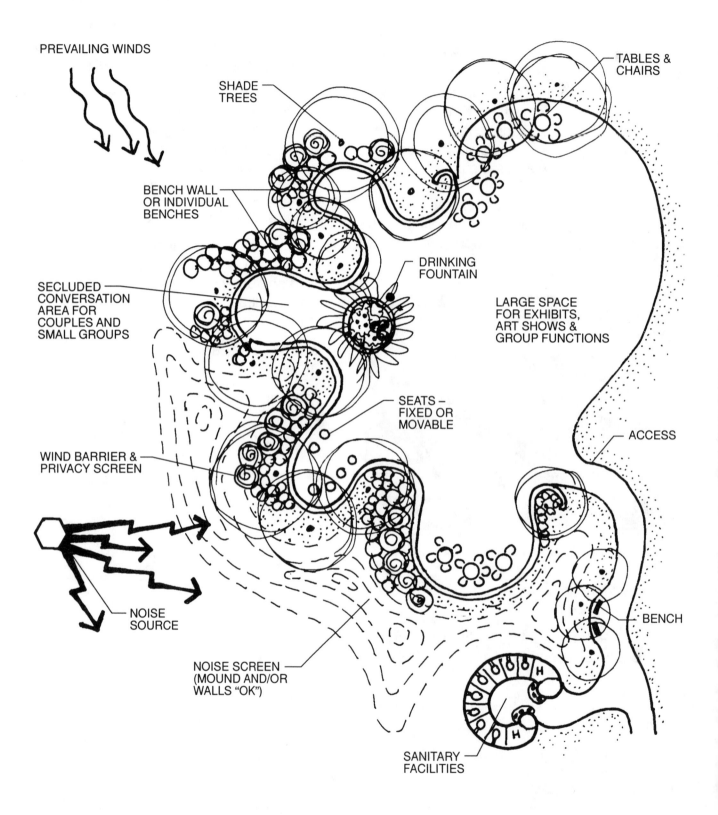

PREVAILING WINDS

SHADE
TREES

TABLES &
CHAIRS

BENCH WALL
OR INDIVIDUAL
BENCHES

DRINKING
FOUNTAIN

SECLUDED
CONVERSATION
AREA FOR
COUPLES AND
SMALL GROUPS

LARGE SPACE
FOR EXHIBITS,
ART SHOWS &
GROUP FUNCTIONS

SEATS –
FIXED OR
MOVABLE

ACCESS

WIND BARRIER &
PRIVACY SCREEN

NOISE
SOURCE

BENCH

NOISE SCREEN
(MOUND AND/OR
WALLS "OK")

SANITARY
FACILITIES

Figure 8.16 *Outdoor Social Space*

MISCELLANEOUS FACILITIES

Swings

Many older people remember with nostalgia the swings on the front porch. Those who are too young to remember the front porch swing can also enjoy the pleasures of a relaxing swing, either solo or with a friend. Planners and operators of parks and other places where older people gather may consider providing swings for them.

General Criteria:

- Design for two people.

- Shade is needed. Trees or, if desired for instant effect or aesthetic reasons, structural solutions are a satisfactory alternative.

- Locate in a quiet space.

- Orient swings with a view of some feature, either active or scenic.

- Design of details must fit overall park detail theme. Off-the-shelf versions of this type of swing are available from Playworld Systems.

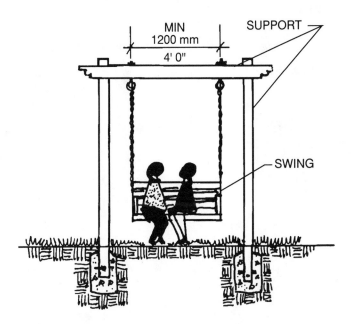

ELEVATION

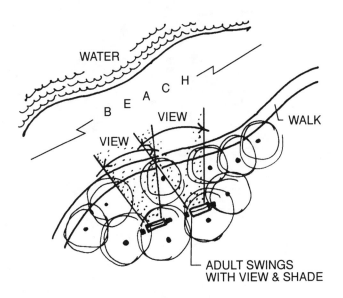

Figure 8.17 *Schematic Swing Location*

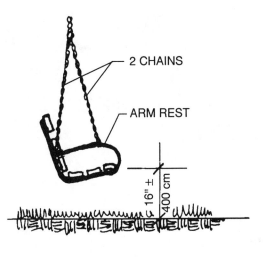

END VIEW

Figure 8.18 *2-Seater Swing*

CHILDREN'S PLAY SPACE

Obviously older people do not need children's play equipment. Not so obvious though is the need to provide convenient space at children's play areas for caregivers, especially those play spaces catering to those under the age of six, where older people are likely to be present.

*Caregivers' sitting/visiting space
– downtown Boston, Massachusetts*

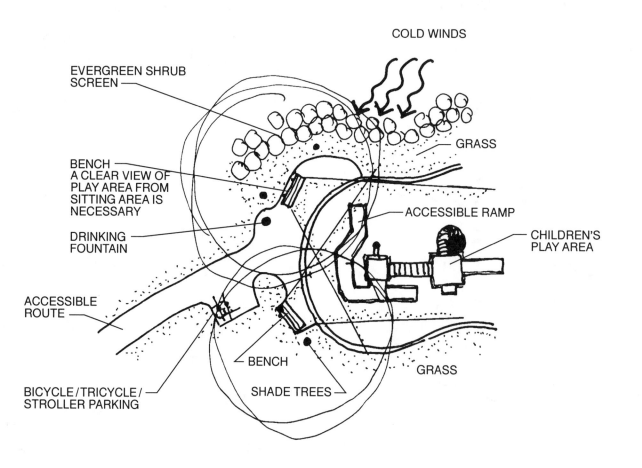

COLD WINDS

EVERGREEN SHRUB
SCREEN

GRASS

BENCH
A CLEAR VIEW OF
PLAY AREA FROM
SITTING AREA IS
NECESSARY

ACCESSIBLE RAMP

CHILDREN'S
PLAY AREA

DRINKING
FOUNTAIN

ACCESSIBLE
ROUTE

BENCH

GRASS

BICYCLE/TRICYCLE/
STROLLER PARKING

SHADE TREES

Figure 8.19   *Caregiver's space at a children's play area.*

The caregivers' space would ideally:

- Have seating with clear view of play area.

- Be shaded by trees (deciduous in north, evergreen in south) or a shade structure. See Chapter 10 – Details–Shade Structures. Where environmental conditions warrant, consider man-made or evergreen windscreens.

- Have a space for "parking" strollers, tricycles, etc. Where users are within biking distance, space should be considered for bike and 3-wheeler parking plus a children's bicycle trailer.

- Have easy access – probably on the accessible route so that strollers, etc., can get to the site easily.

- Have drinking water, preferably chilled, at a convenient location within 30 m (100') of play area, and toilets within 60 m (200').

OUTDOOR COOKING

An outdoor cooking area as discussed here is more than a typical picnic barbecue grill. The intent is to provide an outside "kitchen" where meals can be prepared. Such a cooking area would typically be located in conjunction with pools, outdoor and/or indoor social areas, and in the common areas of condo-type homes and/or apartments. Normally this type of facility would be used in the evening. The ingredients for a successful outdoor cooking area would be:

- A good quality, raised cooking unit – usually gas fired (bottled or piped), down wind from the food preparation and/or sitting area. If a charcoal grill is provided, a suitable charcoal disposal container is a necessity.

- Food preparation space (a table or counter space).

- Good, even night lighting.

- Benches or seats for resting.

- Good, surfaced access to area and within the cooking area. The surface under the cooking area should be one that does not show stains from cooking. Compacted crushed stone choked with fines is suggested. See Chapter 10 – Details–Trails.

- Environmental mitigation – i.e. wind protection, shade if used during the day, and a roofed space where frequent showers may be encountered.

Additional amenities:

- Water is desirable – if provided, good drainage at the source is a necessity.

- Screen the cooking site in areas with insect problems, especially those which are subject to encephalitis outbreaks or other insect-borne diseases.

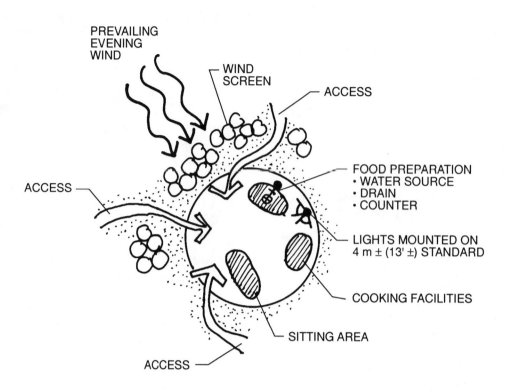

Figure 8.20 *Outdoor Cooking Area*

HORSESHOES AND SHUFFLEBOARD

If you ask a person on the street what should be provided for recreation facilities for older people, they will almost invariably tell you horseshoes and shuffleboard. The authors' survey gives a totally different picture, with most of the respondents hardly ever doing either activity. Partly this was because many did not have access to facilities.

Those who do participate in either shuffleboard or horseshoes usually do so frequently. To make the facilities most usable, the following amenities should be provided in addition to the actual north/south oriented horseshoe pitches and shuffleboard courts.

• Shaded sitting areas for players and spectators.

• Sanitary facilities at the site if there is a sufficient number of users to justify the cost, or within 60 m (200') of the facilities.

• Chilled drinking water.

• Easy, surfaced accessway(s).

• Night lighting, especially useful in warm climates.

• Score recording devices.

• Wind screen where prevailing winds are a problem.

Shuffleboard

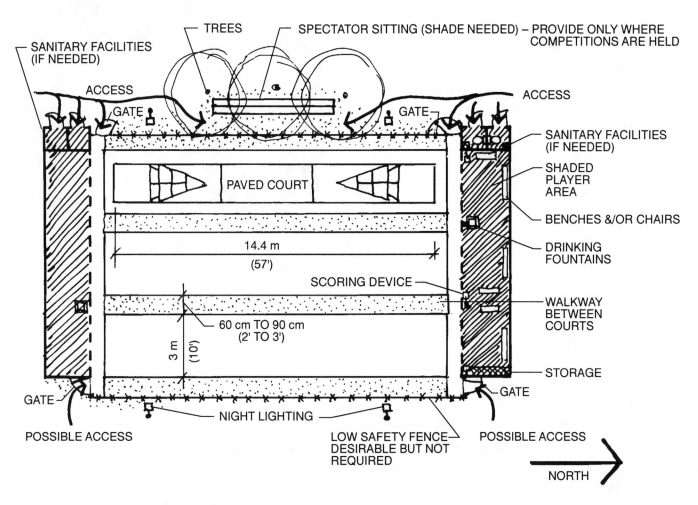

Figure 8.21 *Shuffleboard*

Shuffleboard courts, Fleischmann's Park – Naples, Florida

Additional amenities:

- Bicycle parking for two and three-wheelers – urban areas only.

Horseshoe Pitch

Most horseshoe pitch details are the same as shuffleboard. Special pitch requirements are:

- The shelters/shaded areas will be primarily for spectators and waiting players due to the necessity of all players being on the pitch at the same time.

- Access only at the ends and with a sign warning of the danger to passersby and to spectators.

Horseshoe pitch, Fleischmann's Park – Naples, Florida

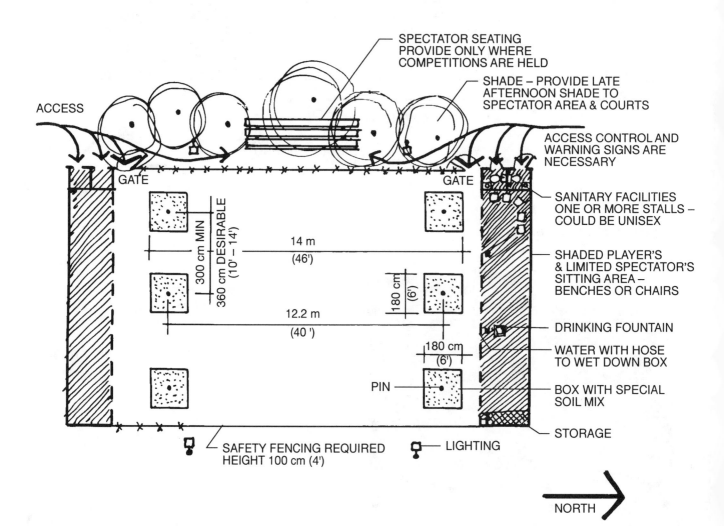

SPECTATOR SEATING PROVIDE ONLY WHERE COMPETITIONS ARE HELD

SHADE – PROVIDE LATE AFTERNOON SHADE TO SPECTATOR AREA & COURTS

ACCESS

ACCESS CONTROL AND WARNING SIGNS ARE NECESSARY

GATE

GATE

SANITARY FACILITIES ONE OR MORE STALLS – COULD BE UNISEX

300 cm MIN
360 cm DESIRABLE (10' – 14')

14 m (46')

180 cm (6')

SHADED PLAYER'S & LIMITED SPECTATOR'S SITTING AREA – BENCHES OR CHAIRS

12.2 m (40')

DRINKING FOUNTAIN

180 cm (6')

WATER WITH HOSE TO WET DOWN BOX

PIN

BOX WITH SPECIAL SOIL MIX

STORAGE

SAFETY FENCING REQUIRED HEIGHT 100 cm (4')

LIGHTING

NORTH

Figure 8.22   *Horseshoe Pitch*

ATTENDING CULTURAL EVENTS

Going out to local arts and craft shows, attending concerts in the park or on the lawn at local businesses, going to the museum or an Indian pow-wow, or going to a historic building or a nature center, etc., are all events which may be heavily attended by people over 55. The authors' survey indicates that older people participate in these types of activities more than two times per year and as often as monthly. This section, Attending Cultural Events, and the following two, Educational/Interpretive Facilities and Outdoor Performance/Assembly Areas, are similar in their needs, but also have unique problems.

Three primary factors need to be considered in making all of these facilities more user-friendly for older people: (1) access to and circulation within the site, (2) comfortable places to rest at the event, and (3) water and sanitary facilities. Facilities for cultural events, like most other sites, must consider the ability levels of the users.

Access and Parking – Cultural events often attract large numbers of users and are held in parks or on private property where there is insufficient parking for these infrequent activities. Under these conditions, adequate drop-off space (with an attendant to keep it free of parked cars) is needed! On-site overflow parking capacity would be a desirable feature if space permits.

Shade – Events and activities that take place in warm seasons must have shade! The shade can be either natural (trees) or man-made, temporary fabric-type, or permanent.

Outdoor art show – Naples, Florida

Pedestrian Circulation – Shade! Shade! Shade! It is critical for the very young and the older users (as well as beneficial to others). The walk/pathway surface should be suitable for walkers using assistive devices. See Chapter 10 – Details–Walks/Patio Surfaces.

Rest Place(s) – The spirit may be willing, but the body needs more frequent rest as it ages. Shaded and, where appropriate, environmentally modified spaces for sitting, resting and people watching are critical for older people's enjoyment and sometimes even for their health. Benches should have arms. See Chapter 10 – Details for benches and shelters.

Sanitary Facilities – Most cultural events take a number of hours to see and enjoy. As such, either permanent or temporary sanitary facilities are required. They should be located within 60 m (200') of the users. If the site is large, then they should be located within 120 m (400' ±) of each other.

Drinking Water – Overheating and dehydration are common problems of older people. Water, preferably chilled, is needed at frequent intervals within the event area. It is desirable every 60 m (200') but, at a minimum, at the sanitary facilities.

Operations – On-site information on what is being presented is very helpful. This can be in the form of signing, information booths and/or handouts. As for all gatherings, adequate security and emergency services must be arranged for prior to the event.

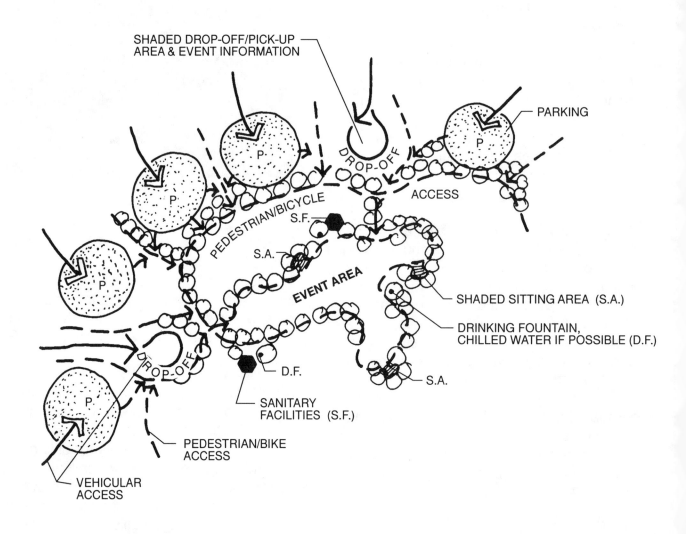

Figure 8.23 *Cultural Event Site*

EDUCATIONAL / INTERPRETIVE FACILITIES

As used here, the section on visiting educational/interpretive facilities is related to museums and natural and cultural sites, both private and public. See also Attending Cultural Events and Outdoor Performance/ Assembly Areas for information on additional similar activities.

Going to the museum, The Smithsonian – Washington, DC

Arrival / Departure Space:

One of the most overlooked aspects of facility design for educational/interpretive facilities is the arrival/departure space. There are two general types of facilities – museums, which are frequently in urban areas, and historic/ natural sites, which are located at the resource. Museum buildings frequently tend toward the monumental. This has often in the past led to a daunting mountain of sun-baked and wind-swept stairs to climb. See Chapters 6 – Circulation–Arrival and 9 – Activities–Indoor–Arrival/Entrance Area for suggestions on how to plan/design this important part of any museum visit to be more user-friendly for older people. Historic and natural areas should have a drop-off area and a comfortable waiting space. Toilets are needed for sites with stays of more than one hour or which are more than one hour's time from the last site with facilities.

Signs / Information:

Information on the facilities must be provided, along with any comfort or safety precautions, i.e. normal length of stay, distance and difficulty of tour, etc. In particular, any safety precautions should be clearly pointed out.

All signs must follow the graphics direction in Chapter 3 – Current Guidelines, Figures 3.22 and 3.23 and Chapter 10 – Details–Graphics. Information should be interesting, clear and concise. If brochures/pamphlets are provided, they should, as a minimum, be in typeface of this size (12 point).

National Park Service interpretive facilities and interpretive ranger specialist – Castillo de San Marcos National Monument, St. Augustine, Florida

Rest Areas – Provide frequent rest areas. As a minimum, they should be climatically tempered (see Chapter 10 – Details–Shade Structures) to fit the situation and have sitting areas of some type at a suggested minimum of every 100 m (330'±). Water is also desirable. Hilly terrain and hot season use will require more frequent rest stops. If the tour is more than one hour long, then additional small sanitary facilities will be needed at these rest areas at one-hour intervals.

Drinking Water – At a minimum, it should be provided at all sanitary facilities. On trails or other exhibits subject to warm weather, provide extra water at frequent intervals, preferably in conjunction with rest areas.

Trails and Pathways – Shade as much of the tour/exhibit areas as possible. This design direction must be tempered with a clear understanding that the feature(s) being interpreted must take precedent over the need for shade.

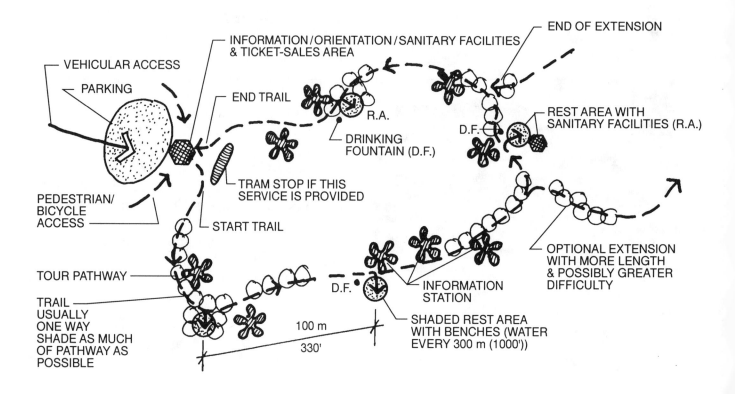

Figure 8.24 *Interpretive Trail Concept*

Driving Trails:

Many large park/cultural sites can only be seen effectively by driving and stopping along the way. Stops may range from a simple pull-off and looking from the vehicle window, to areas for getting out and observing. See this chapter's section Driving for Pleasure for details on how to plan these stopping points. In addition, a self-guiding tour package, either written or audio or perhaps both, is needed at the trail/tour start or visitor information building.

Trams And Other Mass Transit Tours:

One successful and enjoyable way of seeing and learning is by tour tram, bus, train, etc. This means of seeing and learning is particularly well-suited for older users. Special consideration is needed in some aspects to make the tour experience more enjoyable and understandable for the older user.

Waiting Area – Shaded, with drinking water and plenty of seating with backs.

Sound System – A good sound system is needed in the waiting area if one is provided, and more importantly in the tour vehicle.

OUTDOOR PERFORMANCE / ASSEMBLY AREAS

This is the third (see also Educational/Interpretive Facilities and Attending Cultural Events) of a cluster of similar activities requiring many of the same design features. Reference is also made to ADA 4.1.3 (19) Assembly Access (this book Chapter 3 – Current Guidelines), Chapter 6 – Circulation– Parking & Walkways, Chapter 7 – Utilities– Lighting, and Chapter 10 – Details–Benches.

The required handicapped accessible route will provide good, easy ingress and egress to/from the assembly area. There are, however, some additional considerations that will make these facilities more enjoyable for older people. Extend the accessible route to include more parking spaces (Chapter 4 – What is Needed?–Site). Rethink the traditional way of lighting the access walk with aesthetically attractive pools of light for a more even level of illumination (Chapter 7 – Utilities–Lighting). Make more seating accessible without the need of stairs and, where possible, make those seats with sturdy arm rests to assist older people in getting out of the seat or off of the bench.

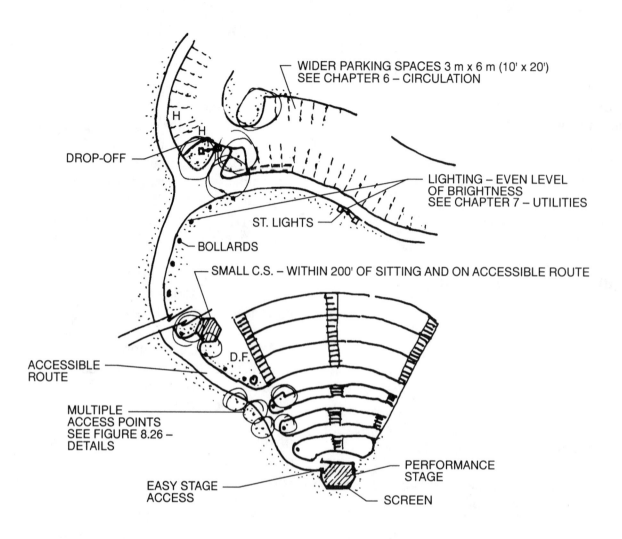

WIDER PARKING SPACES 3 m x 6 m (10' x 20')
SEE CHAPTER 6 – CIRCULATION

DROP-OFF

LIGHTING – EVEN LEVEL
OF BRIGHTNESS
SEE CHAPTER 7 – UTILITIES

ST. LIGHTS

BOLLARDS

SMALL C.S. – WITHIN 200' OF SITTING AND ON ACCESSIBLE ROUTE

ACCESSIBLE
ROUTE

MULTIPLE
ACCESS POINTS
SEE FIGURE 8.26 –
DETAILS

D.F.

PERFORMANCE
STAGE

EASY STAGE
ACCESS

SCREEN

Figure 8.25 *Accessibility Enhancing Ideas*

Spring baseball – Fort Myers, Florida

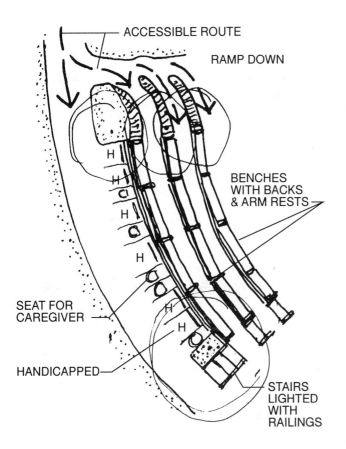

ACCESSIBLE ROUTE

RAMP DOWN

BENCHES
WITH BACKS
& ARM RESTS

SEAT FOR
CAREGIVER

HANDICAPPED

STAIRS
LIGHTED
WITH
RAILINGS

Figure 8.26 *Details*

NON-CONSUMPTIVE NATURAL AREA USE
(Bird Watching / Animal Watching / Nature Study)

Nature and wildlife observation share much of the characteristics of educational/interpretive activities. Many of the site recommendations made for the preceding section also apply here. There are, however, some special modifications that are desirable for the birders and animal watchers. Wildlife watchers may be more critical than most people of the natural appearance and visual quality of their environment and the man-made facilities built on them. **EXTREME** care must be taken to make **ALL** improvements very unobtrusive and environmentally sensitive.

The primary interest of people going out to observe birds and animals is, obviously, the birds and animals. There are techniques available to enhance these viewing opportunities. Please note that these site modifications do not necessarily meet with the approval of some conservationists and naturalists who believe that the natural site should remain untouched. Notwithstanding the possible objections, the following are several suggestions for enhancing the older viewers' and others enjoyment of watching wildlife. *Park Planning Guidelines – 3rd Edition*, Chapter 25 – Non-Consumptive Wildlife Observation covers many of the issues and needs for this activity. See also Chapter 9 of this book, Activities–Outdoor, for around-the-house nature and wildlife viewing.

Bird watching, Ding Darling Preserve – Sanibel Island, Florida

Requirements:

Visual screening – from wildlife being viewed.

Shade – at all view areas and where possible along pathway.

Benches – shaded and at all view areas and at intervals along pathways. See Chapter 6 – Circulation.

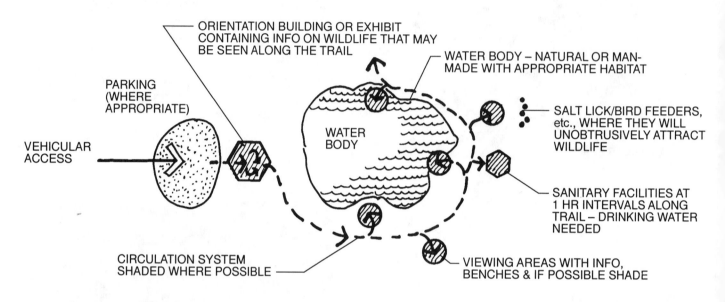

Figure 8.27 *Conceptual Wildlife Trail Layout*

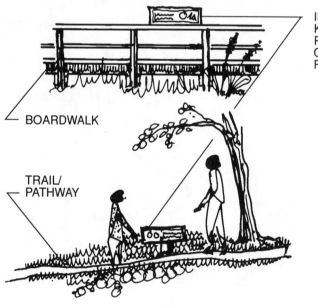

Figure 8.28 *Pathway Information*

All types of trails and viewing areas have certain universal requirements.

Swamp Lily
– Big Cypress National Preserve, Florida

Information – Usually provided at an orientation building or display, plus on-site information. It should be provided as a starting point for trails with viewing areas and, most importantly, at the places to see the wildlife.

Sanitary facilities – Locate at one-hour intervals – distance depends on method of viewing wildlife, i.e. on foot, biking, vehicular.

Habitat Modification – As a reminder, this is possibly the most controversial aspect in preparing a wildlife viewing area for use by people. Items to consider are salt licks to attract animals, feed plots (corn and other grains) and seed plants, fruiting trees and shrubs, habitat modifications for cover – e.g., brush piles, understory, perching spaces, mast (nut) producing trees, water bodies, drinking areas (especially in arid climates), meadows for grazing animals, flowers for butterflies, etc.

Trails

Vehicular:

Many animals are not frightened by people in vehicles. Those same people outside the vehicles may, however, cause them to disperse immediately. Owner occupied cars and tour vehicles of various kinds are, therefore, very effective methods for wildlife viewing. The vehicular trails normally would be narrow, one-way 4 m to 5 m (12' to 15') wide roads with frequent pull-offs, or they could be wider 6 m (20') leaving room for continuous stopping and viewing of the wildlife.

Vehicular/Bike/3-Wheeler:

Some trails, if wide enough, can serve a variety of types of users. Vehicular use of the same space as bikers normally is not recommended. *Slow* traffic and sufficient width do make it possible with a reasonable degree of safety.

Bike/3-Wheeler/Pedestrian:

Separation of vehicles from bikers and pedestrians is, of course, desirable. A further separation of bikers and pedestrians normally might be even better, but again a low speed makes the mix acceptable. The main concern is to make the trail wide enough to handle the various intended uses.

Pedestrian:

The most satisfactory method for intimate contact with nature is on foot even though people may disturb much wildlife. Special viewing areas can make it possible to see the birds and animals and still be out in the *natural* environment.

*Mule deer buck in velvet
– Olympic National Park, Washington*

Viewing Areas

Platforms:

They should be located in prime viewing areas. Easy access, preferably by ramps, but stairs if necessary, is a requirement for use by older people. Platforms, as a minimum, need –

• Shade

• Benches

*Great Blue Heron
– Everglades National Park, Florida*

• Information on what normally can be seen from the viewing platform.

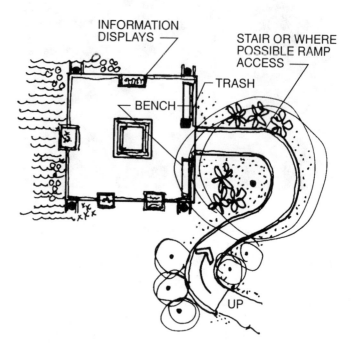

PLAN

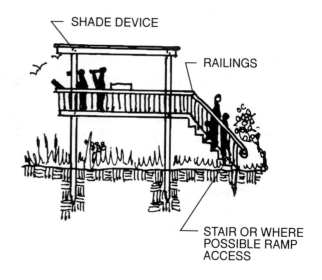

SECTION

Figure 8.29 *Raised Wildlife Viewing Platforms*

Viewing Blinds:

Their design and location are dependent on the wildlife being viewed and the terrain. No blind should be intrusive.

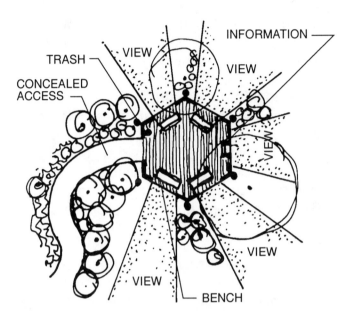

PLAN

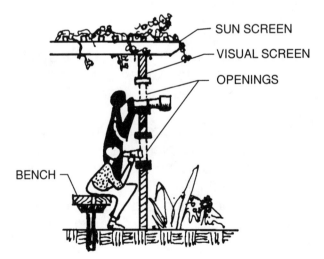

SECTION

Figure 8.30 *Wildlife Viewing Blinds*

GARDENING

Many people like to garden. Some people (the authors included), confine their green thumb activities to small patios and indoor gardening. Others have more substantial appetites and develop and maintain beautiful home grounds and/or wonderfully productive vegetable gardens. As we grow older, it becomes more difficult to do some of the more physically demanding gardening tasks. One older person in Sequim, Washington, planned ahead by raising his gardening beds to reduce his need to bend.

Raised planter for ease in gardening – Sequim, Washington

Some gardening tasks can be made easier by incorporating the following suggestions. These suggestions will be helpful for private homes as well as public, community-type gardens.

Raised Gardening Plots – Raising gardening plots make gardening easier, provides good drainage, and contains the areas where special soil mix needs to be provided.

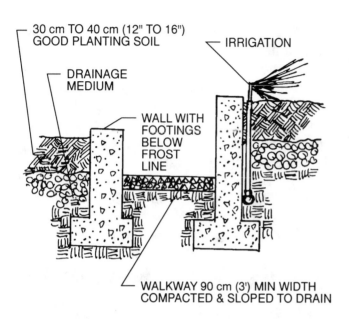

30 cm TO 40 cm (12" TO 16")
GOOD PLANTING SOIL

IRRIGATION

DRAINAGE
MEDIUM

WALL WITH
FOOTINGS
BELOW
FROST
LINE

WALKWAY 90 cm (3') MIN WIDTH
COMPACTED & SLOPED TO DRAIN

Figure 8.31 *Raised Planting Areas*

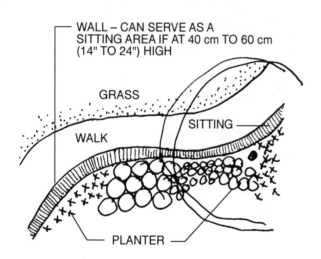

WALL – CAN SERVE AS A
SITTING AREA IF AT 40 cm TO 60 cm
(14" TO 24") HIGH

GRASS

SITTING

WALK

PLANTER

Figure 8.32 *Informal Raised Planters*

Good, Well-Drained, Easy-to-Till Soil –
This makes the tilling of the soil easier and
increases the success rates of the gardens.

Irrigation System – A necessity and should,
as a minimum, contain a hose bib(s) and
hose(s) on a reel(s) located within 15 m (45')
of every area to be watered. An under-
ground, automatic irrigation system with individually adjustable stations and a moisture
sensor override is the preferred solution.

Shaded Sitting Area(s) – If the area to be
gardened takes more than a few minutes of
care, consider putting in a sitting area. This
could be part of other spaces (patio, pool,
etc.) in the garden. This sitting space could
also be used as a place to view the garden.
Bench walls can be very beneficial in garden
places.

Walkways – They must be firm, well-
drained and easy to walk on, including by
those people using assistive devices such as
walkers and canes. In gardens that are part
of a public use space, at least some (a minimum of 25%) and as much more as possible
of the area should be accessible for the
wheelchair-bound.   A minimum desirable
width of 900 mm (36") is recommended.
Smaller ways only 300 mm (12") can be useful for access to garden areas during and
more likely immediately after a rainfall.

Tool and Supply Storage Area – An easily
accessible, convenient space in the gardening area is desirable for storage of tools and
gardening supplies. The structure could also
be used for potting and other garden tasks.
See Figure 8.33 – Layout of Gardening Plots.

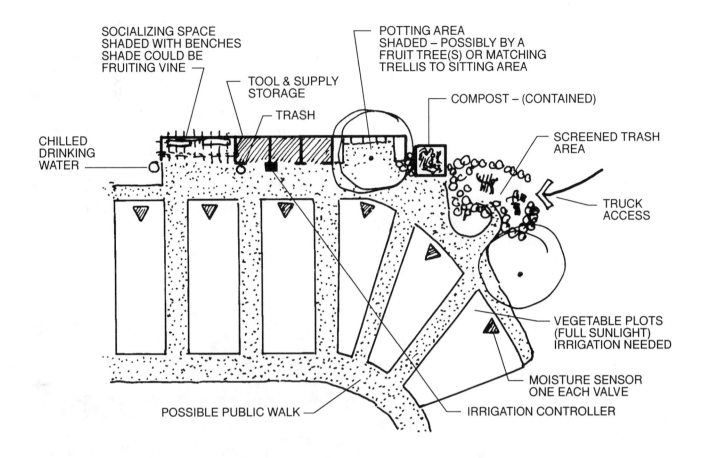

Figure 8.33 *Layout of Gardening Plots – Community Gardens*

Trash/Debris Storage – An on-site trash container (dumpster) for non-compost material is needed. For neatness and to reduce some of the physical gardening work needed, vehicular access is needed for the community trash disposal truck. Trash disposal should, of course, be environmentally sensitive, i.e. recycle!

Compost Area – A raised, contained space for use in turning plant parts into suitable/usable soil is required. This necessary space will be fairly large and should be located in an unobtrusive, but easily accessible, place near the garden.

Sanitary Facilities – Sanitary facilities are needed in larger estate gardens and in public gardening spaces where available facilities are more than 60 m (200') away from the site. They could be combined with the toolshed and potting area.

Night Lighting – Lighting is desirable where gardening is done during the short winter days in the south and where evening gardening is likely to occur.

Group and Community Gardens – Not all of the plots are normally kept-looking, well-maintained, and attractive. The gardens must be located away from the more manicured public areas but where people can get to them easily and safely. Security and off-hour access are additional concerns and must be taken into consideration when locating the gardening area. Finally, telephone emergency 911 service would add a great deal to older users' feeling of safety.

Staffing – At least some staffing time will be needed for community garden spaces for security, educational purposes, clean-up (especially during off-season periods), irrigation maintenance, and possibly tilling.

CAMPING

The authors' survey showed that most people over 55 do not go camping. For those that do, however, camping is a way of life. Some people, on reaching retirement, buy a motor home or camper equipment of some sort and spend much of the year traveling around the country camping, as attested to by the numerous stickers on their vehicles. Other less frequent, older campers are also likely to travel in more upscale camper-type vehicles and are unlikely to be "tent" campers.

Camping at Gifford Pinchot State Park, Pennsylvania
– Photo courtesy of Pennsylvania State Parks

"Upscale" and "long-term" campers will need certain camp modifications to make their stay more enjoyable. These following suggestions are not intended as an endorsement to include in all "public" park settings, but rather as ideas that can be utilized to make campgrounds more suitable for older campers. For a variety of "standard" campground planning information, please refer to *Park Planning Guidelines – 3rd Edition*, Chapter 13 – Overnight Use.

Vehicular Circulation – Larger radius curves are needed to accommodate larger vehicles. Use one-way camp loops. Roads should be a minimum of 4 m (13') with a minimum of 90 cm (3') shoulders. Camp Spurs – Provide more spurs capable of accommodating vans and campers. It is suggested that 25% car/tent spurs and 75% multi-use and capable of accommodating vans/campers be provided. Drive-through sites are the easiest-to-use type of sites for the larger vehicles and for towed camping trailers. They are seldom provided due to higher development costs and additional damage to the site.

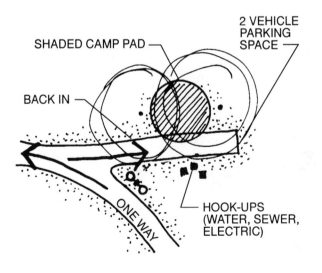

Figure 8.34 *Camp Spur/Pad Layout*

Camp Pad – An area is needed for eating, cooking and sleeping (some older users come with extended family groups with the younger numbers sleeping outside in tents or under the stars).

Water Hydrants – The number needed and their location is dependent on the availability of "hookups." If individual hookups are available, locate as per standard design within 45 m (150') of each site. If hookups are not available, locate within 30 m (100') of each site.

Trash Receptacles – Locate them at every fourth site as in standard designs.

Night Lighting – This is one of the few night use facilities where only limited lighting should be provided. Emergency phones and sanitary facilities should be well-lighted, of course, but otherwise, no lights. For many campers, older campers included, the campground is thought of as an outdoor bedroom under the stars, and they wish to have their bedroom free of lights. Campers typically carry flashlights to find their way about after dark.

Hookups – The travel trailers and self-contained campers all would find water, sewer and electricity hookups desirable. As a minimum, electricity should be provided to eliminate the noise of electric generators.

Sanitary Facilities – The location of sanitary facilities is dependent on the availability of on-site hookups. With hookups available, locate as per normal design – 90 m (300') from farthest campsite. If no hookups are available, then shorten the distance access – 60 m (200') from farthest camp site suitable for older users. All campgrounds serving older people should, if possible, provide wash houses – i.e. a comfort station with showers and laundry facilities. These facilities should be located, when possible, within 120 m (400') of the farthest site to be served.

Provide three or four parking spaces at each wash house. As an alternative, a central "concession" shower/laundry facility could be provided.

Campground Dump Stations – Need for dump stations depends on the availability of on-site "hookups." If hookups are not provided, then the standard dump stations are a necessity. The normal ratio is one per 100 camp sites. The location should be between the entrance/check-in and the first and last trailer sites – i.e. where both the leaving trailer/camper and the entering trailer/camper can get to the facility easily.

Emergency Phone Service – Access to a 911 emergency line is critical for older people, both health-wise and for the feeling of security. Locate it (them) at entrances and, if possible, at sanitary facilities.

Interpretive/Campfire – Educational facilities, i.e. interpretive trails, an amphitheater or "campfire," and interpretive programs, i.e. guided nature walks, evening lectures, etc., should be provided at the campground. See sections on Educational/Interpretive Facilities, Non-Consumptive Natural Areas and Outdoor Performance Areas for more information on these facilities.

Recreational Facilities – Some facilities, such as children's playgrounds, open play fields, volleyball and court games, are not needed for older campers. Other facilities for dancing and socializing, horseshoes, shuffleboard and tennis would be an asset. Locate campsites most suitable for older people in proximity to the latter (social space, etc.) and away from the former (active play).

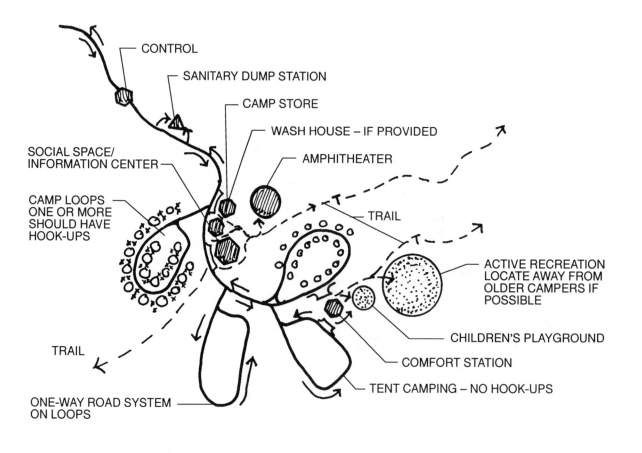

Figure 8.35   *Conceptual Campground Layout*

PICNICKING

Picnicking is part of American culture. It is one of the activities participated in by most families and frequently becomes a focus of weekends, especially good weather holidays (summer in the north and sometimes winter in the hotter southern areas). Older people, according to the authors' 1992-1993 survey, continue to "go on picnics" on the average of once or twice a year. Some of these picnics are "group" activities with their fellow "retirement" home friends, community or senior citizen's groups, and some are with family and/or friends.

General Planning Considerations

The closer a picnic table is to parking, the better. Obviously not everyone can be close to his or her car. Placement of picnic tables with good views (scenic or activities) and/or close to other activities likely to be used (beach, pool, boat rental, etc.) will encourage picnickers to walk further to their table. Do not locate tables along the immediate edge of a beach or view since this then makes it very difficult for the other resource users to get to the beach, have a view, etc.

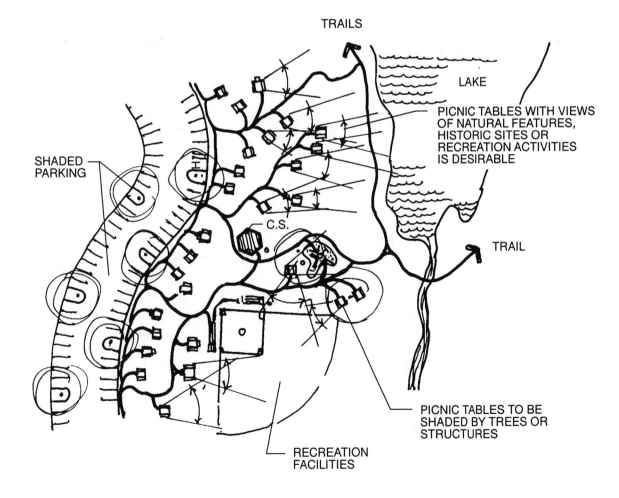

Figure 8.36 *Plan of conceptual picnic area*

Picknicking
– Little Buffalo State Park, Pennsylvania

Design Criteria Considerations:

Sanitary facilities – Locate toilet buildings within a maximum of 60 m (200') of every site.

Site accessibility – The maximum slopes of access walks to picnic facilities should be 8% to 10%. See Chapter 6 – Circulation. Proximity to parking is important with 60 m (200') maximum – 30 m (100') or less is more desirable.

Climate modifications – Shade is critical to older users. Shade can be provided by trees or man-made structures. Normally manmade structures with solid roofs are better for areas where it is likely to rain during the use periods. See Chapter 10 – Details–Shelters. Extreme weather conditions may require strong solutions, i.e. strong prevailing winds would necessitate a wind break (plants or structural), or in cold environments there may be a need for a heating fire.

Views – The opportunity to enjoy views, scenic and/or activities, are of even more importance to older people than for many younger families with children.

Surface – A firm, non-slip, non-erodible surface is required under the tables. This would make it possible for all, including older people and physically challenged, to use the facilities.

% grades – It is best to build picnic areas on gentle slopes of between 4% to 10% where possible. This enables more picnickers to enjoy the view. See Figure 8.37 below.

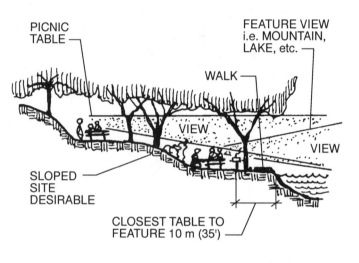

Figure 8.37 *Section through an ideal picnic area slope*

Cooking facilities – Raised charcoal grills at stove height with a firm, non-stain surface under the unit are needed. Locate them down wind from the eating space and possibly shared with one or more other table units.

Picnic tables – See Chapter 10 – Details–Picnic Tables.

BOATING

Boating is an expensive activity, especially if you own a boat. This, except for limited affordable boat rental opportunities, confines boating activities to the affluent and their guests. Another characteristic of boaters derived from unpublished user surveys in Pennsylvania during the 1970's is that they almost always do something other than just go boating.

Boating is not, as a rule, a physically demanding leisure activity. Modifying existing accepted design criteria to accommodate older users can still enhance older boaters' safety and enjoyment.

Boating is for all ages – Naples, Florida

Suggestions for boating are confined primarily to on-shore and marina facilities.

Sanitary Facilities – Provide sanitary facilities at boat ramps and other people-gathering places. See Chapter 7 – Utilities. Maximum distance from use area to sanitary facilities should be 60 m (200').

Shade – Shaded parking and shaded people waiting/shaded observation spaces will add to the users' comfort, and the non-boaters' enjoyment of the facilities. Some marinas have provided shaded in-water boat storage.

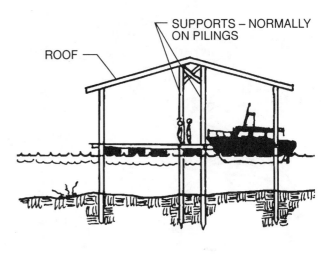

Figure 8.38 *Covered Boat Docks*

Boat Ramp / Launching – Boat launching takes between five to seven minutes after the boat has been prepared for launching. As can be seen at any boat ramp, it is necessary to have a pier to secure boats to while waiting for some boat party member to park or retrieve the car/trailer. See also "Docks" following this section.

Shaded picnic table(s) should be provided for those party members who do not wish to boat the entire duration of the outing. They should be located with a view of the launching and/or boating activity and should be served with a boat dock or smooth sandy beach to load/unload passengers.

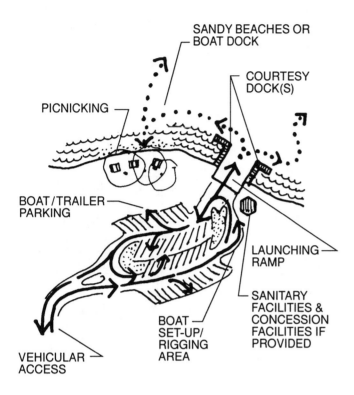

Figure 8.39 *Boat Launch*

Docks – Docks, piers and access gangways should be designed to meet the needs of people with diminishing capabilities. At a minimum, railings on dock access ramps and curbs of 5 cm (2") high on dock edges should be provided. See Chapters 3 – Current Guidelines, 6 – Circulation, and 10 – Details for additional information.

Safe access to marina docks is critical – Naples, Florida – Photo by Robert F. Fulton

Shore–Related Picnicking – Some family members may not wish to go boating or there may not be room in the boat for all the group's members. Provide shaded on-shore picnic facilities with views of boating activities.

Clubhouse and/or Food Service Facilities – A social space with its attendant outdoor sitting/gathering/visiting areas combined with food service facilities serves two of the foremost activities of older people — visiting and dining out for pleasure. These facilities should be provided at any marina large enough to support financially such activities.

Security – As in all facilities, the real and perceived personal safety must be addressed effectively in the design. Access to free emergency 911 service is necessary. Many phone companies will set up a free 911 line if requested.

Lighting – Early morning and late evening fishermen and late-in-the-day social activities make artificial lighting a necessity for usability and a sense of safety. See Chapter 7 – Utilities–Lighting for more information. A pole-mounted "beacon" light is needed at boat ramps and docks to guide the night boaters back to their home port.

FISHING

Not a very high percentage of older people go fishing. The authors' survey shows this as an infrequent activity. A 1985 fishing survey by the U.S. Department of the Interior, Fish and Wildlife Service found that people over 65 fished only one-half as much as younger people (16±% over 65 to 32% under 65). The 1985 survey also found that the most fishermen (90%) also participated in non-consumptive wildlife activities.

There are two basic locations where fishing takes place: (1) Shore fishing – fishing from the shoreline/stream banks, piers and docks, and (2) Boat fishing – in private and party boats.

The co-author showing his tail-catching fishing technique – Photo by Michael W. Fogg

Habitat Enhancement – Most fishing areas can be improved with underwater habitat enhancement, i.e. fish shelters or artificial reefs. See Figures 8.40 and 8.41.

Fish Cleaning – Facilities for cleaning fish should be provided, and they must meet local health codes. These areas can attract birds. This is a desirable feature to some – the ones not doing the cleaning. Other clearly non–desirable critters and odors can also occur if these facilities are not designed and built properly.

Shoreline Fishing

Pathways – Utilize Type I or, where necessary, Type II pathways (refer to Chapter 6 – Circulation) to get to the various fishing spots along the shores of lakes and streams.

Fishing Spots – Benches should be provided at more popular sites. Shade is needed! Preferably it should be natural but, where necessary, man-made structures are acceptable.

Sanitary Facilities – Locate small one or two-seaters within a maximum of 100 m (330') of fishing sites – 60 m (200') is the desirable maximum distance.

Docks / Piers

Access – On-shore parking for bicycles and cars is needed. Pedestrian ways to the fishing structure may be controlled by an access control structure.

Railings – These need to be high enough to lean on and have a large railing cap. Pole holders would be a desirable bonus.

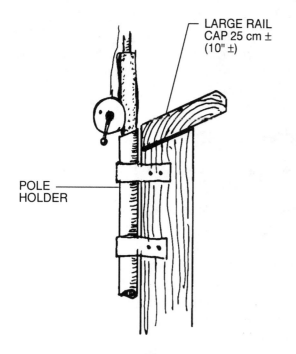

Figure 8.40 *Rail Details*

Sanitary Facilities – Locate them within 60 m (200') of all users.

Trash Cans – Locate them at frequent intervals. It is suggested that they be located at 10 m (30'±) intervals in conjunction with the benches.

Bait/Supplies/Food – Larger fishing piers can support a concession operation which can help pay for operations and maintenance.

Benches – Provide benches at frequent intervals – suggested every 10 m (30'±).

Lighting – Early morning (sometime before dawn) and night fishing are common activity periods for avid fishermen. Good, even, quality lighting is a necessity. See Chapter 7 –Utilities–Lighting.

Shade – Shade is a critical amenity for many older people and should be provided at good fishing spots. See Chapter 10 – Details– Shade Structures. A shade structure is also good place for the non-fishing companions to sit/read/socialize.

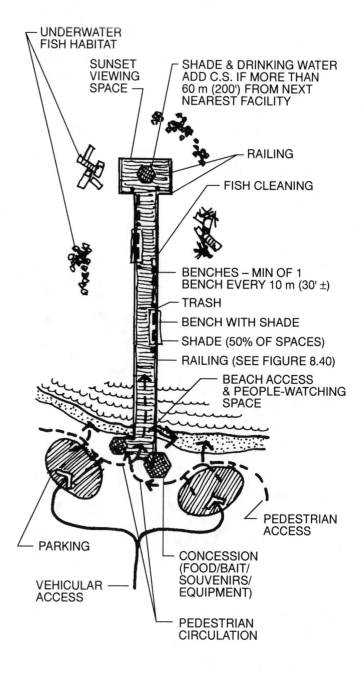

Figure 8.41 *Fishing Pier*

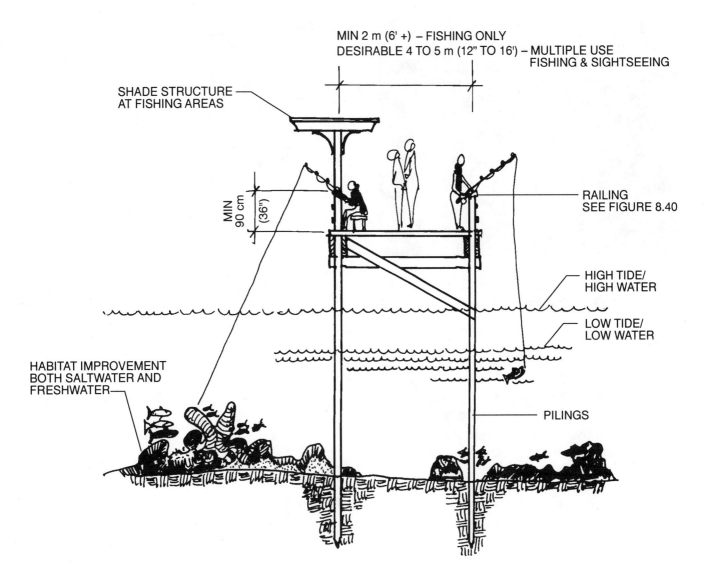

MIN 2 m (6' +) – FISHING ONLY
DESIRABLE 4 TO 5 m (12" TO 16') – MULTIPLE USE
FISHING & SIGHTSEEING

SHADE STRUCTURE
AT FISHING AREAS

MIN 90 cm (36")

RAILING
SEE FIGURE 8.40

HIGH TIDE/
HIGH WATER

LOW TIDE/
LOW WATER

HABITAT IMPROVEMENT
BOTH SALTWATER AND
FRESHWATER

PILINGS

Figure 8.42 *Pier Details*

Boat Fishing

Access – Before going boat fishing you have got to get to the boat. See Chapter 6 – Circulation for parking information. Pedestrian access ramps to fluctuating-level boat docks, and around the areas on the dock where people might congregate before boarding the boats, should have protective railings.

Shade – Shade is needed at waiting/boarding space at the boat dock and on-board ship.

Sanitary Facilities – Facilities appropriate for both men and women are needed at the marina and, most critically, on the boat.

Sitting – Sitting space is needed at waiting/boarding areas and, of course, on-board the boat.

*Indoor fishing on a floating dock
– Lake Texoma, Oklahoma*

Indoor Fishing

A truly unique idea is a floating indoor, climate-controlled fishing area. This facility would be especially well-suited for use by older people by reducing temperature and climate extremes. It could also be a profitable business.

SUMMARY

The following is a summary of suggested guidelines for design of user-friendly facilities for people over 55. The details for these items can be found in preceding pages of this chapter and in Chapters 6 – Circulation, 10 – Details, and 11 – Operations and Maintenance.

SUMMARY OF SUGGESTED GUIDELINES FOR THE DESIGN OF USER-FRIENDLY LEISURE FACILITIES FOR PEOPLE OVER 55

Function/Facility	Recommended Requirements for over 55
ROADS	
Sight Distance	Greater than standard road criteria.
Pull-offs	Provide pull-offs every 1-2 miles on two-lane roads.
Signs	Large clear lettering, well-lighted where possible and high contrast.
Stacking lanes	Needed at intersections.
Acceleration/deceleration lanes	Desirable on any intersection where traffic is over 75 kph (45 mph) or traffic is congested.
Roadside planting	Continuous shade or continuous sun. Do not put in planting which will give alternative sunlight and shadows.
PARKING	
Space width	10' desirable all parking.
Drop-off	At major entrances, shaded with benches.
Bus parking	Near drop-off area where buses and large vans are likely.
Barriers	None between parking and/or drop-off.
Slope	0.5" minimum/1% desirable – 2% desirable maximum.
PEDESTRIAN TRAILS & PATHWAYS	
Running slope	1:12 (8.3%) maximum desirable – 1:8 (12.5%) maximum
Cross slope	2% desirable maximum, 3% maximum.

Width	120 cm (48") desirable – 80 cm (32") minimum.
Walk edges	Railings at dangerous or perceived dangerous locations.
Rest stops	Level areas – shaded with benches at 1–hour intervals.
Surface	Very firm, non-slip – compacted, no loose stone or other similar material.

BIKEWAYS

Intersections	Warning signs or texture. Clear vision space of 10 m ± (33' ±).
Alignment	Curves to discourage high speeds.
Rest areas	Shaded with benches.
Slope	Level to gently rolling – 12% maximum with runout at bottom.
Cross slope	2%
Width	2-way 200 cm (6.7') minimum desirable, 260 cm (10') desirable.
Surface	Hard, all-weather.

HIGH-SPEED/COMMUTER BIKING

Not permitted on trails. Locate at edge of streets in right-of-way only.

RAMPS

Benches in rest areas every 240 cm (18') vertical rise.

Slope	<1:12 to 1:16.
Landings	Every 120 cm (48") of vertical rise.
Edges	Curbs and railings at difficult locations.

TENNIS

Resilient surfacing. Shaded sitting area. Environmental modification. Drinking water (chilled if possible). Phone for emergency. Sanitary facilities within 60 m (200').

GOLF

Clubhouse space where golfers can meet and socialize. Extra tee(s) closer to green. Sanitary facilities at greens 5 and 15. Improved course aesthetics.

CHILDREN'S PLAYGROUNDS

Shaded areas with benches with backs.

Caregivers' observation space

Clear view from benches to play equipment. Drinking water (chilled if possible). Bike/3-wheeler/tricycle parking.

BEACHES

Provide easy access to water. Space to walk along beach. Shade at beach. Drinking water. Sanitary facilities within 60 m (200') of use areas. Food concession with eating area. Foot washing.

POOLS

Possible screened area where insects are a problem. (D)

(N) = Needed

Shower for cooling off, etc. (D)
Chilled drinking water. (N)

(D) = Desirable

Plenty of shaded sitting areas. (N)
Sunny sitting areas. (N)
Deck to pool ratio of 2:1. (N)
Lap swimming space. (N)
Aquasize area. (N)
Adjacent lighted cooking/eating area. (D)
Lighted pool and deck. (N)
Fenced. (N)
Spa. (N)
Sanitary facilities within 50 m (160' ±). (N)

EQUESTRIAN FACILITIES

Desirable to have ramp for mounting horses. Shaded waiting areas with sanitary facilities. Variable length loop trails with shaded rest stops at 1-hour intervals.

DRIVING FOR PLEASURE

Cleared views into the forests or to significant natural and man-made features. Provide frequent overlooks at interesting features with interpretive information and sanitary facilities. Provide pull-offs at 1-mile intervals for slower cars.

SOCIAL SPACE	Protection from harsh environment. Small and large group spaces. Seating. Shade. Sanitary facilities within 50 m (160' ±). Separation from active recreation.
HORSESHOES/SHUFFLEBOARD	Shaded sitting areas. Orient north/south. Spectator space. Chilled drinking water. Sanitary facilities within 50 m (160' ±). Safety fencing for horseshoe pitch. Night lighting.
OUTDOOR PERFORMANCE/ ASSEMBLY AREAS	Drinking water. Shade if facilities are used during the day. Benches with backs – 25-50%. Good acoustical system. Continuous, even lighting level from parking to seating area.
NON-CONSUMPTIVE NATURE USE	Trails – shaded where possible. Interpretive information. Sanitary facilities at trailhead and along trails as needed – minimum 1-hour intervals.
GARDENING	Raised garden plots desirable. Good, easy-to-till/dig soil. Adjacent irrigation water – preferably irrigation system with timer and moisture sensor. Shaded sitting area with bench and water. Tool and supply storage area. Walkways.
CAMPING AREAS	
Parking spurs	25% cars – 75% vans/campers.
Camp pad	On passenger side of parked vehicle – shade required. Firm surfacing under camp pad, table and cooking unit.
Water	Within 35 m (120').
Trash	At every 4th site.
Sanitary facilities	Within 60 m (200'). More women's facilities than men's.
Cooking unit	Raised.

PICNIC AREAS

Drinking water. Views of natural features or activities. Shaded. Firm surfacing under site furniture and equipment. Sanitary facilities within a maximum of 60 m (200') of picnic tables. Parking within 60 m (200') max. – 30 m (100') desirable.

BOATING FACILITIES

Docks, piers, gangways to meet pathways and pedestrian ramp requirements. Curbs and railings at access ramps to floating docks. Sanitary facilities within 60 m (200') of all use areas.

FISHING FACILITIES

Access by Type I Trail preferred, Type II maximum difficulty. Natural shading and/or shelters. Benches, preferably with backs. Pole holders desirable. Sanitary facilities within 100 m (330') of fishing sites.

Deep water

Railings for docks and piers.

Shallow water

Curbs around fishing area.

HISTORIC SITES

Buildings and grounds

Provide highest level of accessibility feasible without damage to the historic resource.

Grounds

Provide shade, sanitary facilities at site and at 1-hour intervals along extended tour ways.

Harold – still fishing at 90
– Sequim, Washington
Photo by Lavinia Graham

Chapter 9 ACTIVITIES–INDOOR

It was pointed out in Chapter 2 that climatic extremes can cause additional stress on people as they age. As a result, more of the leisure time of older people is carried out either within an indoor environment or within one that has the climatic extremes tempered. This chapter will explore the access to some of these indoor spaces and the indoor/outdoor interfaces of others for activities such as dancing, aerobics and physical fitness, social gatherings, dining out, and cultural events. In addition, the aesthetic and environmental quality of the spaces around the buildings will be explored.

Many of the ideas discussed in this chapter are directly related to areas covered in part in Chapters 6 – Circulation, 7 – Utilities, 10 – Details, and 11 – Operation and Maintenance.

Basic themes in this chapter are safety, accessibility and environmental control.

ARRIVAL/ ENTRANCE AREA

The experience of the arrival at and departure from any facility can significantly affect the user's perception of and subsequent enjoyment of the facility/activity. Special care needs to be given then to arrival/departure areas. This ensures that the user's experience is enhanced, not detracted from, during the transition from the vehicle to the use facility and from the use facility back into the vehicle. The following factors should be considered in the planning and design of the older users' arrival at leisure facilities.

Drop-off/pick-up – Unloading/loading places are needed for buses, and especially mini buses, with appropriate waiting areas. See Chapter 6 – Circulation – Drop-off Figure 6.1, and Parking Figure 6.5.

Covered entrance to an upscale shopping center – Naples, Florida

Visual – Aesthetics is an obvious, but sometimes overlooked or neglected, aspect of the arrival sequence. Special care must be taken at the vehicular interface area since older people frequently have to wait for cars and/or other party members at this location.

Valet Parking Service – Parking service would be very beneficial, especially for special events where the parties are specially dressed, i.e. concerts, etc.

Lighting – A high, even level of light intensity is desired. Sequentially, the entrance should be the focal point of light intensity dropping off to lower, but even, levels of lighting away from the arrival space.

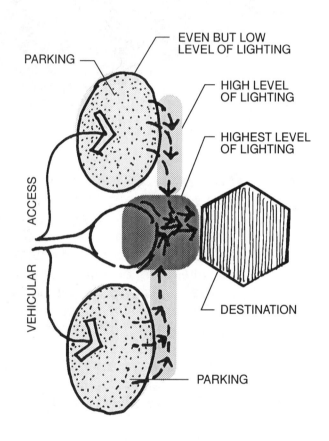

Figure 9.1 *Conceptual Lighting Levels*

Pedestrian Access – Barrier-free access-ways to and from parking are necessary. These should be similar to ADA requirements. A clear, safe, easily-identifiable destination for both day and night is needed to avoid confusion concerning where to go.

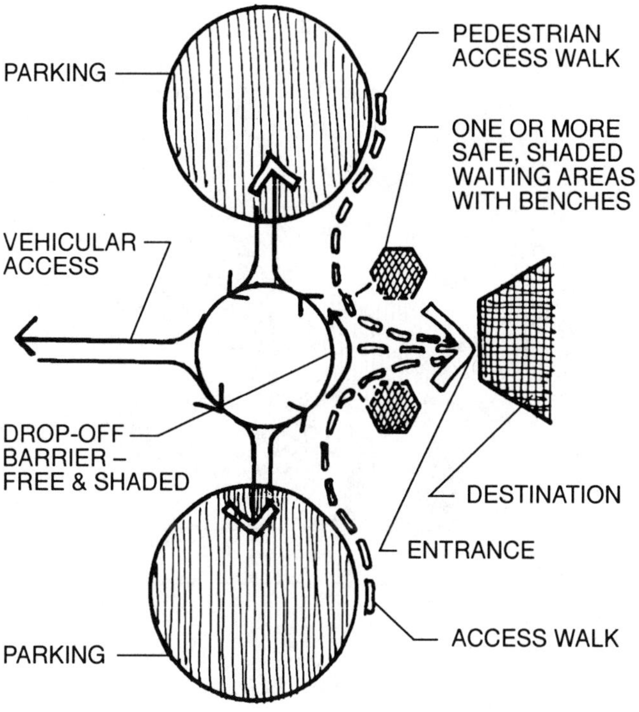

Figure 9.2 *Arrival Sequence*

Gathering Space/Waiting Area – A shaded sitting area with a view of arrival traffic is the necessary minimum. Protection from rain and extremes in weather conditions are also necessary. See also Chapter 6 – Circulation.

Safety/Security – Safety and security are critical. This is achieved primarily by good lighting and a site design which leaves no real or perceived hiding spaces for potential attackers.

MISCELLANEOUS ACTIVITIES/ FACILITIES

Visual Quality

Since many people spend more of their time indoors as they age, it is especially necessary for design teams to plan the environment from the inside out around buildings frequently used by older people. That is, it is more important to design the spaces around the buildings to enhance the enjoyment of the people looking out of the structure rather than for those looking at it. The design then would focus on what can be seen from the windows of places where older people will sit and/or congregate.

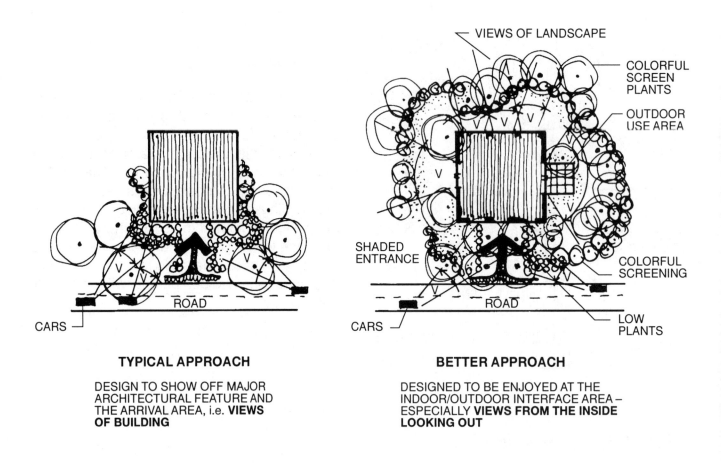

TYPICAL APPROACH

DESIGN TO SHOW OFF MAJOR
ARCHITECTURAL FEATURE AND
THE ARRIVAL AREA, i.e. **VIEWS
OF BUILDING**

BETTER APPROACH

DESIGNED TO BE ENJOYED AT THE
INDOOR/OUTDOOR INTERFACE AREA –
ESPECIALLY **VIEWS FROM THE INSIDE
LOOKING OUT**

Figure 9.3   *Visual Quality of Building Landscaping*

Bird Watching and Nature Enjoyment

People of all ages enjoy seeing and experiencing the natural environment – everything from bird and animal watching, to feeding the birds and animals, to looking at plants (especially flowering plants), to the actual gardening itself. Chapter 8 – Non-Consumptive Natural Area Use describes in some detail the traditional areas of these activities. These can be adapted to the environment surrounding the buildings in which we live, work, and play.

Birding and Animals

Birds and animals can be encouraged to utilize spaces in and around our built environments. Feeding stations are the primary source of attractions. One key to their success is their location. Birds are beautiful, they move freely through their environment, they "sing" and unfortunately, they make a real mess around areas where they congregate, i.e. bird feeders and nesting boxes. The placement of bird feeders and nesting boxes must take this into consideration. Other placement factors for feeders are:

• Safety from predators, especially cats.

Habitat enchancement to improve bird viewing opportunities from interior spaces – Bok Tower Gardens, Florida

• Easy access for restocking the feeders.

• Separation from places frequented by people.

• Location away from walks or other surfaces that should not be "messed."

• Placement where the birds can be seen from inside and outside.

• Provision of perching and habitat areas adjacent to the feeding station(s).

• Feeders do not have to be seen from the viewing area. If they cannot be seen, their perching and habitat areas must be seeable from the viewing space.

Other habitat enhancement features might include:

• Providing a sources(s) of water for drinking and bathing.

• Installing food plants, i.e. fruiting trees, seed flowers, etc.

• Provision of specialized feeders such as liquid hummingbird feeder(s), and holders for suet for woodpeckers, etc.

• Mast-producing trees for squirrels, i.e. oaks, pines, beeches, etc., with nearby protective shrubs, etc., for rabbits.

Please note that squirrels, possums and other animals, including rodents, are likely to frequent the feeders. Although there might be a slight additional cost; designs are available which reduce accessibility to these uninvited guests.

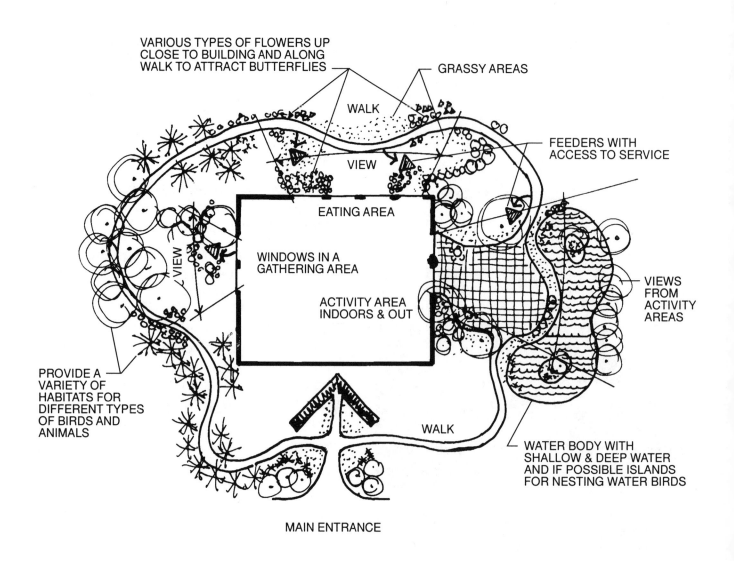

Figure 9.4   *Locations for habitat enhancement*

Butterflies

Butterfly feeding on Goldenrod

A source of constant kaleidoscopic color and motion, butterflies, like birds, can be encouraged to visit building environments. Two things are necessary – the proper type of plant material and an understanding by the maintenance staff, especially the groundskeepers, of what is desired. Butterflies can be seriously affected by herbicides and pesticides by either directly killing the butterflies or the killing of food plants. The preparation and implementation of a management plan as described in Chapter 11 – Operations is almost a necessity to achieving the desired results of numerous colorful visitors.

Flowers

There are **many** plants in addition to the flowers and plants that would be necessary to attract and feed butterflies. People of all ages and backgrounds enjoy flowers, including shrubs and trees. It is extremely important to understand that flowering plants must be chosen that will bloom when the users are there to enjoy them. Many older people, especially when they reach retirement age, have second homes in distant areas of the country. These second homes may be occupied at different times of the year. In Florida the "snow birds" visit in winter, and in Massachusetts the summertime is the big vacation home (or cabin) season.

As in bird watching, people who are confined to spending most of their time indoors would have their lives significantly enhanced with the placement of windows and outdoor gardens so that they can easily view them from inside the buildings.

*Formal gardens
– Downtown Philadelphia, Pennsylvania*

SHOPPING FOR PLEASURE

Shopping for pleasure is going to stores for enjoyment – usually to enclosed shopping centers or malls where there are a variety of things to see and do along with shopping. It is an opportunity to go somewhere, usually with friends or family, away from the home.

The pleasure derived from going shopping is frequently experienced by older people as shown by the authors' survey. The respondents indicated four primary leisure activities in which they participated – walking for exercise, going out to eat, visiting friends and relatives, and shopping. For many people these activities were participated in at least once a week, and frequently much more often.

Several factors can make this frequent shopping experience more enjoyable.

The Arrival – A well-designed arrival/departure area is the best way to begin and end a shopping experience. See Arrival/Entrance Area this chapter and Chapter 6 – Circulation. A reminder: Sitting areas for people with packages is more than a desirable addition – it is a necessity.

Sitting Areas – One of the most important features of a shopping area for older people is frequent sitting spaces out of the main traffic flow. This is true whether it is an enclosed mall or an open area. The sitting space should be attractive and restful.

Sanitary Facilities – Locate public sanitary facilities within 60 m (200') of every shopper. If a large area, then locate them at 120 m (400') of each other. They must be easily found, and if located off the main shopping way, they must be in an attractive, **SAFE** space. Drinking water is a necessity with chilled water desirable.

Window shopping at Waterside Shops – Naples, Florida

Drinking Water – Provision of water is necessary at the sanitary facilities and desirable in other locations if the shopping area is not enclosed.

Safety – Many older people have a heightened concern for safety, and their perception of a place's safety will determine their continued use. This is particularly true in relationship to groups of teenagers "hanging out."

Shade – If the shopping area is not enclosed, provide shade.

Aesthetics – An attractive setting for the older shoppers will enhance their enjoyment and encourage them to return frequently.

Eating Areas – As stated previously in Chapter 2, eating out for pleasure is one of the four top leisure activities for older people. (See the following section, Dining for Pleasure, for more details.) Combining the two activities can enhance the outing for the users and will provide a longer opportunity for the retailers to interface with potential customers. The eating areas should be attractive, with views of the surrounding activity. Some quiet spaces out of the flow of traffic and, if possible, separated from the noise and confusion that sometimes occurs would be desirable.

Most enclosed malls currently are designed as per Figure 9.5. Other features that can be and are often included at enclosed malls are performance areas, special displays and show and, before store hours, wellness walking and fitness programs. All of these "special" events are features which are of strong interest to older people. They should be considered in the mall's planning and design and its ongoing operation.

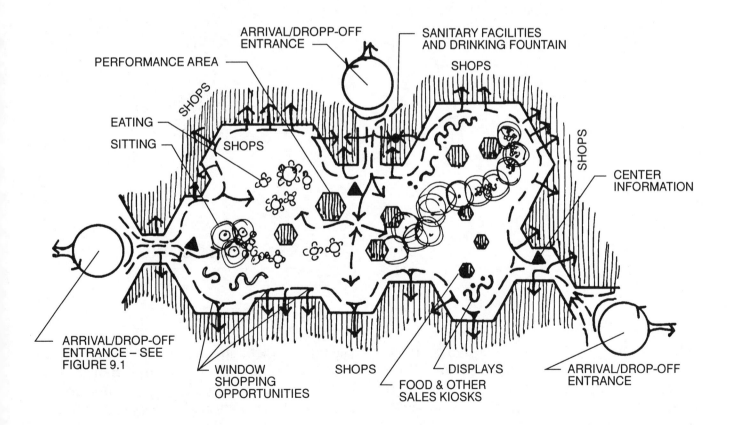

Figure 9.5 *Enclosed Malls*

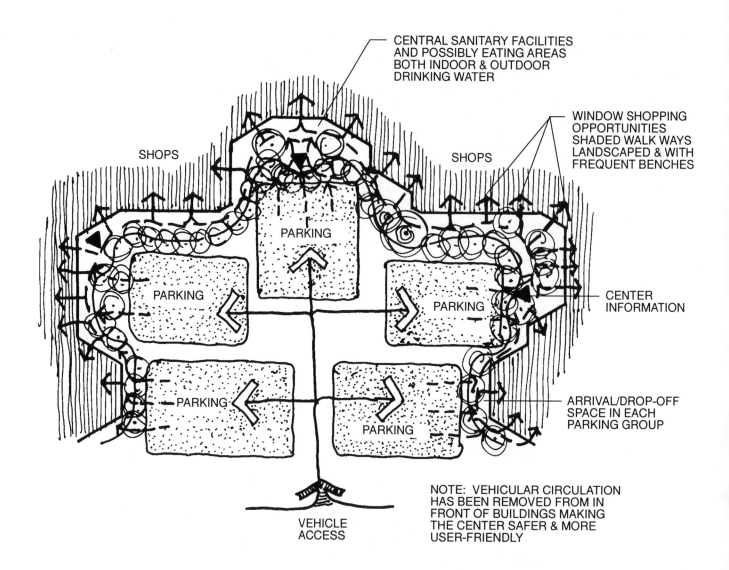

CENTRAL SANITARY FACILITIES
AND POSSIBLY EATING AREAS
BOTH INDOOR & OUTDOOR
DRINKING WATER

WINDOW SHOPPING
OPPORTUNITIES
SHADED WALK WAYS
LANDSCAPED & WITH
FREQUENT BENCHES

SHOPS

SHOPS

PARKING

PARKING

PARKING

CENTER
INFORMATION

PARKING

PARKING

ARRIVAL/DROP-OFF
SPACE IN EACH
PARKING GROUP

VEHICLE
ACCESS

NOTE: VEHICULAR CIRCULATION
HAS BEEN REMOVED FROM IN
FRONT OF BUILDINGS MAKING
THE CENTER SAFER & MORE
USER-FRIENDLY

Figure 9.6   *Shopping Centers*

Most shopping centers are not designed for people to linger or shop for pleasure. The suggested changes are simple and could readily be incorporated into any design, making it possible for older people to utilize the shops in a more leisurely and enjoyable fashion.

DINING FOR PLEASURE

Indoor and Outdoor

Dining for pleasure is one of the top four activities in the authors' survey. Eating is a necessary part of life. Dining for pleasure is more than just eating, it is a leisure experience where the arrival at the restaurant, the restaurant setting and/or ambiance, the service and finally the departure all come together, hopefully to make it a pleasant experience.

Eating in the park, John Pershing Park – Washington, DC

Dining is normally an indoor activity. Some of the most desirable eating spaces are, however, outdoors during comfortable weather conditions, or are situated where the outside view is the primary factor in making the dining an experience, rather than a necessity.

Dining out along the Bay – Naples, Florida

The following are factors to be considered in making the dining more enjoyable for older people.

The Arrival – This is the same as shopping for pleasure, with the exception that the arrival space should have a canopy for use during inclement weather.

Waiting Areas – Where waiting periods for seating are experienced, it is necessary to have sitting spaces because many older people cannot stand for extended periods of time. A bar may be helpful, but many older people feel out of place in bars. Also, many people of all ages do not drink alcohol, prefer a non-smoking environment, or both.

Noise Reduction – Background noise makes hearing conversations especially difficult for older people. Dining areas should, therefore, be designed to minimize noise.

Views or Focal Point – Since *dining for pleasure* is more than just eating, dining areas with views are most desirable. This could even entail putting the eating areas on different levels to afford more good view tables.

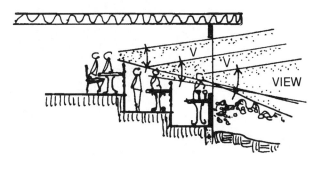

THIS TERRACED ARRANGEMENT ALLOWS MORE TABLES TO ENJOY THE VIEW

VIEW

Figure 9.7 *Terraced Dining Area*

Lighting – A sufficient level of lighting is necessary for older people to be able to see.

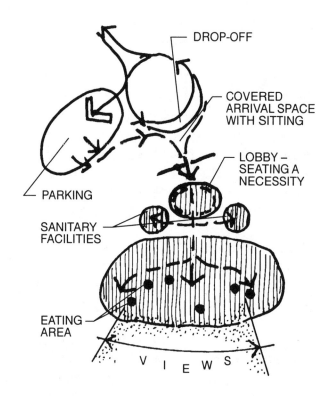

FOCUS OUTWARD

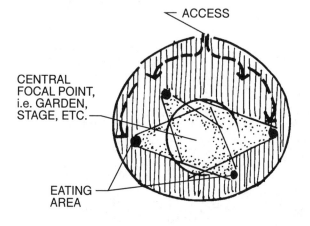

FOCUS INWARD

Figure 9.8 *Conceptual Layout for Dining Area*

Outdoor Dining – For dining outdoors, environmental modifications are almost always necessary. As a minimum, shade is needed during summer. Where rain is frequent, it is desirable to have the shade in the form of a roof. In addition, wind barriers may also be necessary. These can be vegetative or constructed. Where the wind comes from the direction of the view(s), then consider glass or clear plastic/plexiglass screens.

MEETINGS/LECTURES/CONCERTS

Going to meetings, lectures and concerts is done at least two or three times a year by many of the respondents in the authors' survey. In some places and for some events most of the audience may be people over 55, i.e. military band concerts, craft shows, etc. As such, activities/facilities which are likely to attract older users should provide the necessary special accommodations for them. Most of these special needs have been discussed in previous activities. See Chapter 6 – Circulation, and Arrival/Entrance Area in this chapter.

Meetings, lectures, concerts, etc., have concentrated arrival and departure times requiring special accommodations to facilitate the movements of large numbers of people in a short time span.

Vehicular Drop-off Area – These should be sufficient in size to handle the expected number of vehicles. Normally space is needed for more than one car plus at least one van/mini bus.

Valet Parking – Permanent or temporary space may be needed for special events for the desirable service of valet parking. Space will be required to store keys, request car pick-up, etc. Locate this space away from the ticket counter, but close to the vehicular arrival space. If a permanent facility is provided, it must be weatherized, i.e. being heated in the cold season and cooled in the hot season is necessary if events are during the afternoons.

Ticket Sales – If space is provided outside the building, locate the sales booth on the left as you enter the pedestrian arrival area and behind the space needed for those waiting to be picked up.

Outside Waiting Area(s) – Locate these spaces off the main entry path so as not to impede normal pedestrian circulation. Shade only if the facility is likely to be used during the day.

Lighting – Many meetings, lectures and concerts are held in the evening. Even lighting levels will enhance the visual clarity of the space and provide both a real and perceived sense of safety.

BOARD GAMES AREAS

The authors' survey showed many people over 55 played cards and board games frequently, between once a week and once a month. These activities can take place either indoors or outdoors. The space and amenities needed are similar for cards and board games.

Indoor and Outdoor

Space Requirements – 4.2 m^2 to 4.65 m^2 (45 ft^2 to 50 ft^2) is needed for each table with either two or four chairs plus 600 mm (24") space between tables. To determine the number of tables needed, divide the number of expected users by two or four or more (the number of people per table). The tables should not be located in the major pedestrian circulation systems. See Chapter 10 – Details–Tables.

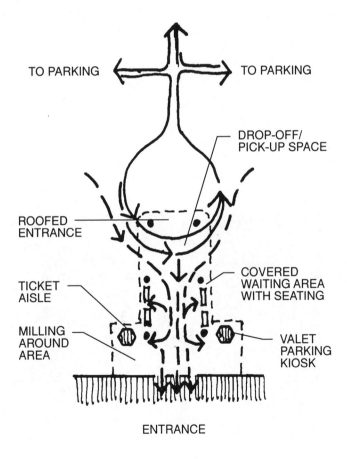

VEHICULAR ACCESS

TO PARKING

TO PARKING

DROP-OFF/
PICK-UP SPACE

ROOFED
ENTRANCE

COVERED
WAITING AREA
WITH SEATING

TICKET
AISLE

MILLING
AROUND
AREA

VALET
PARKING
KIOSK

ENTRANCE

Figure 9.9 *Arrival Area for Meetings/
Lectures/Concerts*

*Board games, North Fort Myers Senior Center
– Lee County, Florida*

Sanitary Facilities – As usual, the sanitary facilities should be located as close to the activity as possible with a maximum distance of 100 m (330') and a desirable maximum of 60 m (200').

Lighting – Good, even reading level lighting is needed indoors and if night use is anticipated, outdoors as well.

Outdoor Only

Shade – Trees, vine-covered trellises or a shade structure of some sort is needed. In the cold season, sunlight is desirable, i.e. deciduous trees and vines to help from warm, sunny southern facing areas.

Wind Barrier – Where there is persistent wind during normal use period from any identifiable direction(s), a wind barrier should be built. Warm and hot season breezes are desirable and should not be blocked.

Playing Surface – Solid, durable, low maintenance tables are needed. A long-lasting built-in game board (usually checkers/chess) is also a good idea. A minimum of two chairs per table are needed when only checkers and chess, etc., are expected to be played. Four or more chairs are recommended for other types of use, and perhaps even more for the likely spectators. Chairs with arms would be more desirable than chairs without arms.

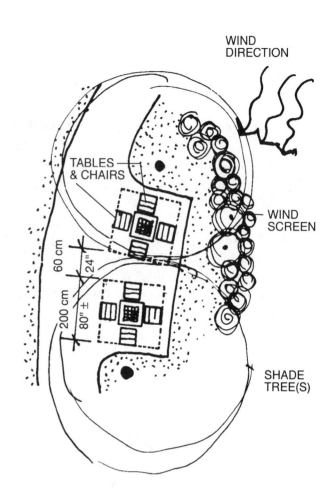

Figure 9.10 *Table Layout Requirements*

Built-in checkerboards
– Hot Springs National Park, Arkansas

Location – It is most desirable to have a space off the main circulation way with some privacy from the passersby. Some additional space around some tables would be desirable to allow onlookers to also enjoy watching the games. An acceptable alternative location is to build the games area adjacent to a secondary walkway.

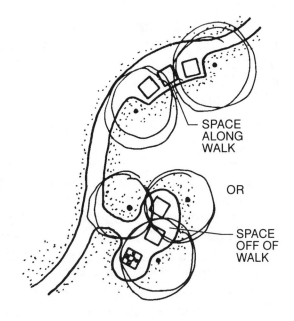

Figure 9.11 *Outdoor Board Game Location*

Indoor Only

Portable tables and chairs can be used; however, some space should be set up and available for play at all times. Table space requirements are the same as for outdoor spaces.

PHYSICAL FITNESS

Awareness of the need for lifetime physical fitness is growing as is evidenced by the large numbers of older people who are walking out along the roadways or in the malls walking for exercise. This contention is further supported by the popularity of physical fitness classes at senior citizen centers and retirement homes.

Information presented in Chapter 6 – Circulation-Pedestrian/Bicycle and Chapter 8 – Activities–Outdoor–Swimming covers the physical facility needs for the walkers, bicyclists, swimmers and water aerobics. This section covers the needs of aerobics, physical fitness equipment, fitness trails and mall walking.

Aerobics (Indoor or Outdoor)

Space – A large open space of sufficient size is needed to accommodate the expected number of participants. Outdoor space must be shaded and visually screened from conflicting activities.

Indoor/outdoor space – dancing, aerobics, etc. – Lee County, Florida

Sound System – An electrical outlet is necessary for the sound system. A quality system is strongly recommended as discussed in Chapter 7 – Utilities.

Background Noise – Minimizing or, better yet, removing background noise will make it possible to better hear and understand the music and instructions for aerobic exercising.

Sanitary Facilities – Include in the standard sanitary facilities *private* shower/change spaces with benches. Since there are many more women than men in most exercise classes, the sanitary/shower facilities should have more fixtures for the women than the men. The ratio might be as much as 2:1 women's to men's fixtures.

Emergency 911 Service – Due to the strenuous nature of this activity, it is critical to have readily available free phone access to emergency service personnel.

Rest Area – Benches and/or chairs are needed for resting.

Dancing

The space for aerobics can be utilized directly for dancing. The only changes would be a need for additional seating and perhaps tables. The number of fixtures, toilets and/or urinals, would need to be approximately equal men to women for this activity.

Physical Fitness Equipment

Space – A room dedicated to this activity is needed. Because of the bulkiness of the equipment, it is not possible to have multiple use of this space. The nature of the equipment precludes this activity from being in an outside location.

Sanitary Facilities – This is similar to aerobics, except that there may need to be more sanitary facilities for men than in an aerobics only area.

Emergency 911 Service – Needed – see Aerobics.

Rest Area – Needed – see Aerobics.

Physical Fitness Trails

Fitness trails are generally not frequently used by younger people, and are rarely used by older people. This is not a recommended facility to enhance usability and enjoyment for older people.

Mall Walking

This activity has become very popular with older people. Enclosed malls are climate-controlled and offer the opportunity for year-round exercise. The mall, as a result, becomes a gathering center for older people early in the day. These walkers frequently stay until the stores open and some may then indulge in a favorite activity of shopping for pleasure as discussed earlier in this chapter.

Chapter 10 DETAILS

Details make or break a project. All of the designers' beautiful ideas are just that if the intended users can't get to them and enjoy them. The walk surface, stairs, railings, benches, etc., that you see up close, that you touch, that you actually use, are the heart of every well done project.

In preceding chapters, you have been shown how to make facilities, and leisure facilities in particular, more user-friendly to older people.

This chapter concerns itself with some of the **details** necessary to make many of the previous design suggestions work, i.e. walk surfaces, ramps, railings, stairs, benches, shade structures and graphics.

WALKS / PATIO SURFACES

The finishes of walks and patios are the only part of the walking surface that directly affect the users. He/she never sees, nor cares, what is under that surface. This finished surface needs special considerations for older users primarily in three areas – (1) color, (2) pattern, and (3) texture. In addition, extreme attention needs to be paid to preventing loose slip-inducing objects from getting onto the walk surface.

- Paving colors and patterns should be continuous or at least not confusing. Patterns that might be construed as being changes in grade (steps) should be avoided.

Avoid confusing paving patterns
– Chatham Center, Pittsburgh, Pennsylvania

- No small loose material, i.e. pea stone or small crushed stone should be placed adjacent to walks. It is too easy for the loose material to get onto the walk and cause a serious slipping/falling hazard. This includes no trees with hard, round fruit or seeds, i.e. some palms, lindens, cherry (pits), etc.

Avoid small stones next to hard surfaces
– private residence, Oakland, California

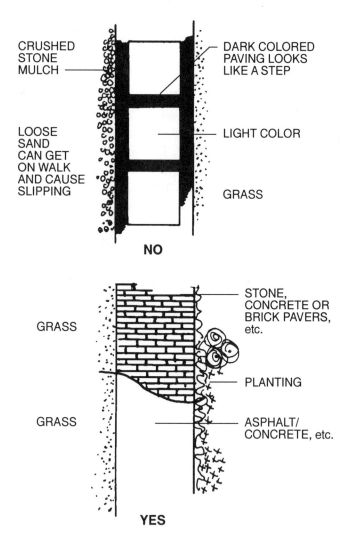

Figure 10.1 *Walk/Patio Paving Patterns*

Continuous pavement color and texture – Washington, DC

In areas subject to snowfall, the following factors should be taken into consideration.

• Dark color on paving will aid in melting snow and ice.

• Space to place removed snow is necessary.

• Good surface drainage is essential to prevent ice buildup.

The following is a list of some of the commonly used walk surfaces. The success of all are dependent on proper grading, drainage (surface and subsurface), and base course preparation.

Concrete – This is the cadillac of walks. It is very expensive, but if properly installed on the correct base it will be long-lasting and virtually maintenance free. It must be finished with a textured surface and the walk must drain to prevent winter ice. Concrete walks are very difficult to patch from an aesthetic standpoint if portions need to be removed for maintenance purposes.

Asphalt – This is a good, moderately priced flexible surface which must be properly "mixed" for the climate in which it is used.

The dark surface is good for thermal heating and subsequent quick melting of ice. In southern climates it is desirable to treat the surface with a light colored finish (i.e. crushed shell or brushed-on dry cement) prior to curing to keep the surface cooler and more firm during summer. Occasional resurfacing will be required.

Pavers on Concrete – These can be an aesthetically outstanding surface that is long lasting and functional. This is the most costly alternative. It is almost impossible to match the material if the walk is damaged for any reason. Special care must be taken to ensure surface evenness as well as providing a non-slip surface, i.e. no polished stones.

Compacted Crushed Stone – A very flexible, cost effective solution. From an aesthetic standpoint, it fits into rural and "park" settings but may look out of place in some urban areas. Occasional top dressing of finish/surface course may be required. It's easy to repair.

Wood Decking (Includes recycled plastic material) – This is useful in environmentally-sensitive areas (especially wetlands and dune areas) and along steep slopes (especially around buildings). Care needs to be taken to make sure there is no warping of wood (or plastic) surfaces, and that the surface is suitably smooth for the purposes (levels of challenge) intended. Wood surfaces require frequent repair and replacement. Recycled plastic wood should be considerably longer-lasting than wood, however, the surface may become smooth and slippery with heavy use.

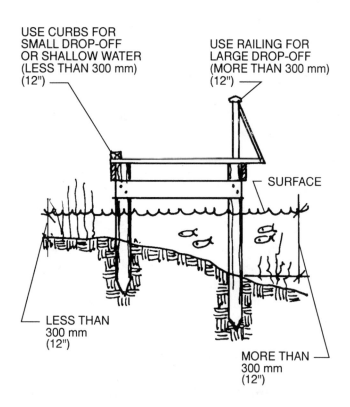

Figure 10.2 *Elevated Walks*

Pavers on Sand – See Pavers on Concrete. This continuous paved surface is much less expensive than pavers on concrete, but just as long-lasting a pathway when property installed. They also are easy to move and replace when any subsurface repairs are needed, and show no signs that a repair in the wearing surface was made.

Wood Chips – This is frequently used as a surface on trails and "natural" pathways. It fits the natural setting but is difficult for some, especially with assistive devices, to walk on. It is inexpensive to install, but requires frequent refurbishing. It is not a good surface for an accessible trail, and is generally not recommended for trails with high numbers of older users.

Grass – This is only suitable in low-use areas. Grass is subject to morning dew and is usually slow in draining. For this reason, it is **NOT RECOMMENDED** except in unusual circumstances. It is also expensive to maintain, and is not generally usable for an accessible way.

Untreated Soil – This should be considered only for low-use areas on "back country trails." It is **NOT RECOMMENDED** except as a last resort, and is not generally usable for an accessible way.

Gravel – Loose gravel and stone are inexpensive but very difficult to use, even by the most able-bodied site visitors. **DO NOT USE**.

TRAILS AND PATHWAYS

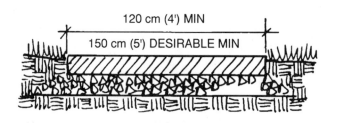

Figure 10.3 *Walk Width*

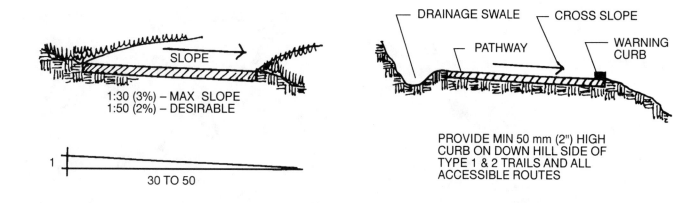

PROVIDE MIN 50 mm (2") HIGH
CURB ON DOWN HILL SIDE OF
TYPE 1 & 2 TRAILS AND ALL
ACCESSIBLE ROUTES

Figure 10.4 *Walk Cross Slope*

Figure 10.6 *Warning Curb on Trails*

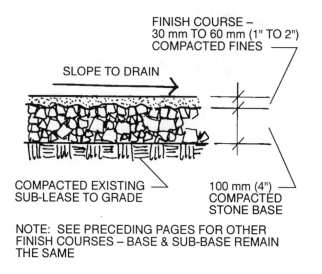

NOTE: SEE PRECEDING PAGES FOR OTHER
FINISH COURSES – BASE & SUB-BASE REMAIN
THE SAME

Figure 10.5 *Unpaved Trail Section*

The finish on non-slip surfaces of pathways
for accessible ways should have a surface
texture of not more than 3 mm (1/8") with
excellent drainage. Other walks should also
be non-slip but may have up to a maximum
surface texture of 10 mm (3/8") with good
drainage.

BENCHES

Benches are one of the most used and visible site amenities or furniture. As such, they
have received much design attention through
the years. There are special designs as well
as "off-the-shelf" benches from numerous
companies for almost any sitting situation
and budget.

– Naples, Florida

– Naples, Florida

– Scotland
Benches – special designs and off-the-shelf

Benches typically are 350 mm – 480 mm (14" – 19") high off ground, and from there everything else is up to the designer or manufacturer.

To make benches/bench walls and other seating more usable for older people the following should be considered:

- **Sitting surface** – bench seats must drain. The surface should be comfortable to sit on – cool in warm climates (light color or wood), and warm in cool and cold climates (dark color or wood). Wood has proven itself to be the most desirable surface in many environments and is easily repairable. Concrete is the least desirable from a comfort standpoint and almost impossible to repair if damaged.

- **Bench height** – install on the higher end of range so the older person does not have as far to leverage his/her body. Also, provision for some sort of optional foot rest is desirable for higher benches. It is uncomfortable to sit with one's feet dangling in mid-air and may also cut off blood circulation.

- **Bench backs** – should be provided where possible.

- **Bench arms** – needed for leverage to assist in getting off of the bench.

- **Benches** should be securely anchored. Sitting on and getting off the bench frequently requires real leverage and any bench movement could be disastrous to those with diminished mobility and reaction capabilities.

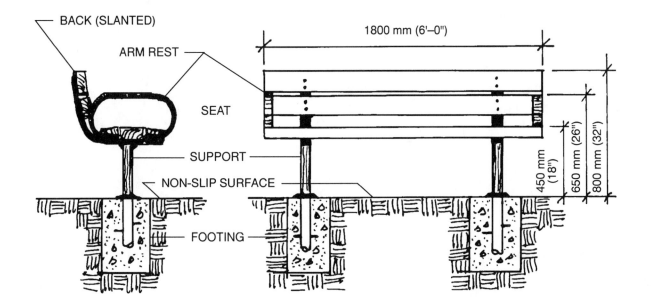

Figure 10.7 *Benches*

"Off-the-shelf" bench
– Tyler State Park, Pennsylvania
– Photo courtesy of Pennsylvania State Parks

• Environmental protection may be needed from the harsh weather conditions of sun and wind.

Particular care must be taken in public places to design the planting to avoid any areas which might provide hiding places for criminals.

BENCH WALLS

Urban parks, especially in heavily used spaces like bus stops, shopping malls and the favorite lunch areas, can benefit from a landscape construction detail called bench or planter walls.

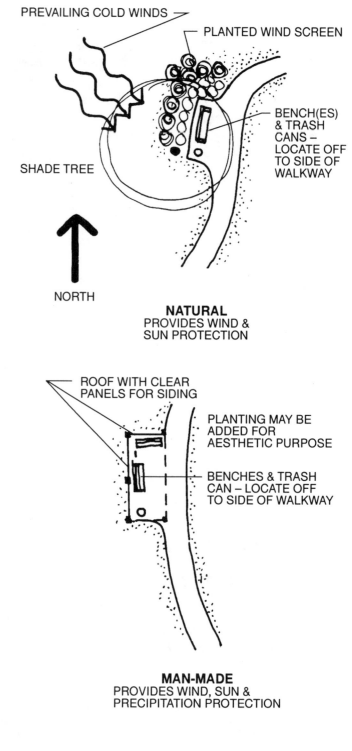

Figure 10.8 *Environmental Protection*

When properly designed, these attractive landscape features provide ideal places for people to rest, people watch and visit.

Bench/planter walls – Victoria, B.C., Canada

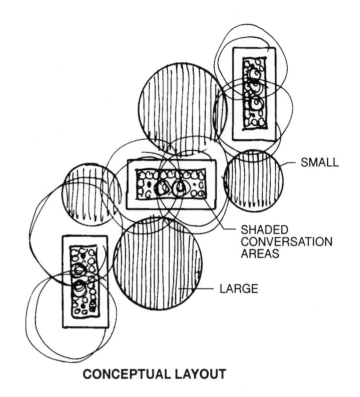

SMALL

SHADED CONVERSATION AREAS

LARGE

CONCEPTUAL LAYOUT

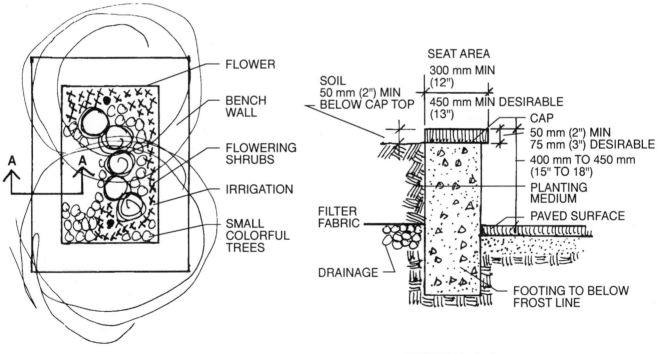

FLOWER

BENCH WALL

FLOWERING SHRUBS

IRRIGATION

SMALL COLORFUL TREES

A

A

PLAN

SEAT AREA
300 mm MIN (12")

SOIL
50 mm (2") MIN
BELOW CAP TOP

450 mm MIN DESIRABLE (13")

CAP

50 mm (2") MIN
75 mm (3") DESIRABLE

400 mm TO 450 mm (15" TO 18")

PLANTING MEDIUM

FILTER FABRIC

PAVED SURFACE

DRAINAGE

FOOTING TO BELOW FROST LINE

SECTION A–A

Figure 10.9 *Bench Wall*

TABLES

Tables of various types and configurations are basic elements in leisure facilities. They can vary from the typical old fashioned "picnic" table to very sophisticated tables for urban areas. Almost any style and size of table is available from one or more of the numerous manufacturers now marketing these and other site products.

Tables can, with a few basic requirements, be enhanced for usability by older people.

Table Design

The size and style of a table are determined by its function and the design theme of the site. There are some common design features which should be avoided and others that work well.

Typical "off-the-shelf" picnic/camp table – Asir National Park, Saudi Arabia

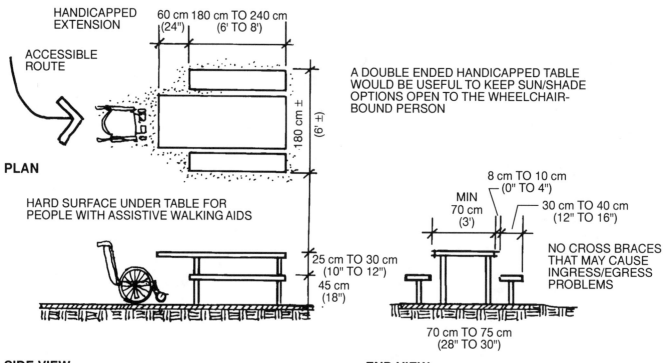

Figure 10.10 *Picnic Table*

Table Supports – Nothing should be put in the way of getting into the seat by people with diminished mobility capabilities.

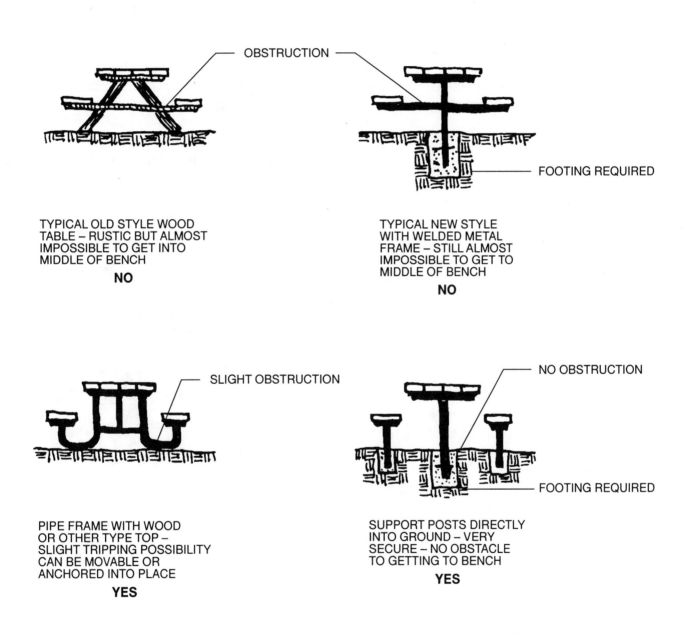

OBSTRUCTION

FOOTING REQUIRED

TYPICAL OLD STYLE WOOD
TABLE – RUSTIC BUT ALMOST
IMPOSSIBLE TO GET INTO
MIDDLE OF BENCH
NO

TYPICAL NEW STYLE
WITH WELDED METAL
FRAME – STILL ALMOST
IMPOSSIBLE TO GET TO
MIDDLE OF BENCH
NO

SLIGHT OBSTRUCTION

NO OBSTRUCTION

FOOTING REQUIRED

PIPE FRAME WITH WOOD
OR OTHER TYPE TOP –
SLIGHT TRIPPING POSSIBILITY
CAN BE MOVABLE OR
ANCHORED INTO PLACE
YES

SUPPORT POSTS DIRECTLY
INTO GROUND – VERY
SECURE – NO OBSTACLE
TO GETTING TO BENCH
YES

Figure 10.11 *Table Supports*

Seat Material

Seats are more important than table tops for user comfort. Some seat materials become hot in the sun and are uncomfortable to sit on, especially during hot weather – metal and plastics in particular. Other seats hold the moisture or cold and are not very pleasant to use during wet and/or cold weather – e.g., concrete and stone. Probably the most comfortable, and fortunately one of the least expensive, most readily available, and easiest to maintain seat material is good quality, treated wood.

Surface Under the Table

The table should be even, drain easily, be weed free and not erode over time. This means that some type of long lasting constructed surface is necessary. Concrete pavers of various types, asphalt and compact crushed stone choked with fines are suggested in descending order of preference.

Specialized Tables

Handicapped Accessibility – At least some of the tables should be handicapped accessible. Consider making both ends of the tables accessible.

STANDARD HANDICAPPED TABLE

DOUBLE ENDED TABLE

Figure 10.12 *Handicapped Accessible Picnic Tables*

Card / Game Tables – These are basically the same as picnic tables, with the exceptions that the tables are square, and seats may be located on all sides. If tables will be used for checkers, chess or backgammon, then the appropriate game board and only two stools are needed, with three or four being more desirable.

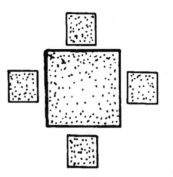

MULTIPURPOSE TABLE
WITH 4 STOOLS –
BOARD OPTIONAL

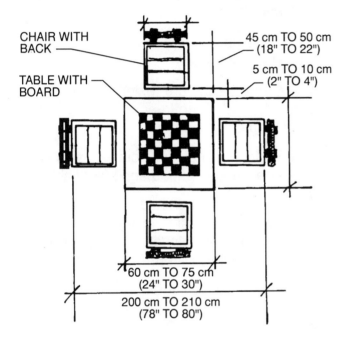

CHAIR WITH
BACK

TABLE WITH
BOARD

45 cm TO 50 cm
(18" TO 22")

5 cm TO 10 cm
(2" TO 4")

60 cm TO 75 cm
(24" TO 30")

200 cm TO 210 cm
(78" TO 80")

Figure 10.13 *Card/Game Table Space
Requirements*

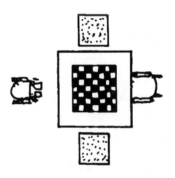

CHECKER/CHESS
BACKGAMMON WITH
2 STOOLS – COULD
ALSO BE USED BY
2 WHEELCHAIRS

HANDICAPPED TABLE
WITH OR WITHOUT
BUILT-IN GAME BOARD

Figure 10.14 *Alternate Stool Arrangements*

STAIRS AND RAMPS

Stairs, ramps and/or mechanical lifts are necessary to move people up and down slopes and between floors of buildings. Only stairs and ramps (with some limited exceptions at pools) are used outside of buildings. Much of the following text shown with an asterisk (*) is derived from an interesting reference on stairs, ramps, etc., by John Templer titled *The Staircase* (see Bibliography). The greater the percentage of slope and/or the greater the vertical separation between two areas to be connected, the more problems there are likely to be.

Most problems result in people losing their balance and falling. Stairs are more likely to be the location of falling accidents than ramps. Ramps are less tiring to use and easier on the joints of older people than stairs. As an example, Section 2.3.4 of *The Staircase* states that 11° ramps are less tiring than 5 1/2" to 7 1/2" risers, and that the lower the percentage of grade on the ramp, the easier it is to use. Conversely, the steeper the grade, the more difficult, with slopes over 20% better served with stairs. Although easier to use, ramps unfortunately take up a great deal more space than stairways (approximately five times as much space).*

People fall on stairs and ramps because they lose their balance. This is caused by user behavior, stair maintenance, stair design and/or poor construction. A well designed facility would be one that minimizes the potential for losing one's balance.* The following design guidelines are recommended.

Stairs

- Provide more than one riser* – a single riser can be missed visually.

- No steps or risers should be in an unexpected place.*

- Make treads wider rather than narrower with 230 mm (9") minimum, 280 mm (11") optimum, and 460 mm (18") maximum.*

- Make risers between 115 mm (4 1/2") and 175 mm (7").*

- ALL treads and risers in any flight of stairs must be uniform.*

- Make sure treads are textured and pitched properly to drain to keep ice from building up during cold weather.*

- It is important that the front edge of each tread be clearly defined and identifiable.*

- Treads and risers should clearly read as a stairway. There should be no confusing patterns on any stairway. Consider making treads and risers different colors.*

- All stairs must be lighted at all times when a facility might be in use. There should be an even level of lighting between 5 and 20 foot-candles.*

- It is finally suggested that unless there is a compelling reason to the contrary, a stairway should not have distracting views to take the users' attention from the task of safely negotiating the change in grade.*

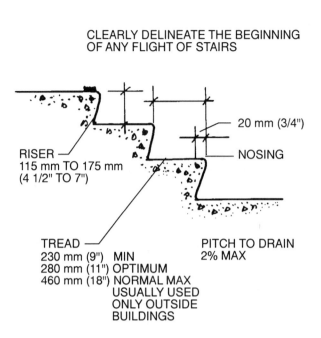

CLEARLY DELINEATE THE BEGINNING
OF ANY FLIGHT OF STAIRS

20 mm (3/4")

NOSING

RISER
115 mm TO 175 mm
(4 1/2" TO 7")

TREAD
230 mm (9") MIN
280 mm (11") OPTIMUM
460 mm (18") NORMAL MAX
USUALLY USED
ONLY OUTSIDE
BUILDINGS

PITCH TO DRAIN
2% MAX

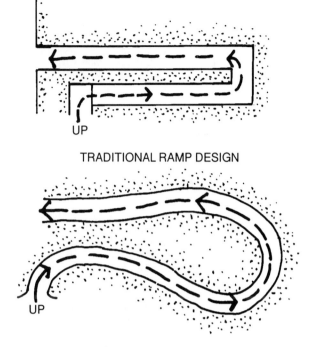

UP

TRADITIONAL RAMP DESIGN

UP

ALTERNATIVE RAMP DESIGN

Figure 10.15 *Stair Detail*

Figure 10.16 *Conceptual Ramp Layout*

Ramps

More people (up to two times more) can use a ramp or walk than can use the same width stairway.*

- Ramps between 1:20 (5%) and 1:16 (6.25%) are the most desirable. Try to keep ramps at 1:14 (7%) if possible. The legal ramp maximum is 1:12 (8.3%) for handicapped accessibility compliance.

- Railings should be included on both sides of all ramps whether or not they are on a handicapped accessible route.

- Surface of ramps should be textured – ***no slippery surfaces!*** See Walks/Patio Surfaces this chapter.

Please note, ramps do not have to be straight lines and may be wider than 915 mm (36").

Railings

Railings help ensure that people can move safely from one level to another. All ramps and stairways must have railings. Use the ADA criteria shown in Chapter 3 – Current Guidelines. In addition, stair and ramp railings should be –

- Circular – approximately 38 mm (1 1/2") in diameter and be finished with a smooth finish* (enamel, steel, vinyl, stainless steel, varnished wood, etc.).

- Easily identifiable, possibly using a contrasting color from surrounding construction and/or landscaping.*

- Rails, to be most effective, should be within reach of stair or ramp users.* Greater spacing is possible, but not desirable.

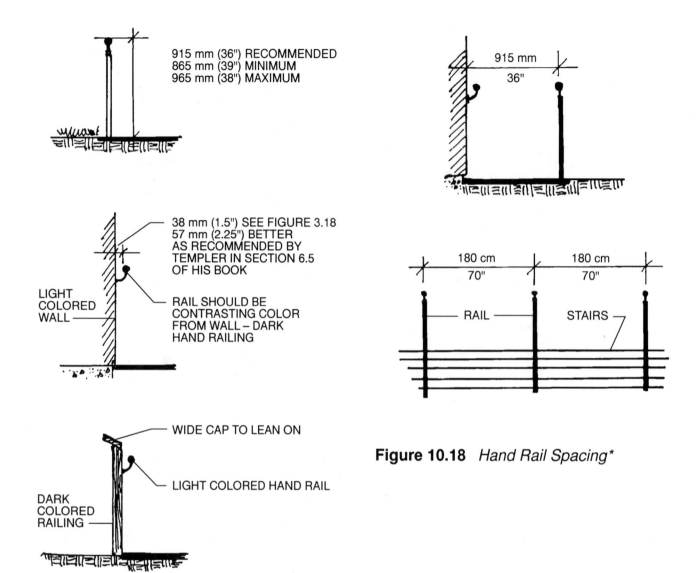

915 mm (36") RECOMMENDED
865 mm (39") MINIMUM
965 mm (38") MAXIMUM

915 mm
36"

38 mm (1.5") SEE FIGURE 3.18
57 mm (2.25") BETTER
AS RECOMMENDED BY
TEMPLER IN SECTION 6.5
OF HIS BOOK

RAIL SHOULD BE
CONTRASTING COLOR
FROM WALL – DARK
HAND RAILING

LIGHT
COLORED
WALL

180 cm
70"

180 cm
70"

RAIL

STAIRS

WIDE CAP TO LEAN ON

LIGHT COLORED HAND RAIL

DARK
COLORED
RAILING

Figure 10.18 *Hand Rail Spacing**

Figure 10.17 *Hand Rail Details*

Ice and Snow Removal

Ice and snow are a serious problem, limiting use of facilities by older people. Stairs and ramps are the most dangerous places on the access route for older people and must be kept clear!

• Provide space for disposal of snow and ice.

• Consider installing heating coils under stairs and ramps to reduce or eliminate ice and snow buildup.

GUARD RAILS AND BALUSTRADES

This section covers all other railings not required for stairways. All raised platforms (decks, observation platforms, fishing piers, overlooks, etc.) need to have railings/balustrades around them for safety. This is especially true for older people with vision impairments. In addition, many people are uncomfortable with heights and these barriers give some of them an increased sense of safety, or at least lessen their discomfort.

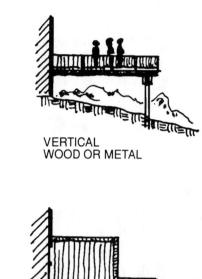

VERTICAL
WOOD OR METAL

ENTRANCE

DECK

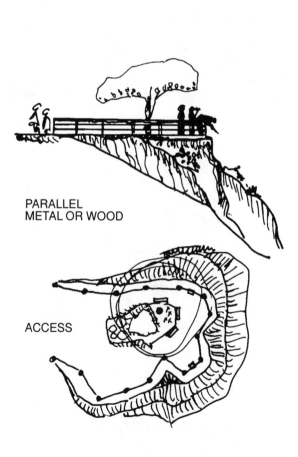

PARALLEL
METAL OR WOOD

ACCESS

OVERLOOK

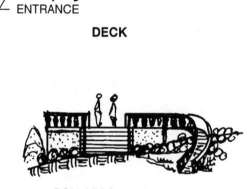

BOLLARDS
STONE OR CONCRETE

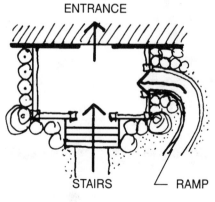

ENTRANCE

STAIRS   RAMP

PLATFORM

Figure 10.19 *Guard Rails*

Railing Height – 1070 mm (40") is the maximum desirable (above waist height); 1015 mm (40") or slightly lower is acceptable if a wide railing is provided, i.e. greater than 150 mm (6").*

Balustrades

Spacing of voids in the vertical elements should be no greater than 890 mm (8 1/2") to prevent children from getting their heads into the openings, or less than 90 mm (3 1/2") to prevent hands or feet getting caught.

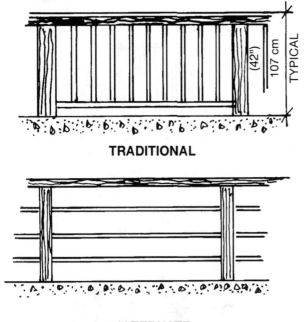

TRADITIONAL

ALTERNATE

ALTERNATE   **RAIL SPACING**

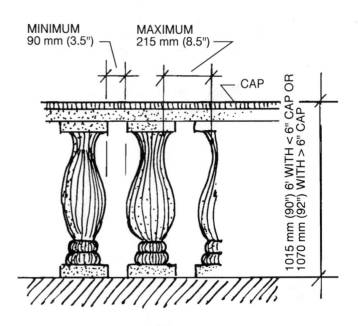

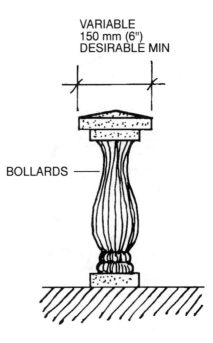

Figure 10.20 *Platform/Overlook Railings*

Figure 10.21 *Balustrades*

SHELTERS

Protection from harsh environmental conditions is important to most older people and becomes increasingly critical as they reach the more senior years. The environment, type of use, and age of the likely users affect the kind and extent of shade/shelter devices needed. In addition, shelters provide a sense of place. They form your home away from home.

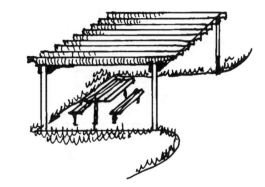

TRELLIS

Vine-covered trellis – Kowloon, Hong Kong

Sun / Shade

Shelters must, as a minimum, protect the user from the sun and may vary in size from a single bench sunscreen to a large group picnic shelter for 100 or more people. The placement of furniture within the structure is dependent upon what time of day and when during the year the facilities will be used. Figure 10.23 shows a desirable placement of a picnic table that would be used during the noon to late afternoon in summer.

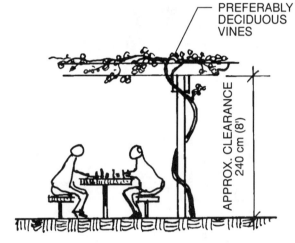

PREFERABLY DECIDUOUS VINES

APPROX. CLEARANCE 240 cm (8')

TRELLIS WITH VINES

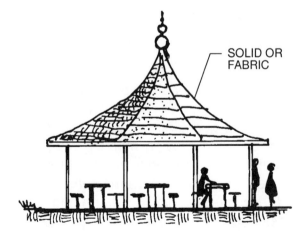

SOLID OR FABRIC

ROOFED STRUCTURE

Figure 10.22 *Shelter Options*

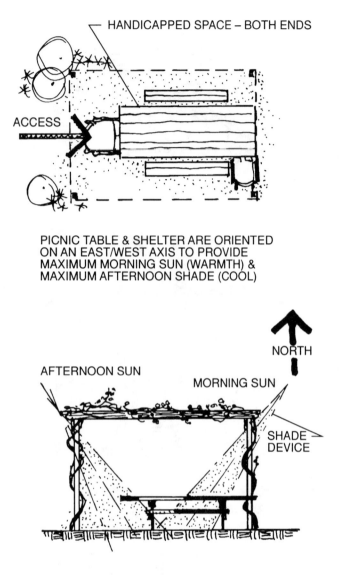

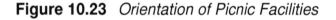

PICNIC TABLE & SHELTER ARE ORIENTED
ON AN EAST/WEST AXIS TO PROVIDE
MAXIMUM MORNING SUN (WARMTH) &
MAXIMUM AFTERNOON SHADE (COOL)

Figure 10.23   *Orientation of Picnic Facilities*

The same picnic table location and orientation would also provide morning sun, when orientation of a rectangular structure on a east/west axis will also permit sunshine during the winter, helping to warm the picnic area during this season.

Figure 10.24   *Sun Angle*

Where shade is needed throughout most of the year, orient the furniture to the northeast quadrant (that is unless the site is in the southern hemisphere).

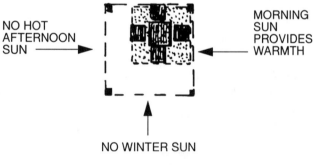

Figure 10.25   *Table Location for Year-round Shade*

Rain Protection

Where rain is expected during the primary use periods, consideration should be given to a roofed structure. The type and style of roof is limited only by the design theme of the overall site and budget limitations.

Wind Protection

Wind can be a very disruptive element in a shelter, especially in eating areas. If there is a prevailing wind, then a windscreen can be installed. There are three general options for screens: Plants (shrubs) – but they can obstruct views and need care – and two types of constructed barriers – opaque and transparent. An opaque screen is relatively easy and inexpensive to construct and maintain, but can obstruct views. Transparent panels are a good solution where the wind is from the direction of the view. Transparent barriers are relatively expensive to build and subject to vandalism. They must also be cleaned frequently. Their use is recommended only where the wind is really a problem and the view must be preserved.

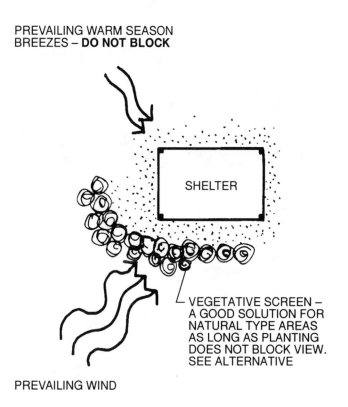

PREVAILING WARM SEASON
BREEZES – **DO NOT BLOCK**

SHELTER

VEGETATIVE SCREEN –
A GOOD SOLUTION FOR
NATURAL TYPE AREAS
AS LONG AS PLANTING
DOES NOT BLOCK VIEW.
SEE ALTERNATIVE

PREVAILING WIND

A GOOD SOLUTION

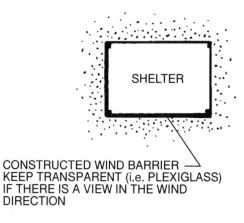

SHELTER

CONSTRUCTED WIND BARRIER –
KEEP TRANSPARENT (i.e. PLEXIGLASS)
IF THERE IS A VIEW IN THE WIND
DIRECTION

AN URBAN ALTERNATIVE

Figure 10.26 *Windscreens*

*Combined wind, sun and rain shelter
– somewhere in the windy Great Plains*

Floor Surface

It is best to utilize a permanent textured surface as discussed in this chapter – Picnic Tables. If eating is expected at the shelter, the floor surface should be one that is easily cleaned or which will not show stains.

GRAPHICS

Graphics, including signs, are of critical importance to all leisure facilities, especially for older people. This includes those who might have seeing and/or hearing impairments. ADA requires that some of all *facilities be available* to people *with various limitations*.

What it comes down to is that the message(s) must be clear, simple to understand, and easily read at the intended viewer distance. Chapter 3 – Current Guidelines spells out the written and graphic requirements that are necessary to meet ADA requirements.

This section of Chapter 10 simply offers some refinements and gives examples of how to improve/adjust the ADA graphics criteria to make the graphics portion of facilities somewhat more usable.

Signs

The key is legibility. This is affected by letter or symbol size and simplicity, and clear contrast with background color. The following photographs clearly illustrate this issue.

NO *Light color on light background
– hard to read – New York City, New York*

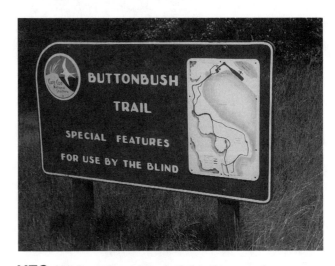

YES *White letters on dark background
– a good, easy to read sign*

YES *Dark letters on white background – easiest to read – Australia*

Text

Usually bigger and clearer/sharper images are better. Previous books by this author have been done in 10-point text. This book was increased to 12-point for easier reading by older people. Consideration should be given to making some text even larger – perhaps even to 14-point as shown by this sentence. All visual presentations, drawings and photos should follow this same theme, bigger and clearer.

Color

Color is an important aspect of any design. Many designers like to use subtle color variations in pastel shades and monochromatic schemes. Chapter 2 – People over 55– Vision states that "yellowing of the eye lens also creates a change in color perception. ... soft pastel colors are difficult if not impossible to distinguish from one another. ... the older person is best able to see bright colors ... and is best able to distinguish between light and dark colors which are placed in juxtaposition." In other words, if color is key to design clarity or direction, the designer must use strong colors and contrasting light and dark values as demonstrated in the previous sign photos.

?   "OK"   BETTER

Figure 10.27 *Graphics – Bigger is Better*

Chapter 11 OPERATIONS

*T*his chapter will focus on operations and maintenance factors primarily as they affect design. There are three operational items that are critical to any facility development.

First, and most important for designers, is to secure the necessary and vital input from the people who are going to operate and maintain the facilities. They know, or should know, what their day-to-day operational and maintenance problems are and how they will handle them. Operational and maintenance staff input from all levels must be evaluated and, where possible, included in the design.

Second, the operational and maintenance policies and procedures to be used after the facility is built are critical to the effective, quality, long term success of any project.

Third, keeping in mind variations on the concept of universal design, how the leisure facility is operated can greatly affect the kind of users that ultimately will be served. As an example, a park designed for primarily family use allows young people (teenagers) to also use the park for cruising. The large number of young people and high traffic volumes discourage families and older people from utilizing the available facilities even though the facilities were designed specifically for families. It is necessary for all staff involved with the operation and maintenance of a leisure facility to have a clear understanding of who the facility is planned to serve. If older people are a component of the user mix, especially if they are a significant percentage of the users (existing or desired), then their special needs must be included in the programming and all other staff actions.

It is strongly recommended that a management plan be prepared and kept current for each developed area. The NRPA publication *Management Planning for Park and Recreation Areas* by George Fogg and Dr. William Shiner can provide guidance on how to prepare such a management plan.

Staff awareness of older needs, however, will not ensure the success of a facility in meeting those needs. **Only with the understanding and strong support of all levels of management will a leisure facility truly be older people user-friendly.**

BUDGETING

All facilities wear out – some sooner than others. Everyone involved with the ongoing maintenance of leisure facilities should be made fully aware of the *costs* of keeping the facilities as they age in good, safe condition. Budgeting for preventive maintenance for major repairs should be initiated in a timely manner to prevent more serious and costly problems at a later date which could cause injury to the users. This is particularly true for facilities used by older people who are frequently susceptible to injuries caused by problems in their environment such as slipping on debris left on walks, tripping over uneven pavement, etc.

SECURITY

As people age, many become more concerned about their security, both from a physical standpoint – falling, slipping, driving – and from the fear of being accosted. These fears, actual and imagined, are real to the many individuals who perceive them.

What Can Be Done Through Design?

Eliminate areas where people who would harm others can hide, i.e. no dark places or screened areas that are near where older people congregate.

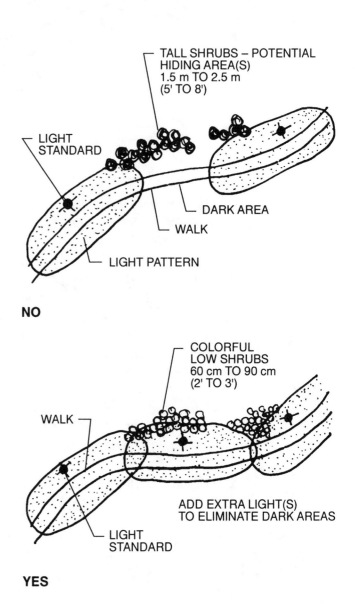

Figure 11.1 *Hiding Places – Walks*

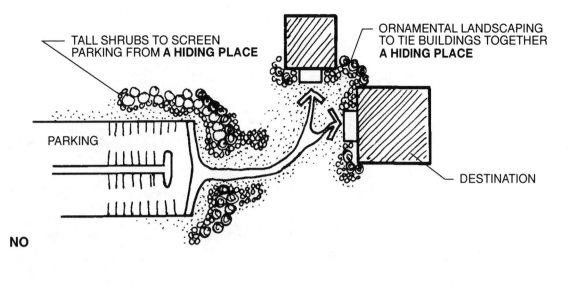

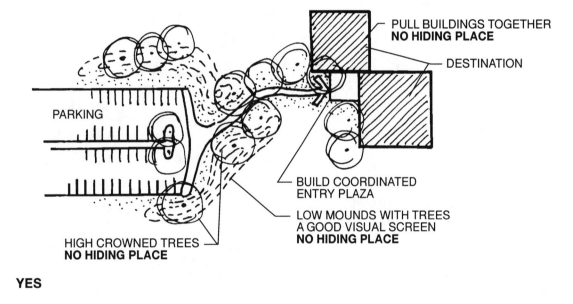

Figure 11.2 *Hiding Places – Parking*

Design all projects so that security personnel can see all areas as they patrol the site. On most areas, large or small, this normally means from their patrol vehicles, i.e. again, no hiding places. This is especially true at facilities in areas that experience or *there is a perception* of crime problems, including drugs, solicitation, etc.

This means, as a minimum, providing clear sight lines from the patrol vehicle route(s) into all site areas where people might assemble or move through.

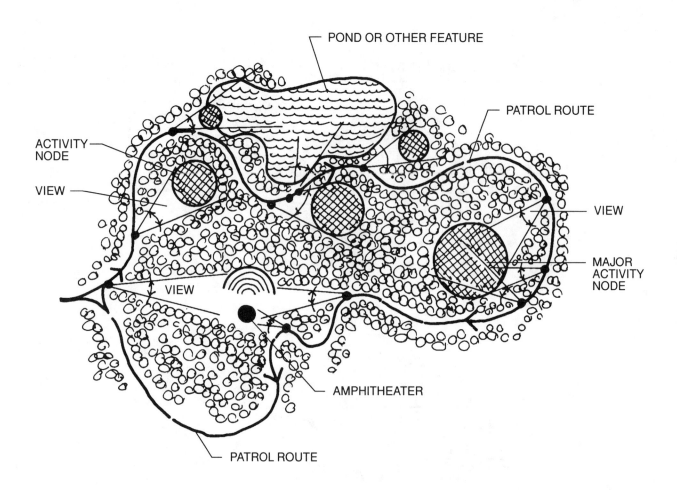

Figure 11.3   *Visibility from Patrol Routes*

It may also be desirable to build roads on higher elevations to give better views into the use areas.   Careful consideration of views may, in addition, enhance the visitor's enjoyment of the leisure facilities through a more interesting and varied driving experience.

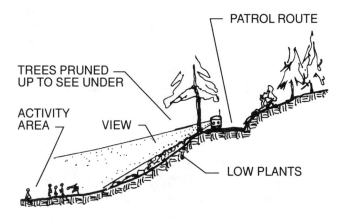

Figure 11.4   *Elevated Road on Hilly Site*

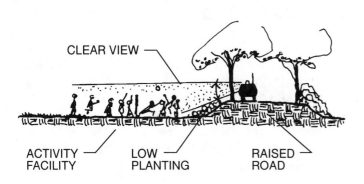

Fencing gives a sense of security and should be included where feasible. Consideration must be given to costs and aesthetics before deciding to fence. Other types of barriers might also be considered to achieve the same results as a fence — water features, thorn-type plantings and buildings themselves. Whatever is done to secure a site for safety purposes must also provide the perception of security as well as the reality.

Figure 11.5 *Elevated Road on Flat Site*

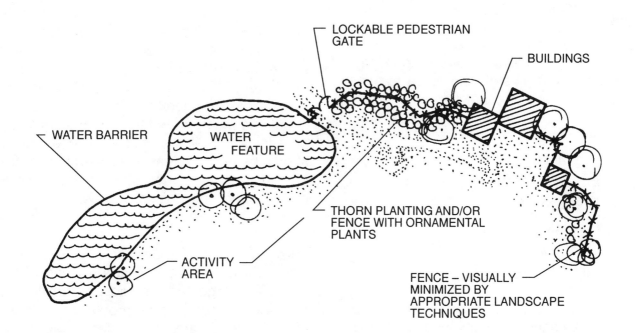

Figure 11.6 *Typical Barriers*

OPERATIONS

Safety Plan

Only so much can be done through design techniques to provide for security and user safety. It is imperative that a carefully thought out and fully implemented safety plan be in effect at all facilities. Such a program should, as a minimum, provide for:

(1) Each staff member should be knowledgeable about the safety/emergency services plan. They should know what their responsibilities are and be current and proficient in their assigned tasks.

(2) Lists of emergency service personnel and/or agencies should be prominently posted and all staff should be aware of who and how to contact the necessary help. The emergency lists should include:
   • First aid personnel
   • Emergency transport service
   • Fire
   • Local police
   • State police
   • Electrical.

(3) Adequate patrols (people and/or electronic) should be implemented. Where users express concerns about safety, provide extra visible patrols on foot, horseback, bicycle, boats or vehicles to give people the added sense of protection.

(4) Adequate and properly maintained equipment should always be available, including patrol vehicles and safety equipment (i.e. first aid kits, oxygen, etc.). This should also include a plan to provide for emergency back-up units should they be required.

ADDITIONAL OPERATIONAL SUGGESTIONS

• Audio warning signals for fire, railroad crossings, storms, etc., must be in the under-1000 hz. range.

• Signals for the beginning of events, whistles, etc., should also be in the 1000 hz. range or lower.

• Messages broadcast over loudspeakers would also be more effective if presented by a lower-voiced person than someone who speaks in the higher frequency ranges.

Verbal messages over sound systems may sound good in the office or control room but may sound very different to an older person at the other end of the speakers due to poor equipment and/or malfunctioning equipment. Regular checks on the audio systems should be incorporated into the management plan for each leisure facility. These checks should be made at least in preparation for the beginning of each use season and periodically during the season – perhaps on a monthly schedule.

Leisure field staff, both public contact and others who might be in areas where older users are expected, should be sensitive to the special needs and problems of these older users. Examples of special needs and concerns are:

• Older people are frequently affected by extremes of temperature. They should unobtrusively be checked on, when possible, to identify obvious emergency situations. The staff, preferably someone wearing a "uniform" and identifiable as a site employee, should not hesitate to inquire in a friendly manner, "Is everything all right?"

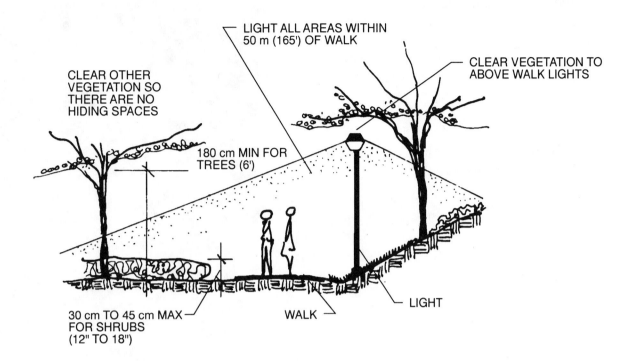

LIGHT ALL AREAS WITHIN
50 m (165') OF WALK

CLEAR OTHER
VEGETATION SO
THERE ARE NO
HIDING SPACES

CLEAR VEGETATION TO
ABOVE WALK LIGHTS

180 cm MIN FOR
TREES (6')

LIGHT

WALK

30 cm TO 45 cm MAX
FOR SHRUBS
(12" TO 18")

Figure 11.7 *Vegetation Maintenance*

PROGRAMMING

Chapter 1 gives an outline of a leisure time life cycle. People's changing needs and abilities are identified. Chapter 2 focuses on people over 55 and identifies their interests and physical/mental capabilities.

The opportunity for older people to participate in leisure activities needs to be provided for by appropriate program modifications as well as the previously discussed design modifications covered in Chapters 6 through 10. As has been stated, older people's leisure interests generally reflect their interest during their younger years. It is often only their capabilities and their available leisure time that have changed.

One of the facts of life for many people as they age is the decrease in family responsibilities and the concurrent increase in the number of leisure hours available. These available leisure hours dramatically increase with retirement. In addition, with retirement the times available for leisure during the day, week and year are different. Vacations can be scheduled any time that's convenient, making it possible to take advantage of slow use seasons. It would also be desirable for leisure providers at destination sites to make their programs more older-generation appropriate. For local leisure providers it would be advisable to program more "older" activities during the day-time hours. This will also make it possible to better utilize the available physical resources.

The long range program planning for leisure pursuits for people over 55 can then be based on current participation in leisure activities by younger people and modified by changes in capability as they age. Using this concept, programs for various communities can and should be adjusted to meet cohort needs and expectations as they progress through their individual leisure life cycles.

In summation, programming for leisure for people over 55 can and should become more older people user-friendly. Some suggestions for programming are:

• Volunteer positions of various types suitable for older people should, where possible, be made available. The local Retired Senior Volunteer Program (RSVP) office usually can be of assistance in securing volunteers.

• In malls where walking is done, perhaps the mall might have special brief programs of interest to older shoppers before the mall officially opens. Some examples could be seminars on health by the mall eye clinic or walking shoes by the various shoe stores, physical fitness equipment by the sport shops, or older fashion models displaying clothing, etc.

• Where a bicycle rental service is available, include 3-wheelers.

• Consider establishing a **special** advisory board composed of older people and people with special needs. This board would address and make recommendations on their own special needs and concerns.

• People over 55 should be represented on the recommending and/or decision-making bodies providing for leisure services and/or facilities.

• Piggyback programs off of one another, e.g., senior meals with a program afterwards.

Docent (volunteer guide), Monticello – Charlottesville, Virginia

MAINTENANCE

The perceived sense of safety requires ongoing maintenance to ensure that the safety features constructed continue to function as intended. Some examples are:

- Vegetation maintenance – keeping areas cleared as needed so that use areas can be observed during patrol. Keeping vegetation and other staff added features from providing hiding places at building entrances and around parking lots, especially isolated parking.

- Keeping the lighting system functional during all dark times when the leisure facilities are in operation, especially the checking and immediate replacement of burned-out light sources.

ADDITIONAL MAINTENANCE SUGGESTIONS

Maintenance of properly constructed facilities is critical for the safe, continued enjoyment of the users. ADA requires this under Section 35.133 Maintenance of Accessible Features published in the *Federal Register/*Vol. 56, No. 144/Friday, July 26, 1991. Section 35.133 provides that "...the public entity shall maintain in operable and working condition those features of facilities and equipment that are required to be readily accessible to and usable by persons with disabilities..." This same admonition is also applicable for the 55 and older segment of society.

Walk and Trail Maintenance

Older people have less capability of seeing and/or avoiding objects on walks and trails. Walks and trails that are utilized by the over 55 age group, and especially by those over 65-70, must be kept free of any material that could cause slipping or tripping. This item should be included in the management plan for checking at appropriate times during the year – i.e. after snows, in the fall, etc. Cleaning and repair, when identified, should be carried out ***immediately***. Three items of particular concern are:

(1) Loose objects on the walk surface such as droppings from overhead or nearby vegetation (seeds, fruit, leaves that could become slippery when wet), downed limbs and trees.

(2) Sand and small stones, etc., that have blown, dropped and/or washed onto the walkway.

(3) Ice and snow.

In addition, walks and trails are subject to damage by settling/heaving, mud slides and washouts. As in cleaning, immediate action to repair the pedestrian way must be undertaken, both from a user enjoyment standpoint and from agency liability.

BIBLIOGRAPHY

Atchley, Robert C.: *Social Forces and Aging - 6th Edition*, Wadsworth, Belmont, CA, 1991.

Bouvier, Leon F.: "America's Baby Boom Generation: The Fateful Bulge," *Population Bulletin, Vol. 35, No. 1*, Population Reference Bureau, Washington, DC, 1980.

Brown, Michael B.: "Older Blacks: No-Nonsense Leisure Activities," *Modern Maturity*, August–September 1993.

Butler, Robert N.: "2020 Vision: A Look at the Next Century," *Modern Maturity*, April–May 1984.

Carstens, Diane Y.: *Site Planning & Design for the Elderly*, Van Nostrand Reinhold Company, New York, 1985.

Colston, Ladd: "An Incentive for Living," *Parks & Recreation*, August 1986.

DeChiara, Joseph and Koppelman, Lee: *Urban Planning & Design Criteria – 2nd Edition*, Van Nostrand Reinhold Company, New York, 1975.

Design Guide for Accessible Outdoor Recreation, U.S. Department of Agriculture and U.S. Department of Interior, September 1990.

Design Guide for Accessible Outdoor Recreation, U.S. Forest Service, Partial Draft for Review, February 1992.

Favaro, Frank J., M.A. CCC-A: Personal communication, Naples, FL, March 1993.

Fogg, George E.: *Park Planning Guidelines – 3rd Edition*, National Recreation and Park Association, Arlington, VA, 1990.

Geraint, John and Heard, Helen (Eds.): *Handbook of Sports & Recreational Building Design –Volumes 1, 2, 3, 4*, Architectural Press, London, 1981.

Gotbey, Geoffrey; Patterson, Arthur; and Brown-Szwak, Laura: "Rethinking Leisure Services in an Aging Population," *Parks & Recreation*, April 1982.

Guidelines to Improve the Aesthetic Quality of Roads in Pennsylvania, Pennsylvania Department of Transportation and Pennsylvania Department of Environmental Resources, June 1978.

Heidenstam, David and Bosanko, Susan (The Diagram Group): *Sports Comparisons*, St. Martins Press, New York, 1982.

Hendricks, C.D. and Hendricks, J.: *Aging in Mass Society – Myths & Realities – 3rd Edition*, Little, Brown and Company, Boston, MA, 1986.

Hiatt, Lorraine G.: "The Environment's Role in the Total Well-Being of the Older Person," *Well-Being and the Elderly: An Holistic View*, (Magan, Geralyn G. and Haught, Evelyn L. Eds.), American Association of Homes for the Aging, Washington, DC, 1986.

Hiatt, Lorraine G.: "Smart Houses for Older People: General Considerations," *International Journal of Technology and Aging, 1, 1*, Spring/Summer 1988, 11-30.

Hooyman, Nancy R. and Kiyak, H. Asuman: *Social Gerontology*, Allyn and Bacon, Boston, MA, 1993.

I.E.S. Lighting Handbook – Reference Volume, Illuminating Engineering Society of North America, New York, NY.

Issues of the 80's: Enriching Lifestyles for the Elderly, A monograph printed from 1981-82 gerontological lecture/seminar series. College of Architecture, University of Florida, Gainesville, FL, 1982.

Kelly, J. R.: *Leisure*, Prentice Hall, Englewood Cliffs, NJ, 1982.

Kelly, J. R.; Steinkamp, M. W.; and Kelly, J.: "Later Life Satisfaction: Does Leisure Contribute?," *Life Sciences 9*, 1987, 189-200.

Lagesse, Jane and Rubinstein, Helge: *Fitness Over 40*, Pantheon Books, New York, 1986.

Lawton, M. P.; Moss, M.; and Fulcomer, M.: "Objective and Subjective Uses of Time by Older People," *International Journal of Aging and Human Development*, 24, 1986-87, 171-188.

MacNeil, R. and Teague, M.: *Aging and Leisure – Vitality in Later Life*, Prentice-Hall, Englewood Cliffs, NJ, 1987.

McGovern, John, Attorney at Law: *The ADA Self Evaluation - A Handbook for Compliance with the Americans with Disabilities Act by Parks and Recreation Agencies*, National Recreation and Park Association, Arlington, VA, 1992.

McPherson, Barry D. (Ed.): *Sport & Aging*, Human Kinetics Publishing, Champaign, IL, 1986.

National Golf Foundation, North Palm Beach, FL, 1987 data.

"Non-discrimination on the Basis of Disability in State and Local Government Services -Rules and Regulations, Department of Justice," *Federal Register – Vol. 56, No. 144*, July 26, 1991.

Ostrow, Andrew C.: *Physical Activity and the Older Adult*, Princeton Book Company, Princeton, NJ, 1984.

Outdoor Recreation in Florida – 1989, State of Florida Department of Natural Resources, Tallahassee, FL, October 1989.

Ramsey, Charles G. and Sleeper, Harold R.: *Architectural Graphics Standards – 6th Edition*, John Wiley & Sons, New York, 1970.

Shea, Edward J.: *Swimming for Seniors*, Leisure Press, Champaign, IL, 1986.

1985 Survey of Fishing, Hunting and Wildlife Associated Recreation, U.S. Department of Interior, Fish & Wildlife Service, November 1988.

Templer, John: *The Staircase*, MIT Press, Cambridge, MA, 1992.

Tennis Buyer's Guide, July 1993, 7 & 24.

Tinsley, H. E.; Combs, S.; Teaff, J. I.; and Kaufman, N.: "The Relationship of Age, Gender, Health, and Economic Status to the Psychological Benefits to Older Persons Report from Participation in Leisure Activities," *Leisure Sciences, 9*, 1987, 53-65.

"Uniform Federal Accessibility Standards" (as part of the implementation of the Architectural Barriers Act, 42 U.S.C. 4151-4157), *Federal Register, Vol. 49, No. 153*, August 7, 1984.

Wilkinson, Jack, Editor (The Diagram Group): *Rules of the Game*, Bantam Books, New York, 1976.

Wolfe, Warren: "Survey Shows Older Americans Love Traveling," *Naples Daily News*, January 1993.

GLOSSARY

Access Aisle: Accessible pedestrian space between elements of a project such as parking spaces, buildings, etc.

Accessible: A site, building, facility or portion thereof which complies with UFAS standards.

Accessible Route: A continuous unobstructed path connecting all the project's accessible elements and spaces.

Accessible Space: Space that complies with UFAS standards.

Activity Day: A measure of recreation use by one person using one facility or area for one day or part of a day. One person may be responsible for more than one activity per day. This measurement is useful for apportioning total resource use to individual uses in sizing the various parts of a given leisure development.

ADA: Americans With Disabilities Act, July 26, 1990.

Age of Frailty: The age where people become frail – usually around 85.

Back Spill: Refers to the area illuminated behind the intended area to be lit, i.e. the neighbor's yard beside a ball field.

Bench Wall: A wall at bench height on which people can sit. It frequently is used around planted areas.

Bidet: A toilet-height fixture in a women's bathroom utilized for washing the external genitals and posterior.

Boat Ramp: The facility where a trailer-pulled boat can put the boat into the water.

Boat Rigging Area: A space before a boat ramp where a vehicle-towed boat on a trailer can stop and prepare the boat for launching, i.e. check fuel, put the food and bait on board, etc. This speeds up use of the boat ramp.

Boat Set-Up Area: See Boat Rigging Area.

Camp Loops: A group of camp sites located on a loop road.

Camp Spurs: The part of a campsite used for parking the car/truck and any camp-related vehicles.

Campground Dump Station: The facility in a campground or other area serving campers where self-contained campers can dump their sewage.

Capacity Day: The maximum number of people who can use an area in one day considering the rate of turnover, i.e. instant capacity times turnover.

Caregiver: The responsible person who takes care of another individual.

Circulation Path: A way of passage from one place to another, normally referred to with a modifier, i.e. vehicular circulation and pedestrian circulation, etc.

Clear: Unobstructed.

Cohort: Term used by sociologists to describe a group of individuals having a common factor(s) in a demographic study and usually related to date of birth.

Comfort Station: Building housing sanitary facilities – term frequently used by park personnel.

Compost: Vegetative material usually generated from gardenning practices which is stored in an area to transform the material into decayed, organic material and normally re-used in the gardening. Frequently used in vegetable gardening where household vegetable scraps may also be added.

Compost Area: Location for storing and processing compost material.

Concession (Stand) Area: That portion of the leisure facility which is operated by a private party not part of the primary owner/organization and may include food, equipment rental, marina, ski school, golf pro, etc.

Courtesy Dock: A boat dock usually for small boats (2 or 3) and used for short stays (minutes), i.e. at a boat ramp.

Cross Slope: The slope that is perpendicular to the direction of travel.

Crosswalks: An identified path intended for use by pedestrians, bicycles, etc., in crossing a vehicular way.

Curb Ramp: A short ramp cutting through a curb or built up to it.

Entrance: Any access point to a building or facility used for the purpose of entering. The principal or main entrance is the primary access by which most people enter.

Fines: Small particles of stone, usually a byproduct of a quarry stone crushing operation. The material can be used as a wearing/finish surface on top of crushed stone roads, and especially walks.

Fixture Units: As used in this text it refers to toilets, urinals, and bidets needed in sanitary facilities.

Frost Line: The depth to which the ground freezes. Footings are normally specified "below the frost line."

Going: The horizontal distance between two successive nosings.

Guard Rail: A device/barrier to keep people from falling off of a raised surface.

Hand Rail: A device to assist people to go safely up or down stairs.

Hookups: Water, sewer, electrical, and possibly cable TV outlets at a camp site that the camper can "hook" (plug, tie) up to when the camper is occupying the camp site.

Horizontal Alignment: The side-to-side path or movement of a road, walk, sewer or other linear type of construction.

Instant Capacity: The capacity in number of people that a leisure facility can accommodate at any given time.

Lumens: The standard unit of light measurement used to measure the amount of light, i.e. one lumen is equal to the amount of light given off by one candle.

Moisture Sensor: A component of an irrigation system which senses or measures the amount of moisture available to the plants and shuts off the water controller if no irrigation is needed.

Nature Trails: Educational trails, guided or self-guided, featuring the natural environment.

Non-Consumptive Wildlife Use: All aspects of enjoyment of wildlife except harvesting, i.e no hunting or fishing involved.

Nose (Nosing): The front edge of a stair tread.

O&M: Commonly used abbreviation for Operations & Maintenance.

Off-the-Shelf: A standard piece of equipment that can be purchased from a manufacturer rather than a specially designed, custom built item. They are usually significantly less expensive than custom designed equipment.

Public Use: Describes spaces that are made available to the general public. They can be at/in facilities that are publicly or privately owned.

Ramp: The inclined plane for passage of traffic – usually associated with handicapped accessibility and greater than a 1:20 slope.

Riser: The upright face of a step.

Sanitary Dump Station: The facility for disposing of sewage from a holding tank in a vehicle, usually a camp vehicle or boat.

Self-Guided Trails: Educational trails with trail information provided in booklet form or in permanent displays along the pathway.

Spill: The lighting that covers more area than intended.

Tactile: Describes an object that can be perceived using the sense of touch.

Three-wheelers: A 3-wheel adult tricycle.

Tread: The horizontal surface of a step.

UFAS: Uniform Federal Accessibility Standards (Code of Federal Regulations 41 CFR 101–19.6).

Unisex Toilets: Toilets that can be used by either men or women.

Universal Design: Design which serves people of all ages, sizes and physical abilities.

Vehicular Way: A route intended for vehicular traffic – normally refers to motorized vehicles only.

Vertical Alignment: The up and down (vertical) path of a road, walk, sewer or other linear type of construction.

Visitor Day: A measure of recreation use by one person for one day or part of a day. One person will be counted only once during the day. The person's day may, however, account for several Activity Days.

Walkover: An elevated constructed walk over a sand dune for beach access in order to protect the dune.

GRAPHIC SYMBOLS USED IN TEXT

● ● ● ● ● ● ● ●   **ACCESSIBLE AREA**

                            BUILDING

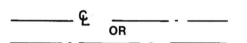   **CENTER LINE**

                            CONCRETE

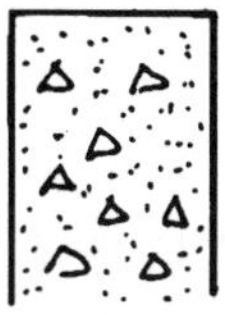

   **DISTURBED GROUND**

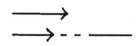   **DRAINAGE FLOW**

H   **HANDICAPPED PARKING**

MAX   **MAXIMUM**

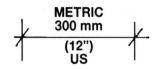

MEASUREMENTS

Meter
(1 m = approx. 3.3')
Millimeter
(25 mm = approx. 1")
Centimeter
(2.5 cm = approx. 1")

Please note that primary measurements are in metric, with U.S. equivalents in parentheses. The metric U.S. equivalents are not exact, but are usable as presented, i.e. 30 cm (12") when actually 30 cm = 11.81".

MIN

MINIMUM

PEDESTRIAN TRAFFIC WITH DIRECTION

UNDISTURBED EARTH

VEHICULAR   TRAFFIC   FLOW WITH DIRECTION

SURVEY SOURCES AND PEOPLE WHO ASSISTED IN CONDUCTING THE SURVEY

Survey Response	Location/Survey Facilitator
# 1 – 61	Harrisburg, PA – Rutherford House, Carol Fogg (61)
# 62 – 66	Golden Gate, Florida – Augustine Alvarez (5)
# 67 – 166	Naples, Florida – Briggs Health Resource Center, Andrea Wheaton and her wonderful center volunteers (conducted by G. Fogg) (100)
# 167 – 224	Manlius, NY – Manlius Recreation Department, Pat Urqhart – Director (58)
# 225 – 274	Lehigh Acres, Florida – Lee County Florida Senior Center, Agnes Prestigiorani – Director (50)
# 275 – 283	Naples, Florida – Miscellaneous, G. Fogg (9)
# 284 – 315	Collier County, Florida – Collier County Parks & Recreation, Mary EllenDonner – Recreation Director (32)
# 316 – 360	Lee County, Florida – North Fort Myers Senior Center, Lyn Trembly, Director and his assistant Kathy (45)
# 361 – 367	Naples, Florida – Emerald Greens Condominium, G. Fogg (7)
# 368 – 392	Sequim, WA – Lavinia Graham (25)
# 393 – 402	Naples, Florida – Emerald Greens Condominium, G. Fogg (10)
# 404 – 500	Oklahoma City, OK – Senior Center (97)

# 501 – 505	Oklahoma City, OK – Community College (5)
# 508 – 516	Pittsburgh, PA – River View Towers (a retirement home), Laura Zimmermann (9)
# 517 – 535	Groton, CT – Senior Center, Linda Parrish (19)
# 536 – 540	Central Pennsylvania – Miscellaneous, Michael Fogg (5)
# 543 – 578	Alaska – Pam Ulsher (36)
# 579 – 584	Montana & Wyoming (6)

George Fogg, an "over fifty-fiver," continues his 35 years of involvement in the field of park planning, design and development with this, his fourth book, *Leisure Site Guidelines for People Over 55*. In the three years of researching the leisure needs of older people, he has become acutely aware of the lack of knowledge by many designers, himself included, on the needs of older people. He has reviewed all the readily available information on older leisure needs and facilities and assisted in conducting a national survey of "over 55" leisure interests. He has also observed, photographed and talked to older people and the providers of their leisure time needs and facilities. Mr. Fogg received his bachelor's degree in Landscape Architecture from the University of Massachusetts and his master's degree in the same subject from the University of California, Berkeley. He has worked in various capacities for the U.S. National Park Service, the Hayward Area Recreation and Park District, California; the East Bay Regional Park District, California; the California State Parks Department; Pennsylvania State Parks, Pennsylvania Scenic Rivers, and Pennsylvania Coastal Zone Management Programs. He also conducted a private practice in landscape architecture and park planning in the United States and internationally. He has taught Landscape Architecture and Park Planning in the Kingdom of Saudi Arabia and the U.S. Mr. Fogg is currently practicing Landscape Architecture and Park Planning in Naples, Florida, in his firm, IBIS.

George Fogg has also published, through the National Recreation and Park Association, *A Site Design Process*, *Management Planning for Park and Recreation Areas*, and most recently *Park Planning Guidelines, 3rd Edition*.

Robert F. Fulton is professor of Sociology and Psychology at Edison Community College, Naples, Florida. He regularly teaches courses in the areas of gerontology, sociology and psychology, and has worked in each of these areas outside of the college setting. His undergraduate studies were conducted at Hershey Jr. College, York College of Pennsylvania, and Penn State University, with a B.S. degree in liberal studies being conferred by the Regents for the University of New York. He continued his studies at Oklahoma State University where he earned an M.S. degree in psychology, and a Ph.D. in sociology with post-doctoral work in gerontology.

Dr. Fulton has assisted with the analysis of leisure research data for the Oklahoma Department of Transportation, and designed an instrument recently used for a national survey sample to examine preferences for leisure activities of the elderly. He was director of an advocacy program for people with developmental handicaps in Montana. Since moving to Florida in 1987 he has supervised a state residential facility for people with developmental handicaps, where he also had experience with access problems to leisure sites for people with special needs. Additionally, he was the district program evaluator for programs for the elderly across a seven-county area for the State of Florida's Department of Health and Rehabilitative Services. He has been presenter on the subjects of special elderly housing and environmental needs at a major conference, and has served with panels and workshops. He is currently working on the development of a program in gerontology at the two-year college level for southwest Florida.